Retail Business in India

Retail Business in India

Edited by

P. Arunachalam

SERIALS PUBLICATIONS
NEW DELHI (INDIA)

First Published - 2011

ISBN: 978-81-8387-431-1

Published by

SERIALS PUBLICATIONS
4830/24, Prahlad Street, Ansari Road
Darya Ganj, New Delhi-110002 (India)
Phone: 23245225 Fax: 91-11-23272135
E-mail: serials@sify.com

CONTENTS

PREFACE

For economic growth and development of each country, the trade and commerce is the spinal cord and every country endeavors to develop the same. It is the trade and commerce in addition to other sectors of development which earn foreign exchange of the country and provide stability for the survival of the country. With the establishment of the world trade organization and its agreements with the member countries, it has become essential to make a position in the world taking in view all the developmental sectors.

Retail business is one of the sectors of commerce which enables to the consumers to buy the consumable articles of their choice in the country at the reasonable rate. Retailing is not a new concept but since times immemorial vis from the ancient times, trade flourished simple because some has a surplus of good and desired goods they did not have or could not produce. The earliest traders were Cretans who sailed the Mediterranean and carried on trade with the people of the area. Thy flourished for 2000 years and their culture influenced other great trading civilizations. Later the Phoenicians, the Romans established a sophisticated form of retailing. Numerous small shops were set up with centres. In fact ancient ruins indicate that the world's first departmental store was in Rome. With the fall of the empire the retailing disintegrated.

The book compiles useful research articles on retail industry in India and created awareness among the consumers the types, country, price tag, brand names, availability in the country. All these articles are very informative and can be further used to supplement other piece of information in the study.

The opening article 'applying total quality management to the educational process' is a research paper which peeps into the management of TQM which was espoused by Dr. W Edwards Deming in the late 1950. The article while dealing with the TQM cites examples of world established business houses like Motorola and Federal Express which have turned failing companies into world leaders. For success or failure of TQM implementation effort is universal endorsement, in particular at top. If management is not completely sold on TQM, it is unlikely that an implementation effort will be successful. TQM is a participation management philosophy and everyone has to participate throughout the effort. It enabled to identify the customer and stakeholders. Dr. W Edward Deming formed a 14 Point framework for the implementation of TQM. TQM can be a powerful tool in the educational setting even though it was developed with manufacturing processes in mind. Therefore for successful implementation of TQM, Deming's 14 point should be used as guide checklist.

Niharika Singh, in her HR Management Study in 21st century, details human resource management striking key features. There was a tremendous focus on the US and UK geographies till a couple of years ago especially in the Information Technology world. But now the scenario is changing fast and most countries in Europe are emerging as potential markets. Asian countries like India and China are redefining the landscape. Many multinational prepare to set up a base in these countries because they provide a beneficial ground on several aspects, be it manpower, skill, knowledge etc. Emerging markets put multifold challenges for human resource management. The article examines comprehensively retailing and management talent.

'Importance and effectiveness of organized retailing' by Priya Agarwal examines organized retailing elaborately. It explains brief history of retailing, History of American retailing, organized retailing, is gaining importance. It is not only offering products at best price but also providing the customer an overall experience in shopping. The phenomenal growth of retail in India is reflected in rapid increase in number of supermarkets, departmental stores, big bazaars and various malls, in the country. As prices climb, organized retail confronts the challenges of local markets. The organized grocery retailers is the preferred kind of store by consumers, even though the customers buy in several establishments and not exclusively in the hypermarket, which indicate that there is not single loyalty. While in the organized retail outlets the consumer buy essentially convenience goods with low level of risks in traditional retails. They by essentially products of more involvement, which requires a more complex buying behaviour, customers are always hungry for modern ways of shopping. Indian retail sector is growing fast as its employment potential could not be neglected. Organized retailing will lead to a greater impact on macro economy by way of accelerating productivity growth. Now all Indian cities have Big Bazaarrs, Food Chains, hypermarkets etc.

Pradeep Shukla's research paper, 'Social Entrepreneurship and Emerging Trends in it' Social Entrepreneurship is an extension of corporate social responsibility. Social Entrepreneurs drive social innovations and transformation in various fields including educational, health, environment and enterprise development. Also details leading social entrepreneurs of the world. Also present day leading social entrepreneurs like Ibrahim Abouleisn (Egypt, founder of SEKEM,) Ela Bhatt, (India-founder of SEWA), Nicholas Chan (Singapore- Co-founder of Project Senso Ltd.) Bll Drayton (US), Dr. Abrahim M George (India) etc. The study also describes major MBA recruiters companies of the world. A marvelous useful study for students of MBA Retail Management.

An article has also been rightly selected for Global Brands in small towns of rural India. Indian Market is broadly divided into- Rural and Urban markets. The middle Class which has the higher income aspirations and growing disposable income so far, has been target of marketers and advertisers. The emerging market consists of the population strata which was erstwhile poor, but it is now steadily making rapid economic progress. Hindustan Lever Limited (HLL), is a pioneer with its successful projects like Project SHAKTI AND OPERATION BHARAT. It is a case of aggressive rural marketing. Other Corporate are slowly making headway in the area are Coca Cola, Colgate, Eveready Batteries, LG Electronics, Philips, BSNL, LIC, Cavin Kare, Britainnia, Hero Honda, TVS, Reliance, Airtel, ICICI etc. The study focus on to explain various marketing tools and advertisement messages being used by Global Brands in small towns, elaborates the unconventional channels and methods, adopted by the global brands in reaching small towns, future of global brands, and preference for global brands. The article is the best retailing methodology piece containing useful information.

In modern days, advertisement on TV and Radio has become essential tool to push up sales in retails, Everyday the consumers are exposed to thousands of voices and images in magazines, newspapers, and on bill boards, radio and televisions. Every brand attempts to steal the attention of consumers. Celebrities act as spokesperson, in order to advertise and promote products. These celebrities belong to art scene, modeling, sports, and movie industry. The article 'Comparison of Celebrity and non-Celebrity in advertisement in Madurai City, is an informative study which can be treated as a component to retail business of consumer goods. Indian advertising has now established well in advertising which has been converted into a strategic tool that enhances sales, more profits, and helps in the process of brand building and product production. The study analyses critically the buying behavior of customers on the basis of celebrity advertisement.

D. Ravindran's study entitled, ' Retail Revolution in Fast Moving Food Products (FMFP), is timely study on the topic and right article in the direction of retail business for food products. With vast population base growing middle class and growing macroeconomic environment in Food Retailing has emerged as one of the fastest growing segments in the Indian retail industry. Rapid Lifestyle transformation, particularly urban areas, has resulted into a dramatic increase in the demand for processed or health food, packaged and ready to eat food products. Arrival of food multinationals and proliferation of fast food outlets have further added to the growth.

Retail revolution all over the world including India is tremendous with the emergence of new formal stores as corporate retail, supermarkets, retail chains, shopping malls, retail outlets within the organization etc. The study tabulates fastest growing related segments in India, Malls and Mall Space in 2008. Also provides details of related companies in India. It studies the organized retailing trends in India.

Other articles of useful topics related to retail business directly or indirectly also have been selected for the volume to impart complete information on retail business as far as possible. These articles are – Policy Planning for Quality Improvement in Technical Education-System Dynamic Approach, Debit cards vis-à-vis Credit Cards in India-A critical approach, A Study on Quality of Service on a Tool for Enhancement of Customer Satisfaction in Banks, The Journey of Venture Capital and Private Equity in India, A Study on Financial Awareness on Investors, A Study of Brand Preferences of B Segment Cars (with special reference to Maruti Cars), Manifestation of Quality of Work Life Pattern: Empirical Study of Indian Managers, Saving and Economic Growth in South Asia, Is Corporate Governance Really a Key to National Development.

In view of the above quoted details of articles and other research studies conducted by eminent authors and research scholars in the field of retail business in India and world at large, the volume will prove valuable for students of Commerce and research scholars pursuing studies on the subject and allied subjects related to the retail business. It is hoped that the articles will prove their worth.

P. Arunachalam
M.A (Loyola, Madras), M.Phil and Ph.D
(CUSAT, Cochin), PDT (Tilburg University, the Netherlands),
Faculty Member, Head (2004-07), Department of Applied Economics,
Cochin University of Science and Technology, Kochi-22.

APPLYING TOTAL QUALITY MANAGEMENT TO THE EDUCATIONAL PROCESS

Pradeep Shukla[*] *& D. K. Tripathi*[**]

INTRODUCTION

Total Quality Management (TQM) was first espoused by Dr. W. Edwards Deming in the late 1950's. His ideas were not accepted by US industry but were heartily endorsed by Japan in their recovery from World War II. Largely as a result of the implementation of TQM, 'Made in Japan' has changed from a derogatory term to high praise. In the 1980's, US industry began to sec the value of a TQM approach. Such company as Motorola and Federal Express have turned failing companies into world leaders. Motorola now does a good deal of business selling to Japan. Universities, however, have been slower to see the value of using TQM in their business, although several schools are now using TQM to improve the administration of the university. In 1990, Oregon State University endorsed TQM as its management philosophy and has experienced outstanding success in improving the operations of the university. For example, using TQM they reduced the average duration of remodeling projects by 23%. In 1990, the Air Force Academy, Hyderabad, began an attempt at applying TQM to curriculum development and, in 1990, offered a course that was designed and conducted using the principles of TQM. The course that we chose as the target of our TQM efforts was Energy Systems, a first course in thermodynamics. This course is a core course and is therefore taken by almost all of the cadets at the Academy. Cadets from every major discipline take the course as a graduation requirement, so it differs from traditional thermodynamics courses in that the classes have a large portion of students who are not engineers. Thermodynamics is a difficult subject for technically inclined students and is even more so for students whose interests lie in the humanities or social science. We chose Energy Systems as our target for TQM implementation for two reasons. First, Energy Systems was not a very popular course among the cadets, not unlike thermodynamics courses anywhere else

* Faculty, Lord Krishna College of Management, Ghaziabad, (*pradeepks35@rediffmail.com*)

** Professor, Lord Krishna College of Engineering, Ghaziabad in the country. We felt that if we could improve this course in the eyes of the students, we will have made a significant step. Second, the people charged with running this course, the authors, had been strong advocates of implementing TQM at the Academy from the very beginning. Several papers have been published which describe just what we did to implement TQM in our course. In those papers, we reported impressive improvements in many areas of the course. The students liked the course much more than before and felt they learned more as well. Quantitative measures of student performance increased significantly as well. The purpose of this paper, however, is not to rehash the details of one specific implementation. Rather, it is to make some observations and recommendations based on that experience that can be applied to any university situation. For readers that are interested in the details of our particular implementation, we refer them to the other papers or suggest that they contact the authors directly.

TQM PRINCIPLES

The one factor that is the most influential in the Success or failure of a TQM implementation effort is universal endorsement, in particular at the top. If management is not completely sold on TQM, it is unlikely that an implementation effort will be successful. Endorsing TQM represents a fundamental change in the way one does business. Less than full support by anyone in the chain of authority essentially condemns the effort to failure. In our case at the Air Force Academy, we had the support of everyone above us in the chain of command, from our department head, through the dean, all the way to the Secretary of Defense. That is not to say that there were no opponents on the faculty. Faculty members are a very independent group of people, and consensus on any issue is unlikely. Because those who opposed TQM implementation were not in our chain of command, they did not prevent us from implementing TQM; however, if one of the opponents happened to be in our chain of command, we would have had a much more difficult time. It was also very important to get the endorsement of the students as well as those up the chain. To earn the student's endorsement, we had to make them part of the solution. TQM is a participative management philosophy, and the students had to participate throughout the effort. We therefore had to teach them about TQM and then show them how we were changing things in the course. Without that education process, we would not have had the support of the students that we enjoyed. Once the commitment is made to implement TQM, one of the first steps is to identify the 'customers' or stakeholders. To do this, you must treat the educational process as a system; all elements and the interactions between those elements must be addressed. Process improvement should begin and end with the customer. A systems approach to industrial process improvement is relatively common now. In an industrial application, the customers will include the purchaser of the product or service, suppliers, subcontractors, etc. A careful identification of the customers in the university setting needs to be accomplished. It can rightly be argued that there are many customers of the university including the students, the employers of the school's graduates, the parents of the students, the taxpayers, the whole of society, the Board of Regents, the State Legislature, etc. We have found that by identifying our students and the employers of our graduates (the Air Force) as our primary customers, we would end up satisfying all of the other customers. On the other hand, by focusing on a customer that is too far removed from the operation, it is very easy to overlook the needs of the more immediate customers.

It is not uncommon for universities to address the needs of industry in curriculum development; however, students are usually treated more as a product than a customer. It is likely that many of the problems that plague some universities stem from an effort to make a remote body happy while inadvertently ignoring the students. This is a classic case of improperly defining the system. All relevant participants must be included in the educational system. Once all participants are identified, the relative importance of each participant can be established. Taking a systems approach to education can be a very useful endeavor. If the student is identified as one of your customers, you must try to satisfy that customer, but you must be very sure you know what that customer really wants. An Air Force general may say he wants a fighter that can turn inside a football field at four times the speed of sound, but he really does not want thatÐeven if it was technologically possible, he couldn't afford it, Customers must make an informed decision in deciding what they want, taking into account costs, performance needed, legal issues, etc. Students may say they want an easy 'A' in every class, but what they really want is an education. If high grades were passed out with no learning taking place, prospective employers would quickly learn to avoid hiring the graduates of that university. The perspective we should take is that the students are, at least in principle, paying for the services we provide. We must be sure that we are satisfying their real long-term needs, not simply short-term desires.

DEMING'S 14 POINTS

The 14 points of Dr. W. Edwards Deming form a framework for the implementation of TQM. We have used this list as a checklist of sorts in our effort. These 14 points are general enough that an implementation at one school would probably look considerably different from one at another school. The way that these 14 points should be used is to come to a consensus as to the application of each point to the particular situation at hand. In the following paragraphs, we will present some suggestions on how each point might be applied to the university setting in the administration of the university and in the curriculum. Realize that these are just suggestions, many of which will be totally inappropriate at a particular university. Our purpose here is to give some food for thought and suggest by comparison a methodology one could use to apply TQM to a unique situation.

Create Constancy of Purpose

Develop a mission statement as your corporate purpose or aim. For example, the mission statement for a university might be, 'To develop the skills, attitudes, and motivation in our students so they will become responsible citizens and be capable of making positive contributions to society.' The mission statement for a college of engineering might be, 'To develop the skills, attitudes, and motivation in our students so they will perform in a technically competent, socially responsible, and ethical manner as engineers entrusted with the safety and comfort of their clients.' Developing a mission statement is not a trivial task; it requires a real understanding of just why the organization exists. The mission statement is also hierarchical; the department's mission depends on the college's mission, which depends on the University's mission, and so on. Once the mission statement is developed, everyone (not just the faculty and administration, but everyone employed by the University) must know how they contribute to the mission. The analysis suggested here is to assess the value added by a process. If a process or a position does not add value, that is, does not contribute to the mission, it should be eliminated.

Adopt a New Philosophy

Insist on quality in everything classroom instruction, bookstore service, campus policing, Restroom cleaning, interactions with the legislature everything. To achieve this quality, an atmosphere of cooperation as opposed to competition must be instilled. This is particularly true in the classroom; management must ensure that the processes put in force encourage cooperation at every level student to student and faculty to student. Do away with the 'us versus them' attitude. Instead ask questions like, 'What can we, the faculty and staff, do to make the learning experience in this classroom better?' or 'What can we, the teacher and the students, do to ensure every student has the best opportunity to learn this material?' It is a completely different approach than most of us experienced in school as students.

Cease Dependence on Mass Inspection

Focus on the product or service process. Don't depend on audits, tests, or inspections to build quality. Inspections will only keep bad products from hitting the market, but there are large costs incurred with each bad piece. The analogy in education is that the failed student is scrap that must be either reworked (take the course again or get extra tutoring) or discarded. We need to develop processes in which there is less testing but more focus on progress in learning. For example, ask yourself why you are giving a particular test. If the answer is to evaluate your students, then ask yourself if you need this extra piece of evaluative information. There is evidence that we test far more than is needed to evaluate our students. On the administrative side of the university, are there too many checks and balances? Can a process be changed to make inspections unnecessary or at least to reduce the need for inspections? Statistical process control can be an important tool in developing processes that do not require much inspection.

End the Practice of Conducting Business on Cost Alone

The lowest bid usually does not result in the lowest life-cycle cost. In all our processes, we need to focus on long-term costs and benefits. That may mean that the trendy new course not be offered if it means the failure of a course with more long-term value. Awarding the printing contract to an off campus vendor may have lower first cost, but the inability to get adequate turn-around time or poorer quality may make the overall cost of that decision very high. University professors often complain about the poor job the high schools are doing in preparing students for college. The long-term costs of supplying educated people to society may be less if some of the resources of the university were spent on improving high and junior high schools.

Constantly Improve Processes

Are your customers (the students and their future employers) more satisfied than they werelast semester? Are the faculty members happier? Are the secretaries happier? Are the suppliers of the University happier? If the answer to a question is no, find out why and fix the situation immediately. If the answer is yes, determine what it was in the process that made it so. In any case, analyze the process to determine what changes can be made to make it better. Incremental improvements must be made every semester. This is essentially the Kaizen philosophy encourages innovation, but insists upon incremental improvements, especially after the innovation. The phrase, 'if it's not broke, don't fix it,' does not apply. To help decide where to look for things to improve, use course grades, student performance on 'anchor' problems, student critiques, faculty and staff organizational climate surveys, inputs to suggestion boxes, summaries of complaints, etc. Carefully designed questions on anonymous surveys can be very valuable, but talking directly to the customer is still the best way to find out what the barriers are. There is a side benefit to talking directly to the students about their problems they appreciate it and make the 'us versus them' attitude much less likely.

Institute Training

Everyone needs to know their job. The faculty is certainly well educated in their disciplines but maybe not in the art of teaching. Faculty development programs help teachers know their jobs. Word processing classes help secretaries do their job better. Money spent on faculty and staff training has long-term payback. In addition, you should teach TQM to everyone faculty, staff, and especially students. The more everyone knows about the management principles used on a daily basis, the easier it is for everyone to buy into the idea.

Institute Leadership

Emphasize leadership instead of management. Everyone at the university has a leadership role of some sort. Each person in a supervisory role (including the faculty) should try to be a coach and teacher, not a judge and overseer. As put by Senge, the leader should be a designer, a creator of an environment. Effective leaders will search for barriers to communication and productivity and remove them. A poorly lit classroom can have a significant effect on student performance. A teacher who is an effective leader will see to it that the lighting problems are fixed. A teacher, who will adjust the due date on a project based on special student situations, will probably increase the learning of his students.

Drive Out Fear

In the academic setting, fear is often a big factor in student and faculty performance. For students, any steps that can be taken to reduce the fear involved in taking a test will pay large benefits in student performance and attitude. Allowing for a make-up exam, points for reworking missed problems on an exam, and dropping a low grade are examples of little things that can be done to reduce student fear. Teachers must balance their roles as educators versus evaluators. When asked, most professors will readily say that their job is to educate their students; however, the amount of time they spend on evaluation tends to contradict this view. On the faculty and staff side, fear can also play an important role. If a high price must be paid for failure, few people will be willing to risk experimenting with a promising new innovation, thus keeping a process improvement out of the system. If a teacher would like to try an innovative teaching technique, the effort should be applauded even if it is a failure. Certainly something of value will have come from the experiment. Researchers must have the opportunity to fail without the fear of demotion or lack of promotion opportunity. Fear is a powerful emotion and can have very negative effects on the performance of an organization.

Break Down Barriers

Encourage cooperation, not competition. Encourage the forming of cross-function teams to address problems and process improvements. A team made up of faculty, staff, and students (perhaps from more than one department) will have a broader perspective in addressing issues than a more narrowly composed committee. When addressing a problem in the registration process, address it with a team consisting of representatives from every involved organization faculty, advisors, students, registrar, computer services, etc. A solution devised by only one organization will usually have a negative impact on some other organizations. Bringing everyone in on the decision process will usually result in a better solution, and certainly one that is easier to accept.

Avoid Obsession with Goals and Slogans

Just telling someone to do well is meaningless without the means to achieve that goal. Management must improve the processes so that the goals can be achieved. Stating that 80% is the minimum acceptable score on an exam will not by itself achieve that goal. Stating that goal and then providing excellent instruction, arranging for study teams, giving extra help where needed, etc., will give the students a much better chance for success.

Eliminate Numerical Quotas

It is often said that numbers are the crutches of poor supervision. On the assembly line, this principle is easy to see; in the academic setting, it is not as obvious but just as true. If there are quotas established for 'x' number of papers per year or 'y' number of majors enrolled, quality will decrease. The number one priority should be quality. Only after the process is designed so that quality is assured should the questions of quantity be addressed.

Remove Barriers to Pride of Workmanship

Pride is a strong motivator. In the academic setting, pride certainly flows from personal and group achievements, but there is also a good deal of pride in the institution as well. Often this institutional pride is a result of having survived the program, but it can also stem from having had a part in the development of that program. If the students are included in some of the decision-making processes, they will develop a strong pride of ownership that can have a significant impact on their attitudes. A step as simple as talking to student representatives about their concerns can change an antagonistic faculty/student relationship into a cooperative one. Using some of the elements of cooperative learning also empowers the students by sharing some of the teaching role with the faculty. A secretary who is allowed to choose how the work is to be done and has a voice in some of the administrative decisions that affect secretarial work will be a much more productive and happy worker. Barriers between departments and colleges should be dismantled; each professor can learn a lot by studying the operation of another department.

Organization-wide Involvement

Everyone in the institution must be included in the education process and be aware of and concerned for their immediate 'customer'. Lab technicians who sit in on the courses that they support will have a much better idea of how their work contributes to the mission. Secretaries who learn about new techniques and technologies for use in the office are much more likely to suggest improvements to the processes they are exposed to. Professors should audit courses in other departments, particularly those courses that are prerequisites for their own courses. Faculty members who learn about TQM are much more likely to endorse the concept and to suggest new ways to implement TQM in their jobs. One cannot predict ~~just~~ what piece of knowledge will spark the idea that will lead to a significant process improvement.

Define Management's Responsibilities to Make it Happen

Management, at every level but particularly at the very top, must take and show pride in adopting the TQM philosophy. The meaning of each of the 14 points as related to the mission must be clear to all involved. This is not a trivial process; a good deal of time must be spent in analyzing the various processes and discussing how the 14 points relate to those processes. The time spent in this effort forms the foundation for all of the TQM implementation.

APPLICATION OF THE 14 POINTS

The above 14 points are very general. When TQM is successfully applied, it is a result of a careful study of each point and a clear determination of how each applies to the situation at hand. No two applications of TQM will be the same. The form that a particular implementation takes is dependent on many factors such as the size of the institution, whether the institution is private or public, and the strengths of the people involved, but the most important variables are the maturity of the students and the involvement of the employer. Careful consideration of all aspects of the educational system will help determine just how the TQM implementation will ultimately look. The principles of TQM can also be applied to high school, middle school, and elementary school educational processes as well as to training situations. The principle differences in the implementation of TQM will be the result of the relative weight assigned to each of the customers at the different levels of education. The weighting that is applied is primarily the result of the maturity of the students, but there are other considerations as well. For example, in elementary schools the most important customers, listed in order of importance, are the parents of the students, the students themselves, and the middle school to which the students

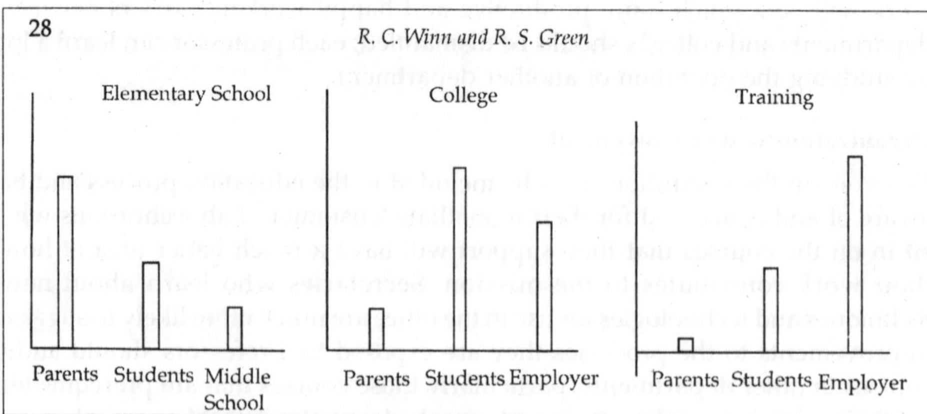

Figure 1 : Relative Customer Importance

are headed. As the maturity of the students increases, the students replace the parents as the most important customer. In a training situation, the most important customer is the organization that needs the individuals trained. Regardless who your primary customer is, it is essential that the students be included in the list of customers. Figure 1 shows a qualitative assessment of the relative importance of various customers in different educational environments. Please keep in mind that only a few of the potential customers have been presented, but students must be considered in each case.

CONCLUSIONS

TQM can be a powerful tool in the educational setting even though it was developed with manufacturing processes in mind. The key elements to a successful implementation are:

- Gain the support of everyone in the chain of supervision.
- Identify your customers.
- Focus on refining the process.
- Use Deming's 14 Points as a guide Checklist during the implementation effort. The final result will be a more efficient operation and a teamwork attitude rather than an 'us versus them' attitude between faculty and students.

References

M. Walton (1986), The Deming Management Method, Perigee Books, New York, NY.

L. E. Coate (1992), Total Quality Management at Oregon State University, Oregon State University, Corvallis, OR, March 1992. Figure 1. Relative customer Importance. 28 R. C. Winn and R. S. Green.

R. S. Green, R. C. Winn, and M. L. Smith (1991), Integrating Total Quality Management into a Thermodynamics Course, Proceedings of the First International Conference on Post High School Technical Education, Jerusalem/Tel Aviv, Israel, December.

R. S. Green, and R. C. Winn (1992), Application of Total Quality Management to Engineering Education, Proceedings of the ASEE Annual Conference, Toledo, OH, July.

R. S. Green, and R. C. Winn, Application of Total Quality Management to a Thermodynamics Course, USAF Academy Technical Report, (Accepted for Publication).

P. Senge (1990), the Fifth Discipline, Doubleday, New York, NY.

R. C. Winn (1990), How Much Testing is Enough? Proceedings of Frontiers in Education '90, Vienna, Austria, July.

G. Bounds, L. Yorks, M. Adams, and G. Ranney (1994), Beyond Total Quality Management: Toward the Emerging Paradigm, McGraw-Hill, Inc., New York, NY.

M. Imai, Kaizen (1986), McGraw-Hill, New York, NY.

HR MANAGEMENT IN THE 21ST CENTURY: CHALLENGES FOR THE FUTURE

Niharika Singh[*] *& Roli Sigh*[**]

INTRODUCTION

If you happen to meet the HR Head of a large organization, just ask him what his biggest challenge is. He will say 'retention of people'. The same person after a few minutes for the same question will answer 'attracting talent'. Probably his answer the next day will be 'staff motivation'. Different answers from the same individual at different times does not mean that he is not sure of what his problem is but it depicts the fact that the priority of HR challenges keep changing from time to time. The biggest challenge for HR in the 21st century is to identify its biggest challenge.

Most of the big companies' values are tied up in intangible assets. The study of intangible assets breaks them into three components. The first is processes. Processes are important for any industry and they determine the output of any activity. Companies should manage their processes well and derive maximum results out of them. Next important intangible is the customer base, or the brand value. Over the last one and a half decades, companies are focusing more on driving maximum value for existing relationships.

The third major intangible is the workforce and the investment made on the employees. The challenge here is to optimize the return in the workforce investment and also ensure that the investment that we make is driving the expected output. It is very important to be significantly different from competitors and always be in the minds of future employees and shareholders. 'People are our biggest assets' has become the buzzword for all organizations and 'how are these great assets managed' remains a million-dollar question! This paper answers such unanswered questions and sincerely attempts to enable

* Lecturer, Lord Krishna Group of Institutions, Ghaziabad, (*30Niharika.singh@gmail.com*)

** Faculty, Amity University,Noida Campus.

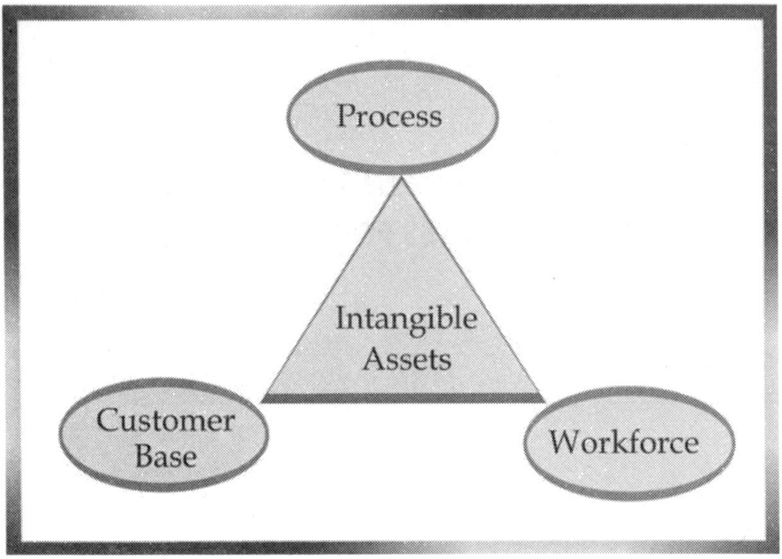

the HR fraternity to overcome their current challenges and make the HR roles interesting.

EMERGING NEW MARKETS

There was a tremendous focus on the US and the UK geographies till a couple of years ago especially in the IT industry. But now the scenario is changing and more countries in the Europe are emerging as potential markets. Asian countries like India and China are redefining the landscape. Many MNCs prefer to set up a base in these countries because they provide a beneficial ground on several aspects, be it manpower, skill, knowledge or anything else. Indian companies are setting up their bases in other countries as well. It is evident from several business reports and articles that the focus is shifting from US, UK to Europe and, of course, APAC. The challenge for HR is multifold in this regard.

> **Emergening Markets**
> **Multifold Challenges for HR**
>
> 1. Retention of manpower (Every company is growing and recruiting)
> 2. Recruitment of (suitable) local citizens in other geographies
> 3. Attracting talent from other organizations both locally as well as foreign geographies.
> 4. Relocation of existing staff from our local geographies to other geographies. Especially moving people to APAC geographies is a 'Herculean' task.
> 5. Diversity Management Customization of HR policies to suit different geographies

These challenges listed in the box above are just a few top priorities, the list grows longer and longer as we get into further details. Another hard fact here is that each one of these items in the list can be broken down into few smaller items, which also serve as big challenges to organizations.

ATTITUDE & BEHAVIOR OF THE WORKFORCE

There is a phenomenal change in the quality of workforce that is available in the market these days. I was interviewing a candidate last week for a position in my team, and this candidate who had two years of experience in HR was giving me electric responses. While I was pleased to note that he had a grip on what he knew and also what he wanted to do next, I was taken aback when he said, "I will start applying to other companies," in response to my question, "What will you do if you feel unhappy with your job profile after a couple of years?" The emerging young workforce is very confident but at the same time too short-sighted. We may argue that the market is good and they just want to make hay while the sun shines, but the fact is these people want to make all the hay in one day. For small hiccups, our people conclude that they got themselves married with the wrong company and they decide on a quick divorce without thinking through, the options for remarriage are plenty though. With the rapidly developing economic conditions and exponentially increasing number of job opportunities across the globe, personnel retention is already a challenge. When you consider the fact too that the attitude and behavior of these new recruits both fresh and lateral entrants are changing drastically, my contention that retention is a nightmare to HR Heads will become obvious

LEADERSHIP DEVELOPMENT

"I want more leaders to carry the organization forward." "We need leaders to meet our vision." These are some of the common statements we would hear from a CXO of any medium or large sized organization. While there is a lot of effort, time and money invested on leadership development initiatives, we

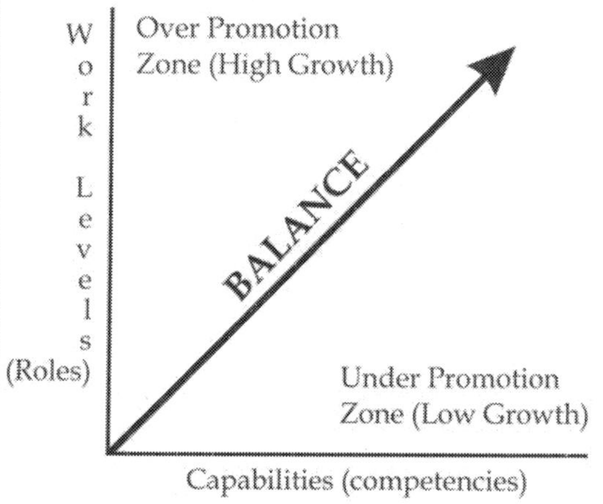

Employee Growth in an Organization

Curtsey : The Healthy Organization - Brian Dive

have very little evidence that these initiatives are driving the expected results. A clear indication that the performance has increased because of these initiatives is still lacking. Hence, many of these initiatives, which do not evidently produce a measurable result, make justifying them for every stakeholder and shareholder a tough task day-by-day. We need to come up with totally new approach for leadership development and that continues to be a big challenge for HR in the current scenario. In our organization, we have come up with certain new approaches for identifying and grooming our leaders, which I would discuss at a later stage in this paper. As illustrated in the figure below, it is very important to ensure a balanced growth, and it is needless to mention that balancing is the biggest challenge in leadership development. Having leaders in either excessiveness or scarcity is not a healthy sign for any organization.

RETAINING & MANAGING TALENT

Many years ago Mckinsey coined a term "war for talent", which is now being looked at as a competition between organizations to attract new talent. What I would like to prescribe here is that we just have to shift gears and focus more on retaining the talent that we have and also come up with new ways of developing talent. It is a good sign that many organizations are moving away from a skill-based approach to a competency-based approach. A system that enables HR to maintain and manage the current competencies and enable employees to plan their development either to higher proficiency levels in their existing competencies or new competencies is a need of the hour. I am talking about a learning and competency management system under retention of employees and I have also clubbed talent management along in the heading because they both go together. At any point in time, an employee who believes that his organization continuously invests in developing his talent and also provides him enough opportunities to deploy his talent in the field will never allow the thought of quitting creep into his mind. But on the one hand, getting more investment into talent development initiatives is currently a challenge, and on the other side creating a career plan for every employee that enables him/her to continuously deploy his/her talent remains a bigger challenge.

INNOVATION & TALENT DEVELOPMENT

It is absolutely beyond debate that 'Innovation' is now mandatory for the success of any business. There are several drivers that can cultivate innovation in an organization and one of them is developing the skills and talents of its employees through various modes of learning. PwC has released a report where the statistics very clearly shows that the investments on training and development activities are much higher in the US than Europe or APAC countries. That could possibly be one of the reasons that most of the innovations come from the US. Japan could be an exception to this but they have restricted themselves to technology innovations while we need innovations in every field.

We still do not have instruments to measure and provide a direct correlation between the investment made on innovation trainings and the number of creative outputs. But what is evident from the PwC report is that the companies that are showing maximum innovations are the companies that invest a lot on training and talent development.

Talent Development Pyramid

CHALLENGES AT DIFFERENT LEVELS OF TALENT DEVELOPMENT

The report also clearly highlights that companies that produce better business results invest a huge sum in training and talent development. I would like to quote my own organization as an example for this. I am proud that I am part of a true learning organization and all of us who work for our organization can loudly say so with due respect to the enormous investment which goes into our learning and development initiatives. Creating an innovative culture within the organization, creating an environment to share ideas, motivating people to innovate are some of the key challenges for HR under this head.

EMPLOYEE ENGAGEMENT & COMMITMENT FROM EMPLOYEES

I remember when this term called 'employee engagement' was introduced into the HR portfolio, it meant including the fun element at work. Rejuvenating the employees with loads of fun activities was the key task of employee engagement personnel. It helped organizations to create a sense of belonging among employees and in turn indirectly demanded a certain degree of commitment from them. Some organizations have gone one step beyond and have included the families in such events. Loyalty to the organization was considered to be the in-thing in every employee's mind.

But unfortunately, today these employee engagement activities just remain as entertainment activities and they do not add any value to the expected outcome. There is again very little evidence in this area too to measure the impact it makes on the organizations. 'Be loyal to your job but never be loyal to your organization' is the definition for loyalty now-a-days among young professionals. We can go on debating whether it is the right thing to do or not, but the bottom line is that we need better employee engagement activities which will create a bonding between employees and organizations.

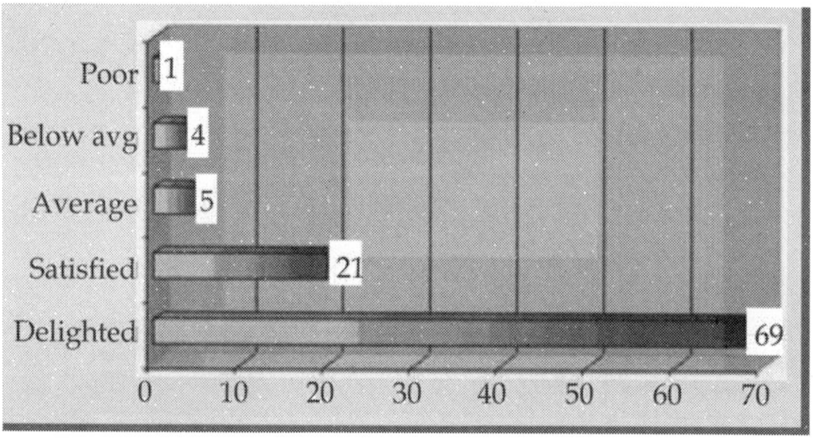

SURVEY CONDUCTED ON EMPLOYEE ENGAGEMENT ACTIVITIES (DIFFERENT IT COMPANIES)

From the above graph, we can see that about 90% of the employees are satisfied or delighted with these initiatives and 5% feel it is average. The dissatisfied percentage is only 5. If we make a direct correlation between attrition rate, which is currently at 14% (industry average), and the dissatisfaction percentage that has come out in this survey (5%), there seems to be a wide gap. We have no visible evidences to prove that our employee engagement activities are helping us to retain our people. The challenge for HR is to come up with innovative HR practices which will make employee engagement activities more interesting and also help us in achieving the objective of retaining people.

WHAT SHOULD WE BE DOING?

After discussing all these challenges at length, I can very well understand that some of you may sigh and ask, "We experience all this but how do we get rid off them." As I mentioned earlier, these issues may sound mundane but they are realistic. We cannot discount the fact that many of us in various HR roles are living with such challenges day in and day out. I would like to quote a traditional proverb here, "Where there is a will, there is a way." It just needs the right attitude or passion, as we may call it, within ourselves. Many experts are talking about HR redefining its strategy to move up the value chain from a supporting function to an enabling function, and then transforming itself into a strategic business partner. To equip ourselves to be a part of this giant leap, all of us need to have certain qualities, competencies, practices, processes, and most important of all, the right people doing the right jobs. An illustration will always help us to understand things better. Along those lines, I would like to site certain initiatives that we had taken in our organization, which makes 'working an exciting experience' for every individual in the organization. We have taken utmost care that all initiatives that we take touch every associate, it really does not matter whether he is the CEO or a trainee who joined just today.

THE TCS PHENOMENON

TCS is a part of the TATA conglomerate, which has a history of over 130 years. This group has a reputation for its people-centric attitude and the intention to contribute back to the society. This company not only says that 'People are our biggest assets' but also exhibits that in every move it makes. Any new HR initiative taken revolves around a people-centric approach. Without getting into too much detail of various HR activities that happen in our organization, I would highlight some best practices, which they follow under every head that I have discussed earlier in this paper. They have been continuously improving and innovating our people practices.

EMERGING NEW MARKETS

The organization strategy for TCS has already been very clearly drawn up for expanding in the maturing markets of Europe and Asia Pacific. They had also announced that they would be recruiting around 5000 associates in China over the next 5 years. Many high performers have been hand-picked to move to these geographies to lay a strong foundation in these maturing markets. These associates have been briefed about the role that they will perform, and have been counseled on why they have been chosen for these roles.

They have selected the right people to move and the employees are also motivated that they have been hand-picked for a challenging overseas assignment; hence, it serves as a win-win situation to both the organization and the individual. They have also decided to recruit local champions to assist these leaders in their respective roles. Hence, they have proactively sought solutions for the emerging challenges, and they have ensured that they are prepared to aggressively enter into these unexplored potential markets.

ATTITUDE & BEHAVIOR OF THE WORKFORCE

As I mentioned earlier, we can debate whether it's a good sign or not that the attitude of young workforce is changing, but what we need right now is to accept the fact that there is a drastic change in the behavior of employees, and quickly come up with counter measures to address this issue. The TCS, has done the same. Their induction program introduces the participants to the various initiatives of the organization and makes them feel that they are a part of the family right from Day One. This creates a sense of belongingness for every new entrant. They also put their associates through a lot of learning programs, which brings about a behavioral change, maybe not overnight, but definitely over a period of time. Moving one step ahead of all these traditional measures, they have created a standard rotational plan for all associates at almost all levels barring a few senior level positions. This helps them to break the monotony of job profiles and energize people. Knowledge and expertise keeps improving and employees begin to understand that the organization is taking maximum care of their career development and, hence, they will want to stick on forever.

LEADERSHIP DEVELOPMENT

"Leaders are not born, they are made." The TCS, do believe this strongly because they have the experience of create leaders for the past many years. Their leadership development program is not just a mere training program but a lot more. They have empowered their associates to nominate themselves as leaders and also select the stream in which they want to move ahead. Then these leaders are hand-picked or interviewed or assessed, followed with an extensive workshop. These workshops not only train them, but also enable them to learn. They live the life of the role that they aspire to take.

The success of this initiative depends on the deployment and, hence, they ensure that these people are quickly deployed into those roles for which they were chosen. Over a period of time, these leaders along with other seniors of the organization share their experiences in the field with the next set of identified leaders. Thus, it is ensured that field experiences are ploughed back into the minds of the next generation leaders. They may still not have measures on ROI on this initiative, but they do have some metric on number of employees trained against number of employees deployed.

RETAINING & MANAGING TALENT

We discussed the need for a learning and competency management system in the previous column on this topic. TCS has been a fore-runner in this aspect and they have developed a system to mange their learning deployment, planning and their competencies. Various features like gap analysis, role tagging, competency mapping, learning plan creation, and so on, makes learning so exciting for our associates. They have the liberty to choose from a huge volume of learning objects, which are divided into Technical, Process, Domain and Soft Skills subject areas. Well-defined career paths for every individual and the corresponding learning interventions are some of the salient features of this system. In the long run, this system will also help us in the process of moving towards a role-based organization. As long as an employee is clearly shown the way, he will move ahead, he will be happy enough to prepare himself to move that way, and take all the necessary help required rather than trying to branch-off elsewhere. Most employees move out for better growth opportunities. If the same is assured at home turf, will anyone quit?

INNOVATION & TALENT DEVELOPMENT

TCS is a learning organization, which spends over 4 per cent of its revenue in its learning & development initiatives. The fact is also obvious from the business results it produces consistently. Referring back to PwC report again, TCS comes up with remarkable innovations, which serve as a benchmark in the industry. They also invest a lot in their R&D initiatives. They do not want to quantify our investment in this area and calculate the ROI. Their actual intention is to be thought leaders in the area we chose, and they have proved to be thought leaders in several unique fields. Talent management is monitored through individual learning plans and personalized career development plans.

CONCLUSION:

"I never predict. I just look out the window and see what is visible – but not yet seen" **(Peter Drucker)**

The management has to recognize the important role of Human Resource Department in order to successfully steer organizations towards profitability. HR managers have to manage all the challenges that they would face from recruiting employees, to training them, and then developing strategies for retaining them and building up an effective career management system for them.

Different companies are using different strategies for facing these challenges and for getting success in this competitive era.

Trends in Human resource management have changed the way we work, as organizations are more depended on HRM to increase the success ratio in today's competitive global environment.

References

Argyris, C. (1993), Overcoming Organizational Defenses: Facilitating Organizational Learning (Harvard University, Allyn and Bacon).

Bennis, W. (1989), On Becoming a Leader (Reading, MA, Addison Wesley). Crosby, P. (1986) Running Things (New York, McGraw-Hill).

Dahlgaard, J. J., Dahlgaard, S.M.P. & Edgeman, R. L. (1998), Core Value Deployment: The Need for a New Renaissance, *Total Quality Management,* 9, pp. S45-S50.

Dyason, M. D. & Kaye, M. M. (1995), Achieving a Competitive Edge Through Continuous Quality Improvement. In: G.K. KENJI (Ed.) Total Quality Management: Proceedings of the First World Congress (London, Chapman & Hall).

Jones-evans, D. (1996), Technical Entrepreneurship, Strategy and Experience, *International Small Business Journal*, 14, pp. 15-39.

Juran, J. M. (1989), Juran on Leadership for Quality: An Executive Handbook (New York, The Free Press).

Kanji, G. K. (1995), Quality and Statistical Concepts. In: G.K. Kanji (Ed.) Total Quality Management in Action, 5(4), pp. 337-350. (London, Chapman St Hall).

Keogh, W. & Evans, G. (1999), Strategies for Growth and the Barriers Faced by New Technology-based SMEs, *Journal of Small Business and Enterprise Development.*

Macdonald, J. (1995), TQM-Does it Always Work? Some Reasons for Disappointment. In: G. K. Kanji (Ed.) Total Quality Management: Proceedings of the First World Congress (London, Chapman & Hall).

Morris, D. S. & Haigh, R. H. (1996), Overcoming the Barriers to TQM. In: G.K. Kanji (Ed.) Total Quality Management in Action (London, Chapman & Hall).

Oakland, J. (1995), Total Quality Management (London, Butterworth Heinemann).

Peters, T. J. & Waterman, R.H. (1982), In Search of Excellence: Lessons from America's Best-run Companies (Nw York, Harper & Row).

Scott, P., Jones, B., Bramley, A. & Bolton, B. (1996), Enhancing Technology and Skills in Small - and Medium-sized Manufacturing Firms: Problems and Prospects, *International Small Business Journal*, 14, pp. 85-99.

Seddon, J. (1995), Changing Management Thinking: The Key to Success with TQM. In: G. K. Kanji (Ed.) Total Quality Management: Proceedings of the First World Congress (London, Chapman & Hall).

Senge, P.M. (1990), The Fifth Discipline (London, Century Business).

Smallbone, D., Leigh, R. & North, D. (1995), The Characteristics and Strategies of High Growth SMEs, *International Journal of Entrepreneurial Behaviour & Research*, 1, pp. 44-62.

Wiseman, A. (1995), Turning Strategy into Decisive Action. In: G.K. Kanji (Ed.) Total Quality Management: Proceedings of the First World Congress (London, Chapman & Hall).

Zairi, M. (1994), Measuring Performance for Business Results (London, Chapman & Hall.

IMPORTANCE AND EFFECTIVENESS OF ORGANIZED RETAILING

Priya Agarwal[*•] *& Pradeep Shukla*[**#]

BRIEF HISTORY OF RETAILING

At some time during the beginnings of civilization, groups began to trade with one another. How or why this occurred is not known, but various explanations have been given. Let's take a look at the history of retail. One theory suggests that trade was an instinctive invention based on the need for food, water and bodily comforts. Another is based on human aggressiveness. Another one asserts that trade was an outgrowth of friendly gift giving. Yet another very plausible explanation suggests that people who had more goods than they could consume traded the excess away. Whatever the reason, it became a staple of civilization. Below is a brief history of retailing.

Ancient Retailing

In the ancient world, trade flourished simple because some has a surplus of one good and desired the goods they did not have or could not produce. The earliest traders were Cretans who sailed the Mediterranean and carried on trade with the people of that area. They flourished for 2,000 years, and their culture influenced other great trading civilizations.

The Phoenicians followed the Cretans as civilizations major traders. You could view them as distributors. They distributed the goods of Egypt and Babylonia. Tyre, Sidon, and Carthage were the principal trading cities of this empire.

This group was in turn succeeded by the Romans. The Romans established a sophisticated form of retailing. Numerous small shops were set up with centers. In fact, ancient ruins indicate that the world's first department store was in Rome!! With the fall of this empire, retailing disintegrated.

* Lecturer, **Faculty (Management), Lord Krishna Group of Institutions, Ghaziabad, (*e-mail: •agpriya88@yahoo.com, #pradeepks35@redifmail.com*)

The Dark Ages

During the period after the fall of the Roman Empire, the only retailers were peddlers. They carried their store around on their back. They went from village to village selling their wares. They often offered inferior merchandise. By the 13th century fairs and markets flourished. Early fairs often had a religious foundation. On feast days people would gather at their churches and exchange goods. Larger markets were also called fairs and people traveled long distances to participate. These fairs eventually became amusement and exist in an entertainment form today! By the 12th century artisan and tradesmen began to organize into guilds and opened up small shops. They helped them gain social and economic advantages.

History of American Retailing

Many American retailing institutions orginated after 1850. Prior to that, many Americans lived on farms and were self sufficient. During this time itinerant peddlers and general stores were basically the only retailers in the country. After 1850, department stores became important. For example, Richs was established in Atlanta in 1867 by 4 Hungarian immigrants. Simon Lazarus, an immigrant from Poland, opened a men's clothing store in Columbus, Ohio in 1851. Macy's can be traced to 1858.

ORGANIZED RETAILING

Interaction between an organization and customers through what we sale our own manufactured or outsource products with the help of service providers is called retailing. Organized Retailing is gaining importance. It is not only offering products at best price but also providing the customer an overall experience in Shopping.The phenomenal growth of retail in India is reflected in the rapid increase in number of supermarkets, departmental stores and hypermarkets in the country.

AS PRICES CLIMB ORGANIZED RETAILERS ATTRACT VALUE SHOPPERS:

Despite the rising value of staples, growth in volume indicates there is no cut back in customer spending. "Despite the rising value of staples, we are seeing a growth in volumes (number of units sold). This could mean that there is no cutback in consumer spends or that whilst there is a cutback, the number of people visiting the store is higher and therefore volumes are higher, says Thomas Varghese, chief executive officer, Aditya Birla Retail Ltd, which runs More, a supermarket and hypermarket format retail chain.

According to financial data provider Bloomberg, India's wholesale food prices rose at their fastest pace in 11 years to 19.05% for the week ended 28 November from the previous year, following a 17.47% gain in the previous week. The increase in food costs is largely on account of lower farm output following a weak monsoon. Key items have surged in October from a year ago—onions are 45% costlier, potatoes have risen 97.73%, pulses by 23%, food grains by 13% and sugar by over 45%. Staples, fruit and vegetables account for as much as 35% of the average bill at a supermarket and at least 20% in a hypermarket, says D.V. Ramkumar, vice-president (food and agri) at Spencers Retail Ltd, a division of RPG Enterprise. Across five suburban Mumbai organized retails stores—HyperCITY, D-Mart, Spencers, Star Bazaar and Food Bazaar—prices for vegetables are not uniform but those for staples are very competitive. Additionally, retailers are beginning to stock more private labels over national brands, and the results are showing.

The sale of private labels have grown by over 16% to 18% over a year ago as people are buying cheaper products and private labels are at least 10% to 20% cheaper than the national brands," says Ashutosh Chakradeo, business head, food and grocery, HyperCITY Retail India Ltd., a part of K. Raheja Corp., which also owns Shopper's Stop Ltd. However, he concedes that buyers are shopping smaller quantities of vegetables and cutting back on fruit consumption. At Spencers, which has 230 super market stores and 25 hypermarket retail stores nationwide, the average bill value has increased 5-6% month-on-month for the last three months even as volumes declined by close to 3%," Ram Kumar of Spencers told Mint.

While some of this is inflationary, Ramkumar says that some real growth is also happening as the price of oil has dropped in the last five months even as staples and vegetables increased. "Oil accounts for 35-38% (of the) value of consumers' staples bill," he said.Consumers are also beginning to take notice of price discrepancies and value offerings. Nisha Manwani, a homemaker whose husband is an investment consultant, shops at D-Mart for groceries and buys vegetables at Spencers even though she stays closer to HyperCITY. "The savings is not much at Rs. 30-Rs. 40. But on a monthly bill of Rs. 3,000-Rs. 4,000 it is 10%." While HyperCITY and Spencers are in adjoining buildings, D-Mart is about 2 km away.

Retailers have become more aggressive in benchmarking the key value items (KVIs) like potatoes, onions, tomatoes, oil, sugar as these are tracked by housewives on a daily basis," says Debashish Mukherjee, principal, A.T. Kearney India. We can see an amplified level of communications surrounding these KVIs in the last few months," "With growing food inflation, our communication is focused on offering our consumers better value for the basic commodities," says Damodar Mall, chief executive officer (incubation and innovation), Future Group, which owns the Big Bazaar and Food Bazaar chains. "The consumer franchise is growing as people from the lower-income bracket are aspiring to move up the value chain and frequenting the modern retail format as they look for cereals."Meanwhile, consumers are increasing the basket of items they track as part of their ongoing search for the best deal.

I no longer experiment with my shopping basket and just buy the basics after looking at value savings across retailers," says Shilpa Devra, a resident of the Mumbai suburb of Goregaon who has started buying smaller quantities and has increased her visits to organized retail stores to up to four times a month in search of bargains.

ORGANIZED RETAIL CONFRONTS THE CHALLENGES OF LOCAL MARKETS

Unused to modern, organized retailing, the Indian consumer is still figuring out how to extract value – beyond lower prices – from the stores, supermarkets and shopping chains that are popping up everywhere. Meanwhile, retailers face other challenges: Indian consumers shop frequently and are used to traveling short distances to their stores; brand penetration is lower compared to developed-country markets; and interstate goods movement is fraught with taxes, delays and other inefficiencies.

All that means warehouses have to be closer to stores, which in turn have to be closer to their so-called catchment" areas, where the new retailers have to build store-specific customer loyalties. Training large numbers of employees in such virgin territory, and promoting retailing as a respectable and attractive career path, are other challenges, according to senior executives from Best Buy, Staples and Aditya Birla Retail, who participated on a panel titled, New Paradigms in Indian Retail, at a recent Harvard Business School conference.

Indian consumers themselves don't know what they want, said Sumant Sinha, CEO of Aditya Birla Retail, which has rolled out 500 stores across India in the past year and is part of the $24 billion Aditya Birla Group. They are evolving, he said, especially those in urban settings. You put a hypermarket in front of them; they've never seen it before. So there's no way they can understand the concept. You really have to go with your gut in India and wait for the reaction.

The Aditya Birla Group began considering a foray into retailing after it was approached by Wal-Mart a couple of years ago, Sinha recalled. Those talks didn't progress because they were looking only for a front-end partner. We like to control our businesses. But the group found the numbers compelling. India is a trillion-dollar economy, of which retail accounts for about 40%, he noted. Of that, 40% to [nearly] 60% is spent on food and groceries, and of that, about 60% is rural and 40% is urban. The group recognized that "the food and grocery business was under penetrated from a retailing standpoint," and that drove its decision to enter the business. Within a year of launching operations, the company has 500 supermarkets, employs about 10,000 people and is hiring at the rate of a thousand employees each month, he added.

What struck Sinha right away was the fact that Indian consumers are extremely value conscious. For them, value is not just price and includes other connotations such as quality, convenience and trust. Most other Indian retailers are going after price to build customer loyalties, and are perhaps getting it wrong, he said. It's not as if they haven't been shopping before organized retailing arrived — they have been shopping for decades and decades at mom-and-pop stores. It's about shifting these consumers from their existing shopping behavior into a different shopping behavior; they are also testing the new format. At this point of time, you have to just go with what you think will work. It's very early days to figure out how that will play out.

Lukas Ruecker, who oversees emerging market business as vice president at Staples, the office products retail chain, agreed with Sinha's assessment. "The market is changing so rapidly in India that we haven't even invested in consumer research, he said. This is going to be an ongoing experiment. The Indian consumer doesn't know what he wants; you have to shape his opinion.

Describing Staples as a cautious strategist that would rarely be caught being first at anything, Ruecker noted its first international foray was into China in 2004, followed by Brazil, Argentina, Taiwan and then India about six months ago. He expects Staples to open 11 stores in India by the end of this month. Staples' Indian business is made up of both retail stores and institutional customers it serves with the only pan-Indian delivery system for office products, he said. It partners with the Mumbai-based Future Group, a fast-growing diversified business house with prominent organized retail banners including Pantaloon and Big Bazaar.

When you enter emerging markets like India or China, you really learn only through experimentation, said Kal Patel, executive vice president of emerging business at Best Buy. He recalled that when he worked on Best Buy's China launch a few years ago, we had to throw away consumer research. The assumptions you have from a top-down marketing standpoint don't stand up in these markets. In developed markets, "you can sit down in a corporate office with a whole bunch of analytics and make predictions for next year," Patel said. In [China], we're asking our store managers and store employees to tell us what they think they can grow if we give them more tools and the things they need. They are coming back with three or four times more optimism. That strategy is ideal for Best Buy in its new markets, according to Patel. "The general principle is: The more local you go, the more front-end you go and ask the people who are serving [customers] whether in rural markets in India or in big cities somewhere else the better is your understanding of emerging trends, he said. Fundamentally, we engineer our company based on the demand we get from the very, very different micro segments.

HALF-EMPTY STORES

Harvard professor of business logistics Ananth Raman, who moderated the discussion, asked Patel and the other panelists about their experiments with the design of their stores in India and how that might be different from those in their home countries. Best Buy has yet to enter the Indian market, but Patel recalled a conversation with his company's store designer who was tapped a while ago by an aspiring Indian retail group to replicate Best Buy stores in

India. He refused to do the work, because using an American design in an Indian context made no sense to him. The interesting thing is that Indians in India are bringing American assumptions into India, Patel said.

Ruecker said Staples did not copy its conventional store design for the Indian market, but created a wholly new one to suit local tastes. We used our technology platform and ideas from our experiences in Portugal, Germany, the Netherlands and the U.S., and then modified them for India. He noted that Staples in India has its own logo, different color schemes and other variations to make them a little more Indian. The response has been mixed. Some people in Bangalore said it doesn't feel like the U.S. Staples; some others said it was fantastic and they liked it.

Unlike in western markets, the Indian store cannot be as big as 15,000 to 20,000 sq. ft., said Sinha, explaining that the markets there don't have as many brands to be stocked. That, unfortunately, is the reality of India – you just do not have enough branded products out there. If you put up a big store, it's probably going to be half empty. You have to think of a smaller-size store. Smaller stores also fit in well with the average Indian family's shopping experience.

For many, many decades, Indian housewives have been used to buying things almost on a daily basis. You have vendors who come in push carts to your house," Sinha added. Such observations lead to other questions, he noted. You would assume that this behavior is borne out of a desire to buy fresh food and cook it every day. Or is it because the supply chain for fruits and vegetables is so poor that the food would become spoiled the next day? Other reasons for buying food on a daily basis may include a lack of storage space or ways to keep food fresh for extended periods of time. They don't have big houses or big refrigerators. And even if they have refrigerators, very often the power goes off. Since the daily shopping habit isn't likely to go away soon, Sinha predicted that stores that are far away but have large catchment areas may not work; they have to be closer to customers. Most Indian housewives don't have easy access to transportation, so going long distances to shop doesn't work for them, he said. A supermarket in the Indian context is going to be a lot closer to customers and will have a lot more footfalls on a daily basis with much smaller basket, or ticket sizes.

BUILDING SUPPLY CHAINS FROM SCRATCH

Raman wondered if the supply chain in India is ready for organized retailing, or if a wholly new infrastructure has to be developed. Ruecker said for Staples, it was a major challenge in both India and China to move products from its warehouses to stores. The overall logistics is so much more difficult from a port in Chennai or a port in Shanghai to stores, he said. Yet, unfathomable as it was, the system worked. You rely on the fact that Indians have always figured out a way to do it. Stuff gets into the stores, it gets there in time, and all our stores are well stocked." But he is not taking too many chances. We are willing to live with the faith, but we need modern warehousing (in India).

According to Sinha, the logistics and supply chain infrastructure has to be built from scratch; it's really about creating a new industry. He said his company started by outsourcing the logistics and warehouse management from third party companies, but eventually decided to bring those functions in-house. It turned out that the main problem the third party logistics suppliers faced was not a lack of expertise, but difficulties getting trained people to track and ship orders, which resulted in lost sales and excess inventories, he said. Aditya Birla Retail decided to take on the training responsibilities. Sinha added that it takes about three months to get new hires up to speed with the requirements.

Sinha said Indian municipal taxes (called *octroi*) and other laws governing interstate movement of goods also make things difficult. You can't set up five large warehouses across the country to serve the market," he said. "You have to set up [very small] warehouses wherever you open each store. And so the profitability of each cluster becomes a function of [that arrangement]. The Indian supply chain infrastructure has a ways to go before it becomes efficient. Unless some laws change in India, it is not going to happen in a hurry.

What's more, many Indian companies, including arms of multinationals, are used to inefficiencies in delivering goods, according to Sinha. "In India you had companies always delivering half of what you asked for, and you don't know which half is delivered, he said. They are not used to organized retailing. They recognize the value and benefits of modern retailing, but it's hard to get the discipline that is required."

The reason we are in China and not in India is because of supply chain, said Patel of Best Buy. In preparation for its plans to enter India, Best Buy brought together consumer electronics suppliers and posed them the problem of generating efficiencies. "We told them to give us higher gross margins," he said, adding that Best Buy had bargaining power because it went about its sourcing globally. All the suppliers at the meeting recognized that it was in everybody's interest to bring in efficiencies.

At the consumer level, Patel said he is acutely aware of how customer loyalties work in the Indian market. You have mom-and-pop [stores] that have relationships with consumers — they have a relationship with the family and the community. What we would do differently is we want to leverage that. However, at the back end you have so much inefficiency.Best Buy has a retail academy in China in partnership with a couple of universities, and that's how we are going into India and that's how you create self esteem for a retail job in that country," said Patel, citing Best Buy's 11,000-strong "geek squads" in the U.S. as one of his models. "Essentially, geek squads are about bringing high self-esteem to computer repair," he said. "We are going to use that [model] in India in sales and service.

Factors that contribute to success of Organized Grocery Retailing:

1. Awareness of customers.
2. Location of the stores.
3. Value added services (carryout services, fax ordering by customers , license department, home delivery, internet ordering by customers, customer rest areas, in store banking).
4. Promotions (Every day low pricing, environmentally- friendly products, newspaper ads with coupons private label program-own brand, frequent shopper/Loyalty card program).

In most households grocery shopping is done by women and mostly their choice of store changes according to their education level. It is seen in India that women who have a considerable good education level have different thought process than a women who is not so well educated. The choice of a store is dependent on a number of members who contribute to the household income. Most of the retailers make sure that they are present nearer to the residential areas. Organized grocery retailers have made use of the technologies like GIS (Geographical Information Systems) in deciding their location. Apart from having outlets in some of the residential areas they also take care to be in the locations from where grocery could be picked up while coming back from the office. There are the some retailers who have taken the strategic alliance route and have opened up small outlets in the premise of large organization. This gives them an opportunity to tap all the employees of the company it can therefore be said that the distance and time consumed in the shopping activity influences the consumer choice of where to buy.

CONCLUSION

The organized grocery retailer is the preferred kind of store by consumers, even though the consumers buy in several establishments and not exclusively in the hypermarket, which indicates that there is no single loyalty. While in the organized retail outlet the consumers buy essentially convenience goods with low level of risks in traditional retail, they buy essentially products of more involvement, which requires a more complex buying behavior. Customers are always hungry for modern ways of shopping. Indian retail sector is growing fast and its employment potential could not be neglected. Organized retailing will lead to a greater impact on macro economy by way of accelerating productivity growth, increased export competitiveness and higher job opportunities. The results also show that consumers evoke price and convenience for not buying certain goods in traditional retail, which reveals an attempt to optimize their time and money.

References

See G. M. Lebhar (1983), *Chain Stores in America, 1859–1959* (3d ed. 1963); R. Hendrickson *The Grand Emporiums* (1979); D. Bellenger and J. I. Goldstucker, *Retailing Basics.*

The Columbia Encyclopedia, Sixth Edition Copyright © 2004, Columbia University Press. Licensed from Lernout & Hauspie Speech Products N.V. All rights reserve.

Philip Kotler, (1997), "Principles of Marketing" Syndicate Binders, B-167, Okhla Industrial Area, Phase I, New Delhi, p. 4.

Kotler, Philip. Marketing Management, Millenium Edition, Prentice Hall of India, New Delhi

C.B. Gupta & N. Rajan Nair (2008), "Marketing Management" Sultan Chand & Sons, New Delhi, p. 18.2.

www.marketinginnovation.net

EMERGING TRENDS IN SOCIAL ENTREPRENEURSHIP

PRADEEP SHUKLA[*#] & *AMIT PANDEY*[*]

Social Entrepreneurship is an extension of Corporate Social Responsibility (CSR). Social Entrepreneurship is as old as CSR. Social entrepreneurs drive social innovation and transformation in various fields including education, health, environment and enterprise development.

They pursue poverty alleviation goals with entrepreneurial zeal, business methods and the courage to innovate and overcome traditional practices. A social entrepreneur, similar to a business entrepreneur, builds strong and sustainable organizations, which are either set up as not-for-profits or companies.

A SOCIAL ENTREPRENEUR IS A LEADER OR PRAGMATIC VISIONARY WHO

- Achieves large scale, systemic and sustainable social change through a new invention, a different approach, a more rigorous application of known technologies or strategies, or a combination of these. Focuses first and foremost on the social and/or ecological value creation and tries to optimize the financial value creation.
- Innovates by finding a new product, a new service, or a new approach to a social problem. Continuously refines and adapts approach in response to feedback.
- Combines the characteristics represented by Richard Branson and Mother Teresa.

The Schwab Foundation employs the following criteria when looking for leading social entrepreneurs: Innovation, Sustainability, Reach and social impact.

SOCIAL ENTREPRENEURS SHARE SOME COMMON TRAITS INCLUDING

- An unwavering belief in the innate capacity of all people to contribute meaningfully to economic and social development A driving passion to make that happen.

* Faculty, Lord Krishna College of Management, Ghaziabad (*pradeepks35@redifmail.com*)

- A practical but innovative stance to a social problem, often using market principles and forces, coupled with dogged determination that allows them to break away from constraints imposed by ideology or field of discipline, and pushes them to take risks that others wouldn't dare.
- A zeal to measure and monitor their impact. Entrepreneurs have high standards, particularly in relation to their own organization's efforts and in response to the communities with which they engage. Data, both quantitative and qualitative, are their key tools, guiding continuous feedback and improvement.
- A healthy impatience. Social entrepreneur cannot sit back and wait for change to happen – they are the change drivers.

SOCIAL ENTREPRENEURSHIP

Social entrepreneurship is about applying practical, innovative and sustainable approaches to benefit society in general, with an emphasis on those who are marginalized and poor.

Social entrepreneurship is the work of a social entrepreneur. A social entrepreneur is someone who recognizes a social problem and uses entrepreneurial principles to organize, create, and manage a venture to make social change. Whereas a business entrepreneur typically measures performance in profit and return, a social entrepreneur assesses success in terms of the impact s/he has on society. While social entrepreneurs often work through nonprofits and citizen groups, many work in the private and governmental sectors.

The main aim of a social entrepreneurship as well as social enterprise is to further social and environmental goals. Although social entrepreneurs are often non-profits, this need not be incompatible with making a profit. Social enterprises are for 'more-than-profit,' using blended value business models that combine a revenue-generating business with a social-value-generating structure or component

In 2009, Business Week publishing a review of American's 25 most promising social entrepreneurs, defined as "enterprising individuals who apply business practices to solving societal problems.

WHY "SOCIAL" ENTREPRENEUR?

Just as entrepreneurs change the face of business, social entrepreneurs act as the change agents for society, seizing opportunities others miss and improving systems, inventing new approaches, and creating solutions to change society for the better. While a business entrepreneur might create entirely new industries, a social entrepreneur comes up with new solutions to social problems and then implements them on a large scale.

India is a key country to look for leading social entrepreneurs, says Klaus Schwab, executive chairman and founder of the World Economic Forum, as his Schwab Foundation prepares to shortlist a winner for the Indian Social Entrepreneur Award for the second year.

"India has some of the most advanced and innovative social entrepreneurs. We believe and already see that many of the models developed in India, for instance rainwater harvesting for schools pioneered by Barefoot College, are exported around the world. India is therefore a key country to look for leading social entrepreneurs," Klaus Schwab told IANS in an exclusive interview.

That's what social entrepreneurship is about creating business models revolving around low-cost products and services to resolve social inequities. And the realization that social progress and profit aren't mutually exclusive has led to many social ventures taking root in India as well.

Examples of successful social projects like Amul or SEWA were few and far between. However, with the slowdown taking the shine off urban, higher-income target markets, organizations focusing on 'bottom of the pyramid' audiences have become a reality. But the days of easy funding are over. Given the employment squeeze, it would be natural for aspiring social entrepreneurs to stick to their secure jobs instead. Surprisingly, they continue to launch social enterprises with a vengeance.

In May 2008, 27-year old Rajnish Sinha and his IIM-Kozhikode batchmate Siva Cotipalli started Bangalore-based DhanaX. A fascination with microfinance and the idea of clubbing it with person to person (P2P) lending led them to quit their jobs to launch DhanaX, a platform where people contribute small amounts online as loans. NGOs take up the task of disbursing these loans to needy communities in their areas of operation.

Interest is charged at 24%, of which Dhanax keeps approximately 6%. This model has worked in other countries as well. So far, DhanaX has helped its four partner NGOs acquire loans of Rs. 20 lakh. While yet to recover their initial investment of Rs. 25 lakh, Sinha is confident of success. "In future, we may partner with wealth management companies or treasury departments of large corporations to keep the pipeline running," he says.

Richa Pandey, a marketing MBA, was a media sales professional in New Delhi for eight years. But her calling was rural India, partly because of her roots—her grandfather was a farmer in Uttar Pradesh. "The retail and BPO sectors were creating job opportunities in a big way. I zeroed in on vocational training for rural youth in these areas," Pandey recalls.In October 2007, she approached the Rural Technology Business Incubator (RTBI) at IIT-Madras with a business plan outline. "The RTBI platform helped add magnitude to my plan," Pandey says, adding, "Prof Ashok Jhunjhunwala assisted me in launching a pilot programme in three districts of Tamil Nadu under the banner of eJeevika." Around the same time, she got a lucrative offer to head the marketing division of a large media firm. Pandey turned it down and continued focusing on designing course content and online training programmes in three areas: retail sales, data entry and security services.

eJeevika subjects candidates to psychometric tests to determine where they'd fit in best and trains them accordingly. But Pandey's chosen path hasn't been easy. She currently doesn't take home a salary, preferring instead to plough everything back into the business.

In the past year, eJeevika trained 160 people, is on the verge of signing up four BPOs as partners and is growing both in terms of scale and size, aiming to train 1,500 people by March-end. Experts like Kallol Borah, CEO, Headstart Foundation, feel that social-focus startups will continue to thrive in India. "Bringing low-cost services such as banking, healthcare, finance, etc. to underprivileged sections of society is definitely a big opportunity as well as a necessity. Rural, small-town and lower-income consumers constitute a large market waiting to be tapped, but it is necessary for social entrepreneurs to get past language, literacy and geographical barriers."

HISTORICAL EXAMPLES OF LEADING SOCIAL ENTREPRENEURS

- *Susan B. Anthony (U.S.):* Fought for Women's Rights in the United States, including the right to control property and helped spearhead adoption of the 19th amendment.
- *Vinoba Bhave (India):* Founder and leader of the Land Gift Movement, he caused the redistribution of more than 7,000,000 acres of land to aid India's untouchables and landless.
- *Dr. Maria Montessori (Italy):* Developed the Montessori approach to early childhood education.
- *Florence Nightingale (U.K.):* Founder of modern nursing, she established the first school for nurses and fought to improve hospital conditions.
- *Margaret Sanger (U.S.):* Founder of the Planned Parenthood Federation of America, she led the movement for family planning efforts around the world.
- *John Muir (U.S.):* Naturalist and conservationist, he established the National Park System and helped found The Sierra Club.4 www. Ashoka .org

PRESENT DAY LEADING SOCIAL ENTREPRENEURS

- *Ibrahim Abouleish (Egypt)* - Founder of SEKEM, a biodynamic agricltural corporation, alternative medicine, and educational center located outside of Cairo.
- *Ela Bhatt (India)* - Founder of the Self-Employed Women's Association (SEWA) and the SEWA Cooperative Bank in Gujarat.
- *Nicholas Chan (Singapore)* - Co-Founder of Project:Senso Ltd, the Pledge a Book movement and active advocate for Asian entrepreneurs in incorporating volunteerism and social enterprise into their lives and businesses.

- *Bill Drayton (U.S.)* - Founded Ashoka, Youth Venture, and Get America Working!
- *Marian Wright Edelman (U.S.)* - Founder and president of the Children's Defense Fund (CDF) and advocate for disadvantaged Americans and children.
- *Dr.: Abraham M. George (India)* - Founder of The George Foundation (TGF).
- *Alan Khazei (U.S.)* - Co-Founder of City Year, a leading national service program.
- *Dr. Verghese Kurien (India)* - Founder of the AMUL Dairy Project.
- *Sri Sri Ravi Shankar (India)* - Founded Art of Living Foundation and International Association for Human Values.
- *Muhammad Yunus (Bangladesh)* - Founder of micro credit and the Grameen Bank. He was awarded the 2006 Nobel Peace Prize.

MAJOR MBA RECRUITERS

- *Skoll Foundation:* EBay founder Jeff Skoll chairs the foundation, which awards more than $40 million in grants to social entrepreneurs each year.
- *Acumen Fund:* The investment firm backs socially responsible ventures that find new ways to provide poor communities in Kenya, India, and other countries with healthcare, housing, energy, and water.
- *Ashoka: Founded in 1980,* Ashoka gives up-and-coming social entrepreneurs a living stipend for three years as they launch ventures to address societal needs in developing countries.
- *Teach for America:* The teachers come out of undergrad programs, but TFA values innovative MBA students who can help the organization recruit and retain top talent for the classroom.
- *Bridgespan and FSG Social Impact Advisors:* The leading consulting firms for nonprofit organizations.

GETTING THE SKILLS

Several of the country's top business schools, such as Yale, Duke, Harvard, and Stanford, offer specific programs to prepare MBAs who want to combine traditional business skills with innovative approaches to solving social problems. And unlike the traditional nonprofit curriculum, which typically sticks to the fundamentals of fundraising and grant writing, these programs combine the finance and management training of an MBA with electives that cover everything from how to get venture capital and invest in emerging markets to innovating in healthcare and developing sustainable energy sources.

Regardless of whether social entrepreneurs want to work for a nonprofit or for-profit, they need a "deep understanding of management principles as they apply across sectors and the globe," says Tony Sheldon, executive director of the Program on Social Enterprise at Yale's School of Management.

In addition, the current economy demands MBAs with strong backgrounds in results measurement, performance management, financial models, capital markets, strategic planning, and savvy resource allocation. Experience interning or volunteering in a specific social sector doesn't hurt either.

"The skill set is a lot different when you're trying to sell something and serve a social purpose at the same time," says Suzanne Steffens, an analyst for Community Wealth Ventures, a consulting firm that teaches nonprofit organizations how to create for-profit businesses to fund core missions. Social entrepreneurs typically operate with less capital, says Steffens, so they must be flexible enough to shift resources, learn from mistakes, and even alter entire business plans in a matter of months in order to remain operational.

THE JOB OUTLOOK FOR NEW MBAS

According to Matt Nash, managing director of Duke's Center for the Advancement of Social Entrepreneurship, MBAs tend to follow one of three basic paths: They launch a new venture with a social cause, support an existing venture in strategy or operations roles, or work in consulting to help other nonprofits and for-profits balance their financial and social goals. Despite the recession, many of the large, existing "social enterprise" firms are poised to move back into a growth pattern, says James Weinberg, founder and CEO of Common Good Careers, a hiring firm for social entrepreneurs.

CONCLUSION

Long before the economy tanked, MBAs were in hot pursuit of alternative career tracks - instead of running investment firms, many have aspired to invest themselves in business with a social cause – from nonprofit organizations to overseas startups in developing countries. Top-tier schools like Duke's Fuqua School of Business and Yale's School of Management responded by creating programs to prepare so-called "social entrepreneurs." The down economy, not surprisingly, is driving more MBA students down socially responsible business paths. And while it's not yet clear how much the recession will impact businesses with financial and social goals, social entrepreneurs have what it takes to adapt – even in a strong economy, they learn how to do more with less.

References

Social Sector Entrepreneurship and Innovation by Warren Tranquada; John Baker & John Pepin (Paperback - Jan. 25, 2007)

Social Entrepreneurship's Reference Guide by Warren Tranquada and John Pepin (Paperback - Mar. 2004)

O'Hara, P. & O'Shaughnessy, M. (2004) "Work Integration Social Enterprises in Ireland", *EMES*

Working Papers, no. 04/03.

Vidal, I. & Claver, N. (2004), "Work Integration Social Enterprises in Spain", *EMES Working Papers,* No. 04/05.

Perista, H. & Nogueira, S. (2004), "Work Integration Social Enterprises in Portugal", *EMES Working Papers,* No. 04/06.

Pättiniemi, P. (2004), "Work Integration Social Enterprises in Finland", *EMES Working Papers,* no. 04/07.

Hulgård, L. & Bisballe, T. (2004), "Work Integration Social Enterprises in Denmark", *EMES Working Papers,* no. 04/08.

A STUDY ON THE PROMOTION OF GLOBAL BRANDS IN SMALL TOWNS OF RURAL INDIA

M. Neelamalar[*] *& H. Arun Darwin*[**]

INTRODUCTION

Indian market is broadly divided into rural and urban. The "middle class" which has had the highest aspirations and growing disposable income so far, has been the target of marketers and advertisers. The Emerging Market consists of the population strata which was erstwhile poor, but is now steadily making rapid economic progress. The majority of this new target lives in the remote villages of rural areas and hence, the generalization of the term "rural". What is really being referred to here is the earlier ignored "poor". This segment is present in urban towns and large cities too, where they can easily be identified and reached through mass media. The challenge for marketers lies in reaching out to those that are in remote corners and villages of the Country, where mass media is either not present or ineffective. The term "Emerging Market" is used in the present study to avoid ambiguity.

Rural Market

The Census defined urban India as - "All the places that fall within the administrative limits of a municipal corporation, municipality, cantonment board etc. or have a population of at least 5,000 and have at least 75 per cent male working population in outside the primary sector and have a population density of at least 400 per square kilometer. Rural India, on the other hand, comprises all places that are not urban" *(The Census of India, 1991)* Over 70%, (roughly 670 million) of India's teeming masses live in rural areas. Of these, some more than two million live in almost complete media darkness, without access to TV, radio, and beyond the reach of newspapers and magazines. Widespread illiteracy allied with the multitude of languages and dialects puts most of these people beyond the reach of conventional media planning.

* Lecturer, Department of Media Sciences, Anna University Chennai, (*e-mail: nmalar@yahoo.com*)

** Final year, M.Sc Electronic Media, Anna University Chennai.

Yet the villagers are increasingly gaining importance as consumers. A survey by India's National Centre for Applied Economics and Research revealed double-digit rural growth rates in a cross section of products ranging from scooters to confectionery between 1995 and 1999.

Size and Strength - Rural Market

The Indian rural market today accounts for only about Rs. 800 crore (53 per cent - FMCG sector, 59 per cent durables sale, 100 per cent agricultural products) of the total advertising expense, claiming 6.6 per cent of the total share. According to a study by Chennai-based Francis Kanoi Marketing Planning Services Pvt. Ltd., the rural market potential for FMCG is Rs. 65,000 crore, for durables Rs. 5,000 crore, for tractors and Agri-inputs Rs. 45,000 crore and two- and four-wheelers, Rs. 8,000 crore. In total, it is Rs. 1, 23,000 crore. This could be easily achieved if companies understood the New Consumer's buying behavior and communication needs.

Although marketing practitioners have written extensively about the potential of the Emerging Market, only a handful has launched fully fledged campaigns. Hindustan Lever Limited (HLL) is a pioneer with its successful projects like 'Project Shakti' and 'Operation Bharat'. The highlight of HLL's strategy has been to focus on penetrating the market down the line and focusing on price point and activities, which are in line with the brand itself. Amul is case of aggressive rural marketing. Some of the other corporates that are slowly making headway in this area are Coca Cola India, Colgate, Eveready Batteries, LG Electronics, Philips, BSNL, Life Insurance Corporation, Cavin Kare, Britannia and Hero Honda, TVS, Reliance, Hutch, Reliance, Airtel, ICICI and a few others (*Goutham, (2007)*.

Until some years ago, the rural market was being given a step-motherly treatment by many companies and advertising to rural consumers was usually a hit or miss effort. More often than not, the modus operandi was to take the short-cut route of pushing urban communication to the rural market by merely transliterating the communication content. Advertising that is rooted in urban sensitivities cannot touch the hearts and minds of the rural consumer. The greatest challenge for advertisers and marketers continues to be in finding the right mix that will have a pan-Indian rural appeal. The Emerging Market is growing at a far greater speed than its urban counterpart. "All the data provided by various research agencies like NCAER, Francis Kanoi etc show that rural markets are growing faster than urban markets in several product categories. The share of FMCG products in rural markets is 53 per cent and of durables, 59 per cent market share.

The New Consumer - Rural/Small Towns

The main challenge in the Emerging Market is the basic understanding of the New Consumer who is very different from the urban counterpart. Therefore, campaigns have to be tailor made for each product category and each of the regions where the campaign is to be executed. A thorough knowledge of the nuances of language, dialects and familiarity with prevailing customs in the specific region is essential.

Compared to the Indian urban society, which is turning into a consumerism society; the New Consumer will always remain driven by needs first and will therefore be cost conscious and thrifty in spending habits. The converging of the urban-rural divide will take a while for want of the mindset to change. It is driven by tradition, custom and values that are difficult to shed. Only concepts that are innovative in content and design, media and interactivity will cut ice. Specialized knowledge about the region will be an asset, especially in outdoor media like wall painting and folk art. The sheer size and spread, and its variety of culture, language, polity, religion and customs call for in depth market study.

The New Consumer buys small packs, as they are perceived as value for money. Often this is due to the small amounts of savings at a given time. There is brand loyalty, where a consumer buys a brand out of habit and not really by choice. Disposable income is not low. Per capita annual income in rural areas is Rs. 9,481; in urban, Rs. 19,407 *(Human Development Report 2004-2005)*. But in villages, hardly anybody pays home rent or spends money on drinking water or on primary health care. Buying is a collective decision and the influencer, decision-maker, buyer are often different. So campaigns will have to appeal at different levels.

Buying Process

In villages, because of the lack of mobility among women and their having very little contact with the market, it is the men who make the purchase decisions. Further, while an urban individual is free to take independent purchase decisions, in a village, because of the strong social structures, including caste considerations, and due to low literacy levels community decision- making is quite common.

Companies that took the trouble to understand these needs and peculiarities have tasted success. For instance, some packaged consumer goods companies consider even the remotest regions and tiniest villages as potential targets, and aim to maximize penetration in the rural economy's scattered 3.5 million retail outlets. For example, Eveready, the market leader in batteries and flashlights, operates a fleet of over a 1,000 company-owned vans and has over 4,000 distributors to directly service 600,000 retail outlets; Hindustan Lever Limited (HLL) has pioneered new forms of rural distribution. Its Shakti campaign recruits female members of village self help groups and trains them to become direct to home distributors of HLL products. (*Business World Marketing White Book, 2008)*

Similarly, LG has tasted huge success through its low cost, no-frills, regional-menu driven Sampoorna TV and other relevant offerings in the rural market. In 2003, 35% of LG's Rs. 4,500-crore projected turnover came from rural India which it plans to double to 70% on the Rs 7,000-crore projected turnover for 2004.

Towns and Cities

Based on the latest Indian National Census in 2001, India comprises 5,161 cities and towns in 35 states and union territories and almost 600 districts across the country. MGI has grouped these towns into four tiers, primarily on the basis of population. Over the past two decades tier 1 city such as the national capital New Delhi, commercial capital Mumbai, and IT hubs such as Bangalore and Hyderabad have expanded to become mush larger markets than other populous cities. Most multinational operate only in the eight tier 1 cities, and many have a long way to go before they will have fully penetrated these rapidly growing markets. Among tier 1 cities Delhi and Mumbai are in a class apart in terms of market size. These two mega-metropolises have experienced rapid growth in their suburbs as well as mushrooming satellite towns, many of which are becoming significant markets of their own.

Alternative Media

The characteristics of the Emerging Market have necessitated the development of custom-designed media vehicles. Even mass media is all set to morph into a new, localized form. This process of change is beginning at the grassroots level, where the merchandisers are using the local reach of cable TV to sell their wares in small towns and overgrown villages that are today connected by the television. Catalyzing this change will be the Optic Fiber Cable (OFC) Network that will soon connect the remotest corners of the country. Emerging Markets demand a new genre of communication.

The alternative media, with the business houses keen on building marketing links to the rural world, on the one hand, and the telecommunications explosion allowing cable TV, to reach the remotest corners of the country, is ready to take off. This does not only refer to the "mobile vans", but also newer and more personalized forms of communication.

Selling in the Emerging Market is no longer restricted to using mobile vans with television sets screening Hindi film songs interspersed with messages about a product. New avenues include games (with the product being given as a prize), door-to-door sales, folk dances, wall paintings, putting up shoe racks in temples, tiles in village wells, scarecrows in fields and occasionally painting the horns of cows!

Objectives of the Study

1. To explain the various marketing tools and advertising messages, being used by global brands in small towns.
2. To explain the unconventional channels and methods adopted by the global brands in reaching small towns.

3. To find the preference and usage level of global brands among small town people.
4. To find out the future of global brands in small towns.

REVIEW OF LITERATURE

Mooij (2002) states that in the world of growing media opportunities, distinctive advertising is needed that stands out from the clutter. It is paradoxical that advertisers prefer to develop what is universal instead of what should appeal to specific people in particular. In the age of increasing communication over load, people's selective perception mechanism will work harder.

McCracken (1988) points out that advertising works as a method of meaning transfer by bringing the consumer good and a representation of the culturally constituted world together within the frame of a particular advertisement. A creative director decides how the culturally constituted world is portrayed in an advertisement and the decision makers at the company decide if that view reflects their cultural framework. This begs the question of what advertising represents –the culture of the consumer or the culture of the company.

Mooij (1994) points out that a global brand is one which shares the same strategic principles, positioning and marketing in every market throughout the world, although the marketing mix can vary. It carries the same brand name or logo. Its values are identical in all countries; it has a substantial market share in all countries and comparable brand loyalty. The distribution channels are similar.

Richard, (2006). Worldwide marketers face three distinctive challenges in executing their advertising campaigns. The first is a creative challenge that derives from differences in experience and meaning among cultures. Even the pictures featured in an ad maybe translated differently from one county to the next. The second is a media challenge. Media availability, media coverage, and media cost vary dramatically around the world, adding a second complication to international advertising. Finally, the amount and nature of advertising regulation vary dramatically from country to country and may force a complete reformulation of an advertising campaign.

Yadagiri and Sreenivas (2009) in their research work tilled "Brand strategies for globalization" states that today's brand marketers are facing cut-throat competition in the domestic market. Rising competition on the domestic front forces a company to go for a corporate brand makeover. But a mere change in logo wil not serves the purpose; it requires an overall corporate identity makeover to represent a fundamental shift in the way the companies operate. It is very obvious that brand management at the global level becomes very crucial and important. At a global level, starting from Brand name to Brand relationship, all the strategies should be aligned according to the culture and environment of the concerned country.

Blinn (1999) in his article "Expanding the boundaries in a global context" states that a global brand has a clear and consistent identity with consumers across geographies. It is positioned the same from one country to another; it has essentially the same formula; it delivers the same benefit and is presented consistently to the consumer through consistent advertising and packaging.

Vasudeva (2004) states that marketing can be conceived as an integral part of two processes, technical and social. So far as the technical aspect is concerned, international and domestic marketing are identical. Technical aspect includes non-human factors in marketing such as products, price, band, packaging, warehousing costs, etc. and the basic principles regarding these variables have universal applicability. The social aspect, on the other hand, is unique in any given stratum as it involves human elements, namely, the behavioral pattern of the consumers and the characteristics of the society such as customs, attitudes, values, etc. thus, international marketing is identical to domestic marketing as far as technical aspect is concerned but when it is visualized as a social process, if differs from domestic marketing.

Banerjee (1994) opines that, for most global brands, the product mix will vary to meet local consumer needs and competitive requirements. For example, both coca cola and Pepsi-Cola increased the sweetness of their drink in the Middle East, where consumers prefer a sweeter drink. The issue is not exact uniformity, but rather whether it is essentially the same product that is offered. Other elements of the marketing mix, such as price, promotion, appeal, media, distribution channels and tactics, may also vary.

Moriarty and Duncan (1990) points out that global-versus-local debate is really pointless, because, in reality, the issue is not one of whether an ad campaign for a brand can be completely globalized, by rather of the extent or degree to which a global brands' campaign can be standardized across the world. According to Sandra Moriarty and Thomas Duncan, such advertising standardization can vary on a continuum, if one breaks up an ad into its message strategy and tactical execution components. At one extreme, an advertiser could totally standardize both the advertising message strategy and the tactical message executions. Next on the continuum would be a standardized strategy with translated executions, followed by standardized strategy with modified executions, to totally localized strategy and executions on the other extreme.

Colyer (2006) in his article titled "India a hot brand climate" states that, the market has expanded many-fold in the past few years (than) it ever did during the decades before," says Burges Dandiwala of Brand Catalyst, a brand agency based in Mumbai. "With this has come an inflow of foreign brands that are competing with the traditional, long-established Indian products. Before there was essentially a monopoly: one brand of soap for the low end, one brand for the high end, for example. People now find it difficult—there's a choice for everything. People are just starting to realize the importance of branding."

Karwal (2008) Most marketers confuse the smaller markets as rural markets. It's true that many rural consumers come to these small towns or village melas to buy, but the most successful are those brads which reach out to them. There are brands in the rural market, which may be operating only in one region but still are bigger that most urban brands because they not only sell but provide service and listen to their village customers, the expansion o the word rural should be 'real unexplored rampant adventurous land'.

Razzouk (1991) in his research article titled "Conceptualization of India's emerging rural consuming system" states that while the literature dealing with marketing and development process is extensive and growing, there is very little research attention paid to the rural sectors of developing countries. However, major consumption system changes are taking place in rural sectors of many of the developing countries which in turn may be significant for marketers in these countries. In this paper it is attempted to conceptualize the emerging rural consumption system in the second most populous country, India. The critical factors shaping the emerging rural consuming system were identified. The marketing implications of these emerging trends were identified and discussed.

Kicha (2007) in his article titled "Building brands in rural India" states that, In a market where life has revolved around deep rooted community values, joint families, and social customs and taboos (women, for example, are not allowed to wear trousers), marketers realize that the traditional routes of market entry and brand building employed in urban India are often not feasible. As Adi Godrej, Chairman of the Godrej Group, says, "The challenge [for brands] is to understand the [psyche] of the rural consumer, create better distribution, and [appreciate] the heterogeneity."

METHODOLOGY

Methodology is defined as "the analysis of the principle of methods, rules, and postulated employed by a discipline" or "a particular procedure or set of procedures". Methodology refers to more than a simple set of methods; rather it refers to the rationale and the philosophical assumption that underlies a particular study.

Research Design

Research Design is defined as "the plan used to guide the researcher in choosing the methods and procedures for collecting, analyzing and interpreting data". In this research, descriptive design is used. Survey method is used for the purpose of this research.

Tools of Data Collection

Major tools used for collecting data in this study are questionnaire for the purpose of survey, case studies from Secondary sources and In-depth Interviews from experts.

Sampling

Purposive Sampling method is adopted in this research. Selected samples are selected from the age group of above 25 among small town people. Survey has been done in the region of Chengalpattu to Thindivanam across various age groups which include both genders.

ANALYSIS AND INTERPRETATIONS

Presentation and Interpretation of Data

The results given below reveal the key findings of the survey conducted among the small town people in rural areas.

Medium in which Time Spent more

Almost 80% of them spend their time on television, followed by news paper/ Magazine which accounts for 11% and remaining in radio and stage shows. Time spend on Cinema and Internet is very less.

Table 1
Medium in which Time Spent more

Time spends more	*Percentage of Respondents (n=150)*
Television	80
Radio	4
News paper/Magazine	11
Puppetry/stage/folk shows	2
Internet	1
Cinema	2
Total	100

Though small towns in rural areas have access to most of the medium still, time spent on television is huge compared to any other medium. With the increasing literacy rate in small towns and villages news paper readership is expected to increase in near future. Since the traditional medium like radio which has very less listenership may increase if the frequency of private FM radio channels has been extended to rural towns. Time spend on internet and cinema is very minimum compared to any other medium

Place of Purchasing Groceries and Provisions

41% of the people in small towns prefer to buy in retail shop followed by 36% in whole sale shop. 14% of them purchase their products in Bazaar/Mela's and 7% of them buy their groceries in super markets/branded shops.

Retail shops in nearby homes are the place where majority of the people prefer to purchase their groceries and provisions items for their homes. Most

Table 2
Place of Purchasing Groceries and Provisions

Place of purchasing groceries and provisions	*Percentage of Respondents (n=150)*
Retail shop in your area	41
Super markets/Branded retail shops	7
Bazaar/Mela's	14
Whole sale shop	36
others	2
Total	100

of the important household products are purchased in whole sale shop on a monthly basis followed by the retail shops. Though the bazaar's and melas are famous in small towns but, the percentage of people purchasing is less compared to any other place. The concept of branded super markets has not penetrated well as compared to retail and whole sale shop in small towns.

Amount Spent for Monthly Provisions (Including Vegetables)

45% of the households spent up to Rs. 3000 for their monthly provisions, 25% of them spent up to Rs. 1500, 15% of them spent up to Rs. 4000, 12% of them spent up to 5000 and 8% of them spent more than 5000 rupees.

Table 3
Amount Spent for Monthly Provisions

Amount spend for monthly provisions	*Percentage of Respondents (n=150)*
less than Rs. 1500	25
up to Rs. 3000	45
up to Rs. 4000	15
up to Rs. 5000	12
more than Rs. 5000	8
Total	100

Nearly 50% of the people in small towns spent up to Rs. 3000, it is clear that the spending power is huge in small towns and also willing to buy products. Also there are 25% of people in lower income strata spend up to Rs. 1500; they can be targeted efficiently by introducing more products in sachets or packets with a less price. There are also nearly 20% of the people spent up to or more than 5000 rupees for their monthly provisions and this may increase if the incomes shift in that family increase marginally.

Importance given by the Respondents in Buying Products form any Kind of Shops

47% of them look out for only quality product, 19% of them say they will look for both quality and less price, 13% of them say they look out for brand name/ image when buying products form shops.

Table 4
Importance given by the Respondents in Buying Products from Shops

Importance given by the respondents in buying products form shops	*Percentage of Respondents (n=150)*
Cheap price	15
Quality product	47
Both (a&b)	19
Brand name/image	13
Well packaged/design	7
Total	100

Thought the consumption and purchasing powers is less compared to urban households still majority of the people in small towns look out for only the quality product and price doesn't matters a lot for them. Also 15% of the people says they will look for cheap price of which they can spend; there are also people who prefer both quality and cheap price of about 19%. The awareness of branded products is also on the upscale in small towns, because they particularly ask for those products, few people in small towns are also says that buy a product which has a well package design.

Preference of Global Brands Over Local Brands

56% of them say they will buy global brands, 26% of them say no to it and remaining 18% of them say no opinion in particular about it.

Table 5
Preference of Global Brands Over Local Brands

Preference of global brands over local brands	*Percentage of Respondents (n=150)*
Yes	56
No	26
Can't say	18
Total	100

Majority of the people in small towns say they will prefer global brands due to the quality they offer and also feels pride in purchasing it and also 26% of them say they will not prefer to buy global brands compared to local brands since they are not willing to gain profit by the foreign brands in Indian soil and they are also particular about Indian brands which in anyways going to be better than global brands. Other says they have no opinion in buying foreign or local brands unless the quality of the product is good.

Soaps Used by Respondents for Last 6 Months

33% of them use Hamam, 21% of them use Cinthol, 19% of them use Lifebuoy, 6% of them use Mysore Sandal, 6% of them use Margo, 6% of them use Dettol and remaining 9% of them use other soaps.

Table 6
Soap Used by them Regularly or for Last 6 Months

Soap use by the Respondents	*Percentage of Respondents (n=150)*
Hamam	33
Cinthol	21
Lifebuoy	19
Mysore sandal	6
Margo	6
Medimix	5
Dettol	6
Vivil	2
Power	2
Total	100

Approximately there are more than 20 different varieties of soaps available in the market; still Hamam has been used by 33% of the people in small towns. As far as Cinthol though it is slightly higher price soap compared to others, still many of them use it for its complexion and fragrance. Lifebuoy soap has a huge penetrated in rural villages comapared to small towns but still 19% of them use it and they say they have a strong belief in the brand. Mysore sandal, margo and dettol have been widely used by some of the people in small towns due to the promotions and belief on brand.

Tooth Paste/Powder Used by the Respondents for Past 6 Months

Colgate and close up paste which alone accounts for more than 50% followed by peopsedent of about 13%, 11% of them use Colgate tooth power. Dabur, anchor, aqua fresh tooth paste has been used by 18% of the people. Ayurvedic and Amway products of about 7% are used.

Table 7
Tooth Paste/powder Used by Respondents for Past 6 Months

Tooth paste/powder used by Respondents	*Percentage of Respondents (n=150)*
Colgate paste	30
Colgate powder	11
Close up	21
Peopsedent	13
Dabur	7
Anchor	6
Aquafresh	5
Challenge (Ayurvedic)	4
Glister (amway)	3
Total	100

The global brands like Colgate, Close up, Peopsedent have dominated the small town market than most of the local brands. Still tooth powers like Colgate powder has been used by 11% of the people. Though dabur, anchor, aqua fresh are introducing new product segments and in various price variations, still these major brands have inculcated into the people minds and they are strongly positioned as a brand which meant for masses. Also there is a scope of wide penetration of Amway products in small towns through social and network marketing.

Consumer Durable Products Owned

98% of them own Television in there houses, 35% of them own Refrigerator followed by 13% of them own washing machine in there home. Personal device like Mobile has been used by 85% of the people, Owen, electronic cooker has been owned by 5% of the people.

Table 8
Consumer Durable Products Owned

Consumer durable products owned in your home	*No. of Responses*	*Percentage of Respondents (n=150/variable)*
TV	148	98
Refrigerator	53	35
Washing Machine	19	13
Microwave Owen, electronic cooker	8	5
Mobile	129	85
others	12	8

Television has become a necessary house hold product in every homes of small town, 98% of them own TV, which is more or less equal to urban. Secondly the penetration of mobile phones is very huge in small towns of about 86% which is due to the low cost and more purchase power of small town market. 35% of the households use refrigerator and 13% of them use washing machines in there home, which in near future is going be get doubled. The concept of other modern electronic products like Owen, electronic cooker is very less of about 5% which is due to the less awareness of the product.

Television Brands Owned in Small Town Households

25% of the house holds in small towns own Samsung television followed by LG television sets of about 23%. 16% of them own Philips television followed by Onida of about 12%. Videocon and BPL sets are owned by 16% of the people and the remaining own Aiwa, Sony and Sansui television sets.

Most of the TV brands are present in small town's house holds, in which Samsung television has been owned by the largest percentage of people, most of the brands in Samsung model price range in-between 7-16K followed by LG

Table 9
TV Brands Owned in Home

TV brands owned in home	*Percentage of Respondents (n=150)*
Samsung	25
LG	23
Philips	16
Onida	12
Videocon	9
BPL	7
Aiwa	3
Sony	3
Sansui	2
Total	100

brand of about 23% and LG has a various price variants and has attracted huge people especially with low income groups. Philips, Onida, Videocon, BPL are the ones which kick start there promotions in early 90's and still people use those television sets of about 35%. Sony, Aiwa and Sansui sets are owned by 8% of the households and they are mainly purchased due to the dealers promotion, discounts etc.

Major Reason for Buying a Particular Brand in TV

33% of them say bought due to advertisements, 24% of them say reputation of the company brand image, 18% of them say peer group and 21% of them say cost effective.

Table 10
Major Reason for Buying a Particular Brand in TV

Reason to buy a particular brand in TV	*Percentage of Respondents (n=150)*
Advertisements	33
Reputation of the company/brand image	24
Peer group	18
Cost effective	21
Others	3
Total	100

Majority of the people feel that advertisements influence in buying the television for their home, 24% of them say reputation of the company and brand image makes them to purchase the television. Also 21% of the people in small towns feel that it should be cost effective to buy the television. Peer group influence is also there for about 18%, which normal middle class people tend to believe more in the sayings of peer group.

Refrigerator Brands Owned in Respondents Households

40% of them own Whirlpool brand followed by 26% of them use LG brand, 21% of them own Godrej brand in there homes and a remaining host of refrigerator brands.

Table 11
Refrigerator Brands Owned in Home

Refrigerator brands owned in home	*Percentage of Respondents (n=150)*
Whirlpool	40
LG	26
Godrej	21
Electrolux	2
Kenstar	6
Samsung	4
Videocon	2
Total	100

Though the over all refrigerator market is marginally less than TV or mobile still it has a huge penetration of about 35%. In which majority of them own whirlpool brand followed by LG refrigerator. People in small towns are very cautious about there brand and product value and they expect a good value for there money. Godrej refrigerator is getting penetrated through its recent promotion and re-branding activities. The initial market of refrigerator is mostly cached by these three brands and there is also a huge scope for other brands to penetrate into the small towns.

Reason for Buying a Particular Brand in Refrigerator

43% of them say that they bought refrigerator due to the reputation of the company/brand image and 28% of them say advertisements influence them in buying refrigerator. Also 17% of them feel that they bought due to the cost effective reason.

Table 12
Reason to Buy Particular Brand in Refrigerator

Reason to buy a particular brand in refrigerator	*Percentage of Respondents (n=150)*
Advertisements	28
Reputation of the company/brand image	43
Peer group	9
Cost effective	17
Others	2
Total	100

The reputation and brand name are the most important factors for buying a refrigerator, advertisements and positive sayings by the peer group may be an added value to it. People in small towns are mostly look out for a cost effective and a quality product, so such a compact product should be made and promote in an innovative manner.

Mobile Brands Owned by Respondents

52% of them use Nokia mobile hand set, followed by 19% of them use Motorola, 10% of them use Sony, 9% of them use LG and remaining members use a host of others.

Table 13
Mobile Brands Owned

Mobile brands owned	*Percentage of Respondents (n=150)*
Nokia	52
Motorola	19
Sony	10
LG	9
Samsung	5
Tata Indicom	2
Spice	1
Korean	2
Total	100

Nokia handsets are widely been used by the people in the small towns due to there believability on the product and cost effectiveness. More over people feel that it is very user friendly or comfortable in operating Nokia than other mobile. Though Motorola have a huge market in other countries still it has not adapted to a brand which suits the taste of Indian people, especially small town people. Sony as a brand is seen as a costly mobile by many of people in small town. LG, Samsung has been seen as a mobile which doesn't work well or doesn't suit them. Some of the low end or grey market mobiles are also used by some of them in small towns.

Reason for Buying a Particular Brand in Mobile

47% of them say that the reputation/brand image makes them to purchase the particular mobile, 20% of them say bought due to advertisements, 19% of them say bought due to the cost effectiveness and 12% of them say due to peer group.

Reputation and brand image are the one which people mostly see as a criteria when purchasing mobile phones, advertisements and cost effective factors work in certain cases when there is an immediate need. Most of the people in small towns sees it as a one time investment and should work for last longer.

Table 14
Reason to Buy a Particular Brand in Mobile

Reason to buy a particular brand in mobile	*Percentage of Respondents (n=150)*
Advertisements	20
Reputation of the company/brand image	47
Peer group	12
Cost effective	19
Others	2
Total	100

Buying Products Due to Direct Promotions

57% of the people say haven't bought any product due to direct promotions and 43% says they bought some products due to direct promotions.

Table 15
Bought Any Product Due to Direct Promotions

Bought any product due to direct promotions	*Percentage of Respondents (n=150)*
Yes	43
No	57
Total	100

Majority of the people in small towns feel that the quality and the after sales service will not be good in products purchased due to direct promotions. Majority of the people says direct promotions are sales people coming directly to home and selling their products and they can't come up with examples like promotional activities done by any of global brands. The one main reason is that most of the people in small towns are targeted heavily by mass media. Also there are more people who also prefer to buy products through direct marketing.

Products Bought Due to Direct Promotions

- Detergents
- Soaps
- Dresses
- Aqua guard
- Bed, pillows
- DVD player
- Grinder
- Iron box

Products Bought Due to Promotional Activities Like Discounts/Exchange Offers/ Melas etc.

61% of them say they bought products due to promotional activities like discounts, exchange offers, melas, etc and remaining 39% of them say they have not bought.

Table 16
Bought any Product due to Promotional Activities Like Discounts/Exchange Offers/Melas etc.

Products bought due to discounts/ exchange offers/melas	*Percentage of Respondents (n=150)*
Yes	61
No	39
Total	100

Most of the people in small towns are interested to buy products due to promotional activities like discounts, exchange offers, melas etc. many sees it as an opportunity to buy new products for their home. Though there are people who have not bought any products due to these kinds of promotional activities in future they may change due to the strong campaigns and innovative promotions.

Products Bought Due to Promotional Activities

32% of them have bought dresses, shoes etc due to exchange offers and discounts followed by home appliances like mixer, cooker, stove etc of about 26%, 22% of them bought mobile, 9% of them bought Two-wheelers and remaining bought other products.

Table 17
Product Bought Due to Promotional Activities

Products bought due to promotional activities	*Percentage of Respondents (n=150)*
Dresses, shoes	32
TV	6
Mobile	22
Home appliances like mixer, cooker, stove etc.	26
Two-wheeler	9
Jewellery	2
Washing machine/ refrigerator	2
Total	100

Dresses and allied products which have created curiosity and interest in minds of small town people, where they often look out for discounts and exchange offers but the concept of branding is missing in these area, where people look out for the trendy, colorful, price obviously and giving less importance to the brands. Home appliances like mixer, cooker, stove and host of other kitchen products are the one which people like to update regularly by using the promotions and offers. People have also bought mobile due to promotions though there is a strong believability on mobile brands like Nokia.

Likeability/Preference of Advertisements in TV/Radio

49% of the respondents say they prefer to watch advertisements, 34% of them say they don't prefer and 17% of them have no opinion on it.

Table 18
Likeability/Preference of Advertisements in TV/Radio

Preference of watching ads	*Percentage of Respondents (n=150)*
Yes	49
No	34
Can't say	17
Total	100

Advertisements are the one which keeps informed and makes consumers update about the various products in the market, which has been like by most of them. There are people who say it's a waste of time and creating unnecessary disturbances to them. Also there are certain no of people who don't have any particular opinion in it.

Bought Anything Due to Advertisements

56% of the respondents say they bought products/goods due to advertisements in TV, also 29% of them say they have not purchased any products due to advertisements. 15% of them can't remember or not willing to say.

Table 19
Bought Anything Due to Advertisements

Bought anything due to advertisements	*Percentage of Respondents (n=150)*
Yes	56
No	29
Can't say	15
Total	100

Most of the people in small towns have gone for purchasing a product after seeing advertisements. Also there are people who go by their mind while purchasing any product and not advertisements. The interesting fact is that people who do not prefer to watch ads also have bought products due to the influence of advertisements. 15% of them have no idea about having purchased or not.

Product Purchased Due to Advertisements

- Mobile
- TV
- Refrigerator
- DVD player
- Lays
- Fair & lovely
- Dove
- Complan
- Gold winner
- Dresses form Pothys
- DTH
- Garnier face wash

Types of Advertisements Preferred to Watch by Respondents

29% of them say ads should focus on there utility, 16% of them say ads should focus on the need of the product, 24% of them say ads should come with brand ambassadors, 15% of them say it should focus on price.

Table 20
Types of Advertisements you Preferred to Watch

Types of Advertisements prefer to watch	*Percentage of Respondents (n=150)*
Price	15
Utility	29
Need	26
Brand ambassador	24
Competitors	7
Total	100

It is evident that an advertisement should always focus on its objectivity of the communication but it should also satisfy the consumer needs in communication point of view. Thus utility, need and brand ambassador are the three elements which should be given in a correct proposition in order to reach out to the small town people. Price is always an important factor but consumers are no more looking only on the price of the products rather than the uniqueness and innovation of the communication. It is also clear that the competitors comparison of the products in there ads are not liked by the people in small towns.

Recent TV Commercial which come to Respondents Mind Immediately

- Gold winner
- Colgate
- Aroyoka
- Surf excel
- Castrol
- Pulsar
- Thumps up
- Rin
- Docomo
- Vodafone
- GRT

Thought there are a host of television commercials coming in various formats and types, it is tough to remember or tell the commercial which comes to their mind immediately. But there are ads which is aimed at mass audience for brand building or to make people aware of there brand and some ads are targeted on only on certain market to increase there sales. The ads which remembered by the small town people mostly fall under the category of immediate sales or buying.

Products/Goods Planned to Buy Soon or in Future

23% of them say want to buy a car in the near future, followed by washing machine of about 19% and 15% of them say going to buy Air coolers soon and 13% of them say computers, 10% of the people wants to buy sofa/furniture for their home.

Table 21
Products/Goods Planned to Buy Soon or in Future

Products planning to purchase soon	*Percentage of Respondents (n=150)*
Car	23
Washing machine	19
AC	15
Computer	13
Lcd TV	3
Refrigerator	9
House/land	2
Sofa/furniture's	10
Two wheeler	6
Total	100

Indians have gone crazy about cars, and in coming years the percentage of car owned will get tripled, weather it may be small or compact size car. Just before they do so, they will be selling off their motorbikes. So there will be a huge supply of second-hand motorbikes. Most of the working and non working female population prefers to buy washing machines for their homes to save time and energy. Air cooler are preferred by most of the small town people and most of them feel they will purchase immediately if the price may slightly come down or if it fix to their budget. Most of the people feel computers are necessary for their children to get better education or to update about the latest things in the world. So most of the people in small towns going to buy computers in near future. Designer sofa/furniture are liked by certain percentage of people followed by refrigerator, two wheeler, Lcd tv etc. Since most of the people in small towns own land and house they are less interested in other products.

FINDINGS

1. Car, Washing machine and Air cooler are the products which most of the people in small town are planning to buy soon or in future.
2. Telecom, DTH and Banking are the emerging sectors in small towns and rural areas in near future.
3. Global recession in India doesn't have an impact in small towns and rural markets.
4. Samsung and LG televisions are the global brands owned by majority of the respondents in small towns.
5. More than 50% of the people in the small towns prefer global brands over local brands.
6. Direct promotions in small towns have not made a huge impact and people tend to buy products which are of less (Price) value.
7. Exchange offers/discounts/melas have created a huge impact on small town people and they are willing to spend more on it.
8. Home appliances, mobiles, dresses are the things mostly bought though promotions like exchange offers/Meals.
9. FMCG and consumer durables have a huge penetration in small towns.
10. Brand ambassadors are needed for certain brands to penetrate well in small towns.

References

Banerjee, A. (1994), 'Transnational Advertising Development and Management: An Account Planning Approach and a Process Frame Work', *"International Journal of Advertising"*, 13, 95-124.

Blinn, T. (1999), 'Expanding the Boundaries in a Global Context; Creating a Global Brand, *www.aesgp.org/Berlin1999/12Blinnformat.pdf*

Business World Marketing White Book, 2008.

Colyer, E. (2006), India a Hot Brand Climate *http://www.brandchannel.com/features_effect.asp?pf_id=316*

Goutham, R. (2007), Mindshare Fulcrum in *Indiatelevision.com*

Karwal, R. (2007-08), Marketing White Book, Business World, pp.155.

Kicha, P. (2007), Building Brands in Rural India, *www.Brandchannel.com*

McCracken, G. (1988), Bloomington: Indiana University Press, pp. 71-89.

Mooij, M. (2002), Global Marketing and Advertising: 2nd edition, pp. 9.

Mooij, M. (1994), Advertising Worldwide (2nded.). Hemel Hempstead, Hertfordshire, UK: Prentice Hall International.

Moriarty, S. and Duncan, T. (1990), Global Advertising: Issues and Practices; *"Journal of Current Issues and Research"*, pp. 313-341

Richard, S. (2006), Promotion & Integrated Marketing Communications, pp. 258.

Razzouk N., Conceptualization of India's Emerging Rural Consuming System; *Journal of International Consumer Marketing*, Volume 3, Issue 4, September 1991, pp. 35-50

Vasudeva, P. K. (2004), International Marketing, 2nd edition, pp. 11.

Yadagiri, M., Sreenivas, N. (2009), 'Brand Strategies for Globalization.' *"Indian Journal of Marketing"*, pp. 9.

COMPARISON OF CELEBRITY AND NON CELEBRITY IN ADVERTISEMENT IN MADURAI CITY

P. Raja[*] *& N. Mahesh*[**]

INTRODUCTION

Everyday consumers are exposed to thousands of voices and images in magazines, newspapers, and on billboards, websites, radio and television. Every brand attempts to steal at least a fraction of an unsuspecting person's time to inform him or her of the amazing and different attributes of the product at hand. The challenge of the marketer is to find a hook that will hold the subject's attention. In helping to achieve this, use of celebrity endorsers is a widely used marcom strategy.

Celebrities acted as spokespersons, in order to advertise and promote products, services and ideas. Those celebrities came from the art scene, modelling, sports and the movie industry. The first advertisers used celebrities as pioneers in order to dictate trends. The reason behind the popularity of celebrity advertising is marketers' belief that the viewers' attention level is much higher, which will result in greater sales. Generally, celebrities are used for their unique attributes, accomplishments and expertise which make advertisements more believable to consumers.

Due to the immense availability of media, the emergence of a new stage of commercial communication has taken place. Companies are constantly finding new ways in which they can communicate with their consumers, in both a conscious level and subconscious level, by surrounding consumers with constant brand messages. At a conscious level the consumers choose which communications to be interested in. if they are looking for a specific product or service of interest they will selectively perceives relevant brand messages.

* Senior Lecturer, Department of Management Sciences, Velammal Engineering College, Chennai.

** Professor, Department of Management Studies, International School of Business and Research, Chennai.

The battle for a piece of the consumers "mind space" has lead companies to want to associate their brands with desirable and trustworthy celebrities in order to attract consumer's attention and interest. The use of celebrities as means of communication has been commonly utilized in advertising and branding. This is done because it is assumed that celebrities have a powerful effect on the affluence of the brands they endorse.

Indian advertising started with the hawkers who used to shut out their goods right from the days when cities and markets first began. Since then, advertising has been converted into a strategic tool that enhances sales, more profits and helps in the process of brand-building and product promotion. With this evolved a strategy that tried to benefit from the emotional attachment of the admirers or the fns of the celebrities; in the form of celebrity endorsement. It does help in creating instant awareness and visibility; but for a cost.

Celebrities increase brand awareness and define values and new dimensions of the brand. Marketers use this approach to capture mind and market spaces for their brands. The underlying reason for any celebrity endorsement has to be more sales, with more consumers using the brand. Marketers need to be careful before choosing a celebrity for endorsing their brand, as they spend huge amounts on their brands and also on the celebrity. The use of a celebrity should help in building the brand's image. The pros and cons of using a particular celebrity have to be considered before using them for endorsements; and credibility of celebrity is often one of the basic factors in determining his/her suitability for the endorsement. Marketers have to check if there exists a match between the brand and the celebrity, and whether the deal is worth the investment. With this background, the present study was attempted to compare the celebrity and non celebrity in advertisement in Madurai city of Tamil Nadu.

METHODOLOGY

Among the different cities in Tamil Nadu, the Madurai city is purposively selected for the present study since the Madurai city is the most important market for South Tamil Nadu. Based on the information access and exposure, the Madurai urban is again purposively selected. The respondents were selected by adopting multi-stage random sampling technique.

The data and information were collected from 500 respondents through well-structured interview schedules and it is pre-tested and filed level survey has conducted. Hence, the present study is carried out from the primary data source.

LOGIT REGRESSION MODEL

In order to analyze appearance of celebrities and non celebrities in the advertisement, the binary logit regression model was employed and the functional form of logit model is given below:

$$\ln(ODDS) = \ln\left(\frac{\hat{Y}}{1-\hat{Y}}\right) = a + bX$$

Where,

$\hat{Y}$ = The Predicted Probability of the Event which is coded with 1 (Celebrity) rather than with 0 (Non-celebrity).

1- $\hat{Y}$ = The Predicted Probability of the other decision.

X_i = Predictor variables.

The variables in the logit model are:

Y = Celebrity = 1 and Non-Celebrity = 0

X_1 = Exciting

X_2 = Interesting

X_3 = Appealing

X_4 = Needed

X_5 = Relevant

X_6 - Important

X_7 = Like

X_8 = Favourable

X_9 = Positive

X_{10} = Credible

X_{11} = Effective

X_{12} = Informative

X_{13} = Meaningful

Where

a = Intercept

X_i = Regression Coefficients

The a and b_i are the coefficients which are to be estimated.

RESULTS AND DISCUSSION

Matching of Celebrity with Advertisement

The matching of the celebrity with advertisement was analyzed by computing the mean score and the results are presented in Table 1. From the results, it is clear that the attribute of i stop buying a brand if its celebrity involved in a scandal was the major matching criterion between the celebrity and advertisement followed by celebrity and product are perfectly match to each others, it is more worthy to buy a brand with celebrity endorsement, celebrity gives a positive image to the endorsed brand, i am more confident of the brand with celebrity endorsement i buy a brand if my favorite celebrity advertise the product and it makes me look similar to the endorsing celebrities in the order of preference by the consumers.

Table 1
Matching of Celebrity and Advertisement

Attributes	*Mean Score*	*Rank*
It makes me look similar to the endorsing celebrities	4.94	VI
It gives me a sense of identity	4.38	X
I am more confident of the brand with celebrity endorsement	5.26	V
It is more worthy to buy a brand with celebrity endorsement	5.38	III
I buy a brand if my favorite celebrity advertise the product	4.94	VI
I stop buying a brand if its celebrity involved in a scandal	6.49	I
Celebrity gives a positive image to the endorsed brand	5.30	IV
Celebrity can attract me to buy a product	4.48	VIII
Celebrity and product are perfectly match to each others	5.97	II
Advertisement is increasing the celebrity value	4.41	IX

Besides, celebrity can attract me to buy a product, advertisement is increasing the celebrity value and it gives me a sense of identity was the minor important attributes perceived by the consumers for matching the celebrity and advertisement.

PERSONALITIES OF CELEBRITIES IN ADVERTISEMENT -ANALYSIS OF VARIANCE

The personalities of celebrities in advertisement were analyzed by computing ANOVA and the results are presented in Table 2. The results showed that the F-value was 0.0012 indicating the significance at five per cent level. Hence, it was inferred that there was a significant differences between the personalities of celebrities in advertisement.

Table 2
Personalities of Celebrity in Advertisement–ANOVA

Source		*Sum of Squares*	*d.f*	*Mean Square*	*F*	*Sig.*
Between People		3402.921	499	6.819		
Within People	Between Items	18580.939	18	1032.274	0.0012	.000
	Residual	8262.689	8982	.920		
	Total	26843.628	9000	2.983		
Total		30246.549	9499	3.184		

Grand Mean = 2.6675

CELEBRITY AND NON-CELEBRITY IN ADVERTISEMENT

In order to identify the appearance of celebrities and non-celebrities, the logit regression was carried out and the results are presented in Table 3. The results showed that Cox and Null R^2 was 0.59 indicating the goodness of model.

The likeability, favorable, positive image, creditability and effectiveness of the advertisements were significantly differentiated the celebrities and non-celebrities in the advertisements by consumers.

Table 3
Appearance of Celebrities and Non-Celebrities -Logit Regression Model

Particulars	*Co-efficient(β_i)*	*Wald*	*Sig.*
Exciting (X_1)	.157	1.469	.225
Interesting (X_2)	.025	.040	.841
Appealing (X_3)	-.099	.669	.413
Needed (X_4)	.115	.852	.356
Relevant (X_5)	.125	1.025	.311
Important (X_6)	.045	.145	.703
Like (X_7)	-.472**	8.100	.004
Favourable (X_8)	.661**	17.780	.000
Positive (X_9)	1.281**	56.321	.000
Creditable (X_{10})	1.148**	59.377	.000
Effective (X_{11})	.831**	39.859	.000
Informative (X_{12})	.045	.121	.728
Meaningful (X_{13})	.212	2.912	.088
Constant	-11.295**	185.337	.000
Cox and Null R^2	0.59		
Sample Size	500		

Note: **indicates significance at five per cent level.

ATTITUDES FOR BUYING BEHAVIOUR BASED ON CELEBRITIES IN ADVERTISEMENT

The attitudes for buying behavior of the consumers based on the celebrities in advertisement were analyzed by calculating the weighted mean score and the results are presented in Table 4. In over all, the consumers were agreed with all the attitudinal dimensions. From the table, it is inferred that buying branded products is important to me, i know the price i pay for most of the goods i buy, i make purchase decisions based on advertisement, i buy based on quality, not price, a celebrity endorsement may influence my to consider or buy a product, i buy brands that reflect my style before making a purchase, i prefer products that offer the latest in new technology, my children have a significant impact on the brands i choose and my spouse has a significant impact on the brands i choose with attractive advertisements were agreed.

Besides, the rest of attitudinal dimensions of i like to shop around before making a purchase, my favorite grocery store offers low prices on all products every day, i often seek the advice of others before making a purchase, people often come to me for advice, i always check the ingredients and nutritional content and i like to change brands often for the sake of variety and novelty and also advertisements were neutral with the consumers.

Table 4
Attitudes for Buying Behaviour

Attributes	*Weighted Mean Score*	*Status*
Buying branded products is important to me	4.03	Agree
I know the price I pay for most of the goods I buy	3.84	Agree
I make purchase decisions based on advertisement	3.97	Agree
I like to shop around before making a purchase	3.53	Neutral
I buy based on quality, not price	4.52	Agree
My favorite grocery store offers low prices on all products every day	2.79	Neutral
A celebrity endorsement may influence my to consider or buy a product	4.08	Agree
I often seek the advice of others before making a purchase	3.34	Neutral
I buy brands that reflect my style before making a purchase	4.37	Agree
People often come to me for advice	2.98	Neutral
I prefer products that offer the latest in new technology	3.41	Agree
I always check the ingredients and nutritional content	3.23	Neutral
My children have a significant impact on the brands I choose	3.97	Agree
My spouse has a significant impact on the brands I choose with attractive advertisements	3.62	Agree
I like to change brands often for the sake of variety and novelty and also advertisements	3.23	Neutral
Over all	3.66	Agree

CONCLUSION

The foregoing analysis indicated that the attribute of i stop buying a brand if its celebrity involved in a scandal was the major matching criterion between the celebrity and advertisement followed by celebrity and product are perfectly match to each others, it is more worthy to buy a brand with celebrity endorsement, celebrity gives a positive image to the endorsed brand, i am more confident of the brand with celebrity endorsement i buy a brand if my favorite celebrity advertise the product and it makes me look similar to the endorsing celebrities in the order of preference by the consumers.

The results showed that Cox and Null R^2 was 0.59 indicating the goodness of model. The likeability, favorable, positive image, creditability and effectiveness of the advertisements were significantly differentiated the celebrities and non-celebrities in the advertisements by consumers. In over all, the consumers were agreed with all the attitudinal dimensions.

Consumers are more likely to purchase if the endorsement are described with a strong argument. Before purchase the consumer goes through several stages, they learn something about the product, modify their attitudes on the basis of that learning, and then act on their revised attitudes. Since celebrities have the impetus to market the product quickly, they have the advertisers running behind them for various benefits including brand credibility, creating interest; thereby, creating a win-win situation.

References

Agrawal, J. and Kamakura, W. (1995), " The Economic Worth of Celebrity Endorsers: An Event Study Analysis", *Journal of Marketing,* Vol. 59, (July), pp. 56–62.

Basil, Michael, Identification as a Mediator of Celebrity Effects. *Journal of Broadcasting and Electronic Media.* (Fall 1996), pp. 478-495.

Buhr, T. A., Simpson, T. L. and Pryor, B. (1987), Celebrity Endorsers" Expertise and Perceptions of Attractiveness, Likability, and Familiarity ", *Psychological Reports,* 60, pp. 1307-1309.

Caballero, M. J., Lumpkin, J. R. & Madden, C. S. (1989), Using Physical Attractiveness as an Advertising Tool: An Empirical Test of the Attraction Phenomenon. *Journal of Advertising Research,* 29 (4), 16-22.

Dawra, Jogrook and Katyal, Kanupriya (2006), "Brand–Celebrity Conformance", *The ICFAI Journal of Brand Management,* Vol. III, No. 2, p. 6.

Jagdish, A. & Wagner, K. A. (1995), The Economic Worth of Celebrity Endorsers: An Event Study Analysis. *Journal of Marketing,* 56(3), 56-62. ISSN 0022-2429.

Kamins, Michael A. (1990), An Investigation into the 'Match Up' Hypothesis in Celebrity Advertising: When Beauty May be Only Skin Deep. *Journal of Advertising,* 19, No. 1, p. 413.

Louie, T. A., Obermiller, C. (2002), Consumer Response to a Firm's Endorser (Dis) Association Decisions, *Journal of Advertising,* Vol. 31, No. 4, pp. 41-52.

Ohanian, Roobina (1990), Construction and Validation of a Scale to Measure Celebrity Endorsers' Perceived Expertise, Trustworthiness, and Attractiveness. *Journal of Advertising* 19, pp. 39-52.

Pornpitakpan, Chanthika (2003), "Validation of the Celebrity Endorsers", Credibility Scale Evidence from Asians", *Journal of Marketing Management,* 19 (1/2), pp. 179-195.

Saleem, Farida (2007), "Effect of Single and Multiple Celebrity Endorsement on Low Involvement and High Involvement Product Advertisement", *European Journal of Social Sciences,* Vol. 5(3), October, pp. 125-132.

Sternthal, Brian, Ruby Roy Dholakia, and Clark Leavitt (March 1978), The Persuasive Effect of Source Credibility: Tests of Cognitive Response. *Journal of Consumer Research,* 4, pp. 252-260.

Tripp, C., Jensen, T.D., Carlson, L. (1994), "The Effects of Multiple Product Endorsements by Celebrities on Consumers' Attitudes and Intentions". *Journal of Consumer Research,* Vol. 20, pp. 535-547.

Walker, M., Langmeyer, L., Langmeyer, D. (1991), Celebrity Endorser: Do you get what you Pay for?. *The Journal of Services Marketing,* Vol. 6. Fall, pp. 35-42.

Zafer Erdogan (2001), Selecting Celebrity Endorsers: The Practitioner's Perspective, *Journal of Advertising Research,* Vol. 41, Issue 3, p. 39.

TRENDS AND INSTABILITY OF CAPITAL FORMATION IN INDIAN AGRICULTURE

Ram Kumar Jha[*] & *Hansa Jain*[**]

INTRODUCTION

The constant growth in agricultural production and productivity is important for overall stability of the Indian economy (Prakash, *et al.*, 2006). The growth and development of the agricultural sector is determined strongly by the level of technology and the efficiency of market mechanism. Capital plays an important role for operationalising these two factors. Hence, capital is the important input required for uplifting growth both in the micro and macro units of the economy and agriculture sector. Now-a-days, the investor's interest is decreasing in farm sector as compared to other sectors of the economy. This is because of its higher degree of risk, low productivity and seasonal nature of production coupled with fluctuations in inputs and output prices (Singh, *et al.*, 1996).

The capital formation helps to sustain agricultural growth. The efficiency of capital use and improvement enhances the rate of capital formation (Singh, 1997). But with the process of liberalization and privatization the pattern of capital formation in agriculture has also changed. Gandhi (1996), Bhagwati and Srinivasan (1993), Gulati and Bhide (1993), Ram (1993), Mishra and Chand (1995), Dhawan and Yadav (1995), Mitra (1996), Mani, *et al.*, (1996), Deshmukh and Bhargava (1954), Shukla (1965), Panikar (1969), Kurian (1969), Dantwala (1986), Rath (1989), Shetty (1990), Gandhi (1990), Mujumdar and Menon (1991), Schiff and Valdes (1992), Swaminathan (1992), Rao (1992), Nayyar (1993), Mallick (1993), Rao (1994) and Misra and Hazell (1996) have found that government capital formation in agriculture was almost continuously

* ICSSR-Post Doctoral Fellow, Sardar Patel Institute of Economic and Social Research, Thaltej Road, Ahmedabad, Gujarat (India), (*e-mail: ram_econ@yahoo.co.in*)

** Associate Professor and Senior Social Scientist (ICSSR), Sardar Patel Institute of Economic and Social Research, Thaltej Road, Ahmedabad, Gujarat (India), (*e-mail: hansa@spiesr.ac.in*) rising until the early eighties. After that it showed a decline which continued till 1992. This has caused substantial fluctuations in the private capital formation.

The present study is focused on the present scenario of capital formation in agriculture and the growth of the agricultural production and productivity. It helps to understand the performance of public and private capital formation in agricultural sector. Thus, the objectives of the present study are to calculate the annual and compound growth rates and to frame the instability index for capital formation in agriculture, area, production and yield of food grain and non-food grain crops.

The present study is divided in to five sections. Section 1 contains introduction with objectives of the study while used methodology is presented in section 2. Section 3 presents the data base of the study. Section 4 presents results and discussion and conclusion and policy implications are presented in section 5.

METHODOLOGY

In order to fulfil the objectives of the present study, the time series data are obtained for capital formation in agriculture, area, production and yield of food grain and non-food grain crops for the last 13 years, i.e., from 1994-95 to 2006-07. Annual growth rate (AGR) and compound growth rate (CGR) were obtained for the capital formation, area, production and yield of various food grain and non-food grain crops. Further, instability index (I_I) is calculated to determine the fluctuation in these variables. The AGR, CGR and I_I is calculated in the following manner:

Annual Growth Rate (AGR)

The following linear trend model has been used to calculate AGR.

$$Y_t = a + bt + U_t$$

Where,

Y_t = Variables selected (as shown in Col. (2) in Table 3)

t = Time variable (in years)

a = Intercept

b = Coefficient (dy/dt = rate of change)

U_t = Error term

Further the Annual Growth Rate (AGR) in the linear trend has been defined as

$$Annual\ Growth\ Rate\ (AGR) = \frac{b}{\bar{Y}} \times 100$$

Where, $\bar{Y}$ = Mean value of concerned variable

Compound Growth Rate (CGR)

The following semi-log model has been used to work out CGR.

$$Y_t = ab^t$$

$$LnY_t = a + bt + U_t$$

Where,

Y_t = Variables selected (as shown in Col. (2) in Table 3)

a = Constant

b = Instantaneous growth rates

t = Time variable (in years)

U_t = Error term

Compound Growth Rate (CGR) = [Antilog (b) - 1] x 100

Instability Index (I_I)

Wide fluctuations in crop output brings about sharp fluctuation in prices and also results in wide variations in disposable income of the farmers. The magnitude of fluctuations depends on the nature of technology adopted, its sensitivity to weather conditions, economic environment, availability of material inputs etc. Therefore, instability index is one of the important decisive parameters in development dynamics and in the context of agricultural production.

In the present study, the instability index (I_I) is calculated by the formula used by Parthasarathy (1984) and Wasim (2001) in their study. The formula is as follows:

$$I_I = \sqrt{\frac{\sum_{i=1}^{n} e_t^2}{n-k}}$$

Where,

I_I = Instability index

e_t = Value of residual of tth observations

n = Number of observations

t = Time variable (in years)

k = Number of variables

Relation between Agricultural Productivity and Capital Formation

In order to check the impact of public and private sector gross capital formation on productivity of food gains and non-food grains, simple regression model was build. The agricultural productivity of food grain and non-food grain was regressed on public and private sector gross capital formation in agriculture separately.

Data Base

The study is based upon the secondary sources of data for the period 1994-95 to 2006-07. The data are collected from various published and unpublished sources. Some of them are Different Volumes of Economic Survey of India, URL: *www.indiabudget.nic.in*, RBI Bulletin, URL: *www.rbi.org.in*, CMIE, Mumbai and *www.indiastat.com*.

RESULTS AND DISCUSSION

Scenario of Capital Formation in India

The agricultural productivity is determined from the capital formation in agriculture which itself is composed of capital formation in public and private sectors. The Table 1 shows the trends and composition of capital formation in agriculture (CFA). According to data shown inTable 1, the gross fixed capital formation in agriculture (GFCFA) has increased from Rs. 15562 crores in 1994-95 to Rs. 83421 crores in 2006-07 with some fluctuations. It is also observed that gross capital formation in agriculture (GCFA) has suffered wide fluctuations during the study period. It has increased from Rs. 14969 crores in 1994-95 to Rs. 60319 crores in 2006-07. The share of public and private sector capital formation to total capital formation in agriculture is 33.05 per cent (Rs. 4947 crores) and 66.95 per cent (Rs. 10022 crores) respectively in 1994-95. But in the financial year 2006-07, the share of public and private capital formation to total capital formation in agriculture is 19.77 per cent (Rs. 1192 crores) and 80.23 per cent (Rs. 48392 crores) respectively. The share of public sector capital formation has fallen but the share of private sector capital formation has steadily increased. Less capital formation in agriculture would mean less growth of infrastructure facilities like irrigation, rural roads market, power, cold storage, etc., and this would affect agricultural growth adversely. According to Economic Survey of India (1999-2000), the decline in public capital formation is attributed to diversion of resources from capital formation to current expenditure. A large portion of public expenditure on agriculture is diverted to current expenditure in the form of increased subsidies for food, fertilizer, electricity, credit and other agricultural inputs rather than on creation of assets.

Scenario of Area, Production and Yield in India

Table 2 reveals the area, production and yield of food grain and non-food grain crops. In 1994-95, the gross area under food grain crops is recorded to be 123.71 million hectares (Mha) and their production in the same year is 191.50 million tones (MT), giving an average yield 1546 kg/ha. The gross area under food grains in 2006-07 is 123.48 Mha and their production is 217.28 MT, giving an average yield 1756 kg/ha. This implies that the cropped area has ceased to increase. Only internal adjustments in the cropped area were made. For example, the cropped area for rice and wheat has increased but that of coarse cereals has decreased. Fluctuation is observed in the cropped area of pulses. Same is the case with non-food grain. The cropped area of tea, coffee, cotton and potato has increased by decreasing the area of jute and mesta and tobacco. On comparing the data and agricultural yield for the time series data, it can be said that the percentage increase in yield is much higher than the percentage increase in the cropped area. This implies the excessive use of agricultural inputs

Table 1
Capital Formation in Agriculture in India (in Rupees Crores)

		Gross Capital Formation in Agriculture		
Years	*GFCFA*	*GCFAPuS*	*GCFAPrS*	*GCFA*
(1)	*(2)*	*(3)*	*(4)*	*(5)*
1994-95	15562	4947 (33.05)	10022 (66.95)	14969
1995-96	17665	4849 (30.91)	10841 (69.09)	15690
1996-97	21476	4668 (28.86)	11508 (71.14)	16176
1997-98	25286	3979 (24.96)	11963 (75.04)	15942
1998-99	26613	3870 (25.98)	11025 (74.02)	14895
1999-00	43473	7716 (17.75)	35757 (82.25)	43473
2000-01	40048	7155 (18.47)	31580 (81.53)	38735
2001-02	52009	8746 (18.59)	38297 (81.41)	47043
2002-03	52123	7962 (17.00)	38861 (82.00)	46823
2003-04	51570	9376 (20.77)	35756 (79.23)	45132
2004-05	61173	10267 (21.14)	38309 (78.86)	48576
2005-06	72013	13219 (24.24)	41320 (75.76)	54539
2006-07	83421	11927 (19.77)	48392 (80.23)	60319

Source : (1) CMIE, National Income Statistics July, 2008, (2) Different Volumes of Economic Survey of India, URL: Website: *http://indiabudget.nic.in*

Note : Figures in parenthesis are percentage to GCFA in Col. (6).

Abbreviations : (1) GFCFA: Gross Fixed Capital Formation in Agriculture; (2) GCFAPuS: Gross Capital Formation in Agriculture in Public Sector; (3) GCFAPrS: Gross Capital Formation in Agriculture in Private Sector; (4) GCFA: Gross Capital Formation in Agriculture.

Table 2
Area, Production and Yield of Food Grains and Non-Food Grains Crops in India

Crops	A/P/Y	Years												
		1994-95	1995-96	1996-97	1997-98	1998-99	1999-00	2000-01	2001-02	2002-03	2003-04	2004-05	2005-06	2006-07AE
(1)	(2)	(3)	(4)	(5)	(6)	(7)	(8)	(9)	(10)	(11)	(12)	(13)	(14)	(15)
Rice	A	42.81	42.84	43.43	43.45	44.8	45.16	44.71	44.9	41.18	42.59	41.91	43.66	43.62
	P	81.81	76.98	81.73	82.54	86.08	89.68	84.98	93.34	71.82	88.53	83.13	91.79	93.35
	Y	1911	1797	1882	1900	1921	1986	1901	2079	1744	2077	1984	2102	2127
Wheat	A	25.7	25.01	25.89	26.7	27.52	27.49	25.73	26.34	25.2	26.6	26.38	26.48	28.04
	P	65.77	62.1	69.35	66.35	71.29	76.37	69.68	72.77	65.76	72.15	68.64	69.35	75.81
	Y	2559	2483	2679	2485	2590	2778	2708	2762	2610	2713	2602	2619	2671
Coarse Cereals	A	32.17	30.88	31.81	30.83	29.34	29.34	30.26	29.52	26.99	30.8	29.03	29.04	28.71
	P	29.88	29.03	34.11	30.4	31.33	30.34	31.08	33.37	26.07	37.6	33.46	34.06	33.92
	Y	929	940	1072	986	1068	1034	1027	1131	966	1221	1153	1172	1193
Pulses	A	23.03	22.28	22.45	22.87	23.5	21.12	20.35	22.01	20.5	23.46	22.76	22.39	23.11
	P	14.04	12.31	14.24	12.98	14.91	13.41	11.07	13.37	11.13	14.91	13.13	13.39	14.2
	Y	610	552	635	567	634	635	544	607	543	635	577	598	616
Total Food Grains	A	123.71	121.01	123.58	123.85	125.16	123.11	121.05	122.77	113.87	123.45	120.08	121.57	123.48
	P	191.5	180.42	199.43	192.27	203.61	209.8	196.81	212.85	174.78	213.19	198.36	208.59	217.28
	Y	1546	1491	1614	1552	1627	1704	1626	1734	1535	1727	1652	1715	1756
Total Oilseeds	A	25.3	25.96	26.34	26.12	26.23	24.28	22.77	22.64	21.49	23.66	27.52	27.86	26.05
	P	21.34	22.11	24.38	21.32	24.75	20.71	18.44	20.66	14.84	25.19	24.35	27.98	24.29
	Y	843	851	926	816	944	853	810	913	691	1064	855	1004	917
Sugarcane	A	3.87	4.15	4.17	3.93	4.05	4.22	4.32	4.41	4.52	3.93	3.66	4.2	4.86
	P	275.54	281.1	277.56	279.54	288.72	299.32	295.96	297.21	287.38	233.86	237.09	281.17	355.52
	Y	71254	67787	66496	71134	71203	70935	68577	67370	63576	59380	64752	66928	71081

Contd...

Crops	A/P/Y	Years												
		1994-95	1995-96	1996-97	1997-98	1998-99	1999-00	2000-01	2001-02	2002-03	2003-04	2004-05	2005-06	2006-07AE
(1)	(2)	(3)	(4)	(5)	(6)	(7)	(8)	(9)	(10)	(11)	(12)	(13)	(14)	(15)
Tea$	A	0.43	0.43	0.43	0.43	0.47	0.49	0.5	0.51	0.52	0.52	0.52	0.56	0.57
	P	752.9	756	780.1	810	874.1	825.9	846.9	853.9	838.5	878.1	893	945.97	955.9
	Y	1767	1770	1809	1865	1844	1685	1679	1675	1625	1690	1713	1699	1683
Coffee$	A	0.23	0.24	0.25	0.29	0.3	0.31	0.31	0.32	0.33	0.33	0.33	0.34	0.34
	P	180.1	223	205	228.3	265	292	301.2	300.6	275.3	270.5	275.5	274	280
	Y	788	921	816	799	877	947	959	937	839	931	826	802	820
Cotton**	A	7.87	9.04	9.12	8.87	9.34	8.71	8.53	9.13	7.76	7.6	8.79	8.68	9.14
	P	11.89	12.86	14.23	10.85	12.29	11.63	9.52	10	8.62	13.73	16.43	18.5	22.63
	Y	257	242	265	208	224	225	190	186	191	307	318	362	422
Jute and Mesta*	A	0.93	0.93	1.1	1.11	1.03	1.04	1.02	1.05	1.04	1	0.92	0.9	0.94
	P	9.08	8.81	11.13	11.02	9.81	10.55	10.56	11.68	11.28	11.17	10.27	10.84	11.27
	Y	1760	1712	1818	1792	1722	1836	1867	2007	1960	2008	2019	2173	2167
Tobacco	A	0.38	0.39	0.43	0.46	0.51	0.43	0.26	0.35	0.33	0.37	0.37	0.37	0.37
	P	0.57	0.54	0.62	0.64	0.74	0.52	0.34	0.55	0.49	0.55	0.55	0.55	0.52
	Y	1486	1356	1444	1394	1451	1211	1318	1565	1506	1486	1498	1481	1407
Potato	A	1.07	1.11	1.25	1.21	1.28	1.34	1.21	1.26	1.35	1.28	1.54	1.57	1.48
	P	17.4	18.84	24.22	17.65	22.49	25	22.24	24.46	23.27	23.27	29.19	29.17	22.09
	Y	16272	16991	19391	14613	17571	18643	18363	19417	17300	18113	18925	18592	14903
Total Non-food crops	A	40.08	42.25	43.09	42.42	43.21	40.82	38.92	39.67	37.34	38.69	43.65	44.48	43.75

Sources: (1) RBI Bulletin, URL: *www.rbi.org.in*, (2) CMIE, Mumbai (3) Different volumes of Economic Survey of India, URL: *www.indiabudget.nic.in*

Note: A: Area in Million Hectares, P: Production in Million tones, Y: Yield in Kg. / Hectare, $: production in Million kg, ** production in million bales of 170 kg each, * production in million bales of 180 kg each, AE: Advanced estimates.

like HYV seeds, fertilizers, pesticides and insecticides. All these are met by the current expenditure of the government.

Growth Rates and Instability Index

The annual growth rate (AGR) indicates annual growth of each variable and compound growth rate (CGR) indicates the growth of the variable over the period of time. The analysis of Table 3 shows growth rate of capital formation (CF) along with area, production and yield of food grain and non-food grain crops. The CGR of all components of CF is positively significant at 1 per cent. The CGR of area for food grain crops is estimated negative but for non-food grain crops, it is both positive and negative. It is positively significant at 1 per cent level of significance for Tea (2.55 per cent), Coffee (3.24 per cent) and Potato (2.65 per cent) under non-food grain crops.

The CGR of production for food grain and non-food grain crops is positive for all the crops except for pulses (-0.004 per cent) in food grain crops and Tobacco (-1.20 per cent) in non-food grain crops. The CGR of production is positively significant at 1 per cent level of significance for Tea (1.81 per cent), Coffee (3.05 per cent) and Potato (2.92 per cent) among non-food grain crops. The CGR of yield for total food grain is positive and significant. It is positively significant at 1 per cent level of significance for Rice (0.97 per cent) and Coarse Cereals (1.9 per cent). For non- food grain crops the CGR of yield for sugarcane (-0.55 per cent) is negative but insignificant. It is negative and significant for Tea (-0.70) at 5 per cent level. For Jute and Mesta (1.97 per cent), the CGR of yield is positively significant at 1 per cent level.

Table 3, also presents the result of estimated instability index of capital formation in agriculture, area, production and yield for food grain and non-food grain crops. It is estimated that the components of capital formation in agriculture have high degree of instability. The degree of instability in area is found to be high for total non-food grain crops (0.058) as compared to total food grain crops (0.024). It is very low for all the food gain crops. For the non-food grain crops, the instability index of area for tobacco is found to be comparatively high. The instability index for production of food gains is found to be very low except pulses (0.100). This implies that the food grain crops are found to have faced less variation. It is found to be high for the non-food gain crops like cotton (0.249), tobacco (0.179) and total oilseed (0.167). The instability index for food grain and non-food grain crops are found to be very low for all the crops except Cotton (0.230), Total oilseed (0.109) and Potato (0.096) in non-food grain crops.

This implies that there is a year to year variation in components of capital formation in agriculture. The area of food grain crops is not affected much and it is almost stagnant over the period of time. The internal adjustment in cropped area is found to be high for non- food grains especially tobacco, total oilseeds and sugarcane.

Table 3
Growth Rates and Instability Index of Capital Formation and Area, Production and Yield of Food Grain and Non-food Grain Crops in India

Variables	*Annual Growth Rates (AGR in %)*	*Compound Growth Rates (CGR in %)*	*Instability Index (I_I)*
(1)	*(2)*	*(3)*	*(4)*
(A) Capital Formation			
GFCFA	12.40 (14.965)	14.69 *(15.944)	0.116
GCFAPuS	9.52 (7.755)	10.14* (6.953)	0.187
GCFAPrS	12.17 (7.776)	15.88 *(6.876)	0.289
GCFA	11.60 (8.482)	14.40 *(7.111)	0.255
(B) Area of Food Grain and Non Food Grain Crops			
Rice	-0.09 (0.426)	-0.09 (0.434)	0.029
Wheat	0.36 (1.481)	0.36 (1.485)	0.033
Coarse Cereals	-0.06 (3.210)	-0.83 *(3.132)	0.036
Pulses	-0.03 (0.073)	-0.03 (0.082)	0.050
Total Food Grains	-0.17 (0.954)	-0.17 (0.944)	0.024
Total Oilseed	0.005 (0.008)	-0.03 (0.055)	0.083
Sugarcane	6.95 (1.293)	0.64 (1.168)	0.072
Tea	2.51 (13.267)	2.55 *(12.858)	0.026
Coffee	3.04 (8.664)	3.24* (7.712)	0.056
Cotton	-0.13 (0.256)	-0.13 (0.252)	0.071
Jute and Mesta	-0.61 (1.195)	-0.60 (1.179)	0.069
Tobacco	-1.58 (1.376)	-1.53 (1.266)	0.161
potato	2.63 (5.987)	2.65 *(6.158)	0.057
Total Non Food Grains	0.15 (0.354)	0.13 (0.304)	0.058
(C) *Production of Food Grain and Non Food Grain Crops*			
Rice	0.92 (1.794)	0.90 (1.689)	0.071
Wheat	0.76 (1.935)	0.78 (1.967)	0.053
Coarse Cereals	1.05 (1.650)	1.02 (1.562)	0.088
Pulses	0.005 (0.006)	-0.004 (0.006)	0.100
Total Food Grains	0.82 (1.905)	0.82 (1.828)	0.060
Total Oilseed	0.95 (0.838)	0.79 (0.634)	0.167
Sugarcane	0.34 (0.426)	0.19 (0.239)	0.108
Tea	1.80 (8.455)	1.82* (8.581)	0.028
Coffee	2.74 (3.513)	3.05 *(3.628)	0.112
Cotton	4.17 (2.199)	3.41 (1.815)	0.249
Jute and Mesta	1.27 (2.467)	1.35 (2.518)	0.072
Tobacco	-1.26 (1.040)	-1.20 (0.897)	0.179
Potato	2.81 (3.096)	2.92* (3.167)	0.123

Contd...

Variables	*Annual Growth Rates (AGR in %)*	*Compound Growth Rates (CGR in %)*	*Instability Index (I_I)*
(1)	*(2)*	*(3)*	*(4)*
(D) *Yield of Food Grain and Non Food Grain Crops*			
Rice	0.98 (2.723)	0.97* (2.615)	0.050
Wheat	0.37 (1.438)	0.37 (1.470)	0.034
Coarse Cereals	1.89 (4.352)	1.90* (4.312)	0.059
Pulses	0.03 (0.056)	0.03 (0.071)	0.063
Total Food Grains	0.97 (3.397)	0.98 *(3.372)	0.039
Total Oilseed	0.76 (0.961)	0.69 (0.850)	0.109
Sugarcane	-0.54 (1.419)	-0.55 (1.417)	0.053
Tea	-0.70 (2.826)	-0.70 **(2.836)	0.033
Coffee	-0.03 (0.059)	0.03 (0.043)	0.077
Cotton	4.19 (2.419)	3.56 (2.053)	0.230
Jute and Mesta	1.97 (8.651)	1.97* (8.740)	0.030
Tobacco	0.43 (0.864)	0.43 (0.843)	0.069
Potato	0.27 (0.394)	0.26 (0.369)	0.096

Source: Computed

Notes: (1) Figures in parenthesis are the t-values; (2) *, ** shows the significance level at 1%, 5% respectively. Abbreviations: (1) GFCFA: Gross Fixed Capital Formation in Agriculture; (2) GCFAPuS: Gross Capital Formation in Agriculture in Public Sector; (3) GCFAPrS: Gross Capital Formation in Agriculture in Private Sector; (4) GCFA: Gross Capital Formation in Agriculture.

Relations between Agricultural Productivity and Capital Formation

Table 4 shows the relationship between agricultural productivity and capital formation. The impact of public and private sector gross capital formation on food grain productivity is found to be positive and significant (0.02 and 0.004

Table 4
Relations between Agricultural Productivity and Capital Formation

Model	R^2
(1)	*(2)*
Yield of Food grain crops = 1481.88 + 0.02* (GCFAPuS)	0.518
Yield of Food grain crops = 1516.24 + 0.004* (GCFAPrS)	0.512
Yield of Non-food grain crops[1] = 11788.22 - 0.0301 (GCFAPuS)	0.058
Yield of Non-food grain crops = 11746.70 - 0.007 (GCFAPuS)	0.064

Source: Computed

Notes: (1) * shows the significance level at 1 per cent

(2) [1]Yield of Total Non-food grains is calculated by averaging the yield of eight crops viz., total oilseed, sugarcane, tea, coffee, cotton, jute and mista, tobacco and potato.

Abbreviations: (1) GCFAPuS: Gross Capital Formation in Agriculture in Public Sector; (2) GCFAPrS: Gross Capital Formation in Agriculture in Private Sector.

per cent respectively a 1 per cent change in the amount of GCFAPuS and GCFAPrS would increase the food grain productivity by 0.02 per cent and 0.004 per cent respectively. The impact of GCFAPuS and GCFAPrs on non-food grain productivity is negative but insignificant.

CONCLUSIONS AND POLICY IMPLICATIONS

The study finds wide fluctuations in gross capital formation in agriculture during the period 1994-95 to 2006-07. The share of public sector capital formation to GCFA has decreased from 33.05 per cent in 1994-95 to 19.77 per cent in 2006-07, while that of private sector has increased from 66.95 per cent in 1994-95 to 80.23 per cent in 2006-07. Due to the limitation of the increase in cropped area, some internal adjustments were observed in the cropped area for different crops. The increase in the yield of both food grain and non-food grain during the study period indicates the use of agricultural inputs like HYV seeds, fertilizers, insecticides and pesticides, etc. which are met by the current expenditure.

The CGR of all the variables of capital formation is positive and significant. The CGR of area for food grain crops is estimated negative and significant for coarse cereals. For non-food grain crops it is both positive and significant for tea, coffee and potato. The CGR of production of food grain is found to be positive but insignificant for all the crops while it is positive and significant for tea, coffee and potato among the non-food grain crops. For the yield of food grain, the CGR is positive and significant for rice, wheat and coarse cereals and also for the total food grains. For non-food grains, it is negative and significant for tea and positive and significant for jute and mesta.

The instability index is found to be high for capital formation. About the cropped area, it is high for tobacco and about production; it is high for pulses, total oilseed, sugarcane, coffee, cotton, tobacco and potato. The instability index for yield is high for total oilseed and cotton.

The study shows the importance of gross capital formation both in private and public sector for food grains.

Hence it is suggested that in order to increase the food grain productivity, the capital formation in both the sectors is important. The degree of instability in area, production and yield in food grain is very low. Therefore, the increase in agricultural productivity of food grains would not only solve the problem of food insecurity but would also be able to maintain sustainability.

References

Bagwati, Jagdish and Srinivasan, T. N. (1993), *"India's Economic Reforms: Report"*, Ministry, Government of India, New Delhi.

Dantwala, M. L. (1986), "Strategy of Agricultural Development since Independence", in M. L. Dantwala and others (1986), *Indian Agricultural Development since Independence – A Collection of Essays*, Oxford and IBH Publishing Co. Pvt. Ltd., New Delhi.

Deshmukh, M. B. and M. P. Bhargave (1954), "Capital Formation in Indian Agriculture", *Indian Journal of Agricultural Economics,* Vol. 9, No. 1, January-February.

Dhawan, B. D. and Yadav, S. S. (1995), "Private Fixed Capital Formation in Agriculture: Some Aspects of Indian Farmers' Capital formation Behaviour", *Economic and Political Weekly,* Vol. 30, No. 39, September 30, pp. A–103–A–109.

Economic Survey of India (1999 - 2000), Ministry of Finance, Government of India.

Gandhi, V. P. (1990), *"Capital formation Behaviour in Developing Countries–A Case of Agriculture in India"*, Food Research Institute Studies, Vol. 22, No. 10.

Gandhi,V. P. (1996), "Capital formation Behaviour in Indian Agriculture", *Indian Journal of Agricultural Economics,* Vol. 51, No. 4, October–December, pp. 543–559.

Gulati, Ashok and Bhide, Shashanka (1993), *"New Economic Policy: Likely Implications for Agriculture"*, Proceedings, First National Conference on Agricultural Policy in the Context of New Economic Policy, February 24–25, p. 26.

Kurian, A. P. (1969), "Estimates of Private Capital Expenditure in Agriculture during the Period 1969–70 to 1973–74", *Indian Journal of Agricultural Economics,* Vol. XXIV, No. 4, October–December, pp. 67-70.

Mallick, S. K. (1993), "Capital Formation in Indian Agriculture: Recent Trends", *Indian Journal of Agricultural Economics,* Vol. 48, No. 4, October–December.

Mani, K. P., P. Shaheena and P. Chacko Jose (1996), "Some Reflection on Capital Formation in Indian Agriculture" *Indian Journal of Agricultural Economics,* Vol. 51, No. 4, October–December, pp. 569–578.

Mishra, S. N. and Chand, Ramesh (1995), "Public and Private Capital Formation in Indian Agriculture: Comments on Complementarily Hypothesis and others", *Economic and political Weekly,* Vol. 30, No. 25, June 24, pp. A-64–A-79.

Misra, V. N. and Peter B. R. Hazell (1996), "Terms of Trade, Rural Poverty, Technology and Capital formation: The Indian Experience, 1952-53 to 1990-91", *Economic and Political Weekly,* Vol. 31, No. 13, March 30.

Mitra, Ashok, K. (1996), *" Public and Private Capital formation in Agriculture"*, Paper Presented at the National Seminar on Agricultural Development Perspective for the Ninth Five Year Plan, Indian Institute of Management, Ahmedabad.

Mujumdar, N. A. and K. A. Menon (1991), "Saving and Capital Formation in the Agricultural Sector: A Review", in M. L. Dantwala (Ed.) (1991), *Indian Agricultural Development since Independence,* Second Revised Edition, Oxford and IBH Publishing Co. Pvt. Ltd., New Delhi.

Nayyar, Deepak (1993), "Indian Economy at the Cross Roads: Illusions and Realities", *Economic and Political Weekly,* Vol. 28, No. 15, April 10.

Panikar, P. G. K. (1969), "Capital Formation in Indian Agriculture", *Indian Journal of Agricultural Economics,* Vol. 24, No. 4, October–December.

Parthasarathy, G. (1984), "Growth and Fluctuations of Agricultural Production: A District-Wise Analysis in Andhra Pradesh", *Economic and Political Weekly,* Vol. 19, No. 26, June 30, pp. A-74 to A-84.

Praksh, Gyan, Ram Kumar Jha, R C Sharma (2006), "Estimating Marketing Efficiency of Chicken (Fowl) Farms: An Empirical Analysis" *ICFAI Journal of Agricultural Economics*, Hyderabad, Vol. IV, No. 1, January, pp. 36-42.

Ram, G. S. (1993), *"New Economic Policy and Agricultural Capital formation"*, Proceedings, First National Conference on Agricultural Policy in the Context of New Economic Policy, February 24–25, p. 14.

Rao, C. H., Hanumantha (1994), *"Agricultural Growth, Rural Poverty and Environmental Degradation in India"*, Oxford university Press, New Delhi.

Rao, G.V. K. (1992), "Strategies for Agricultural Development in the Nineties", *Financing Agriculture,* Vol. 24, No. 1, January–March.

Rath, Nilakantha (1989), "Agricultural Growth and Capital formation in India", *Journal of Indian School of Political Economy,* Vol. 1, No. 1, January–June.

Schiff, Maurice and Alberto Valdes (1992), "Capital Formation in Agriculture", *New England Economic Review,* Boston, p. 32.

Shetty, S. L. (1990), "Capital Formation in Indian Agriculture: Brief Review of Recent Trends", *Economic and Political Weekly,* Vol. 25, Nos. 7 and 8, February 17–24.

Shukla, Tara (1965), "Rate of Gross and Net Capital Formation in Indian Agriculture and Factor Influencing them", *Indian Agricultural Economics,* Vol. 20, No. 1, January–March.

Singh, Karam (1997), "Trends and Determinants of Capital Formation on Indian Agriculture", A Rappoteur Report, *Indian Journal of Agricultural Economics,* Vol. 52, No. 1, January-March, pp. 48-51.

Singh, Rachhpal, Bant Singh and Jaswinder Kaur (1996), "A Spatio-Temporal Analysis of Capital Accumulation on Punjab Farms", *Indian Journal of Agricultural Economics,* Vol. 51, No. 4, October-December, pp. 579-586.

Swaminathan, M. S. (1992), "Agriculture for the 21st Century: New Thinking Needed", *Financing Agriculture,* Vol. 24, No. 1, January–March.

Wasim, Mohammad Pervez (2001), "Agricultural Growth and Instability in Major Crops Production: A Province-Wise Analysis in Pakistan", *Asian Economic Review,* Vol. 43, No. 2, pp. 294-314.

INFLUENCE OF GROWTH DETERMINANTS ON BUSINESS INCOME OF WOMEN ENTREPRENEURS THROUGH SHGs IN TIRUVALLUR DISTRICT OF TAMIL NADU

*D. Revathi Pandian** *& G. Vasanthi***

INTRODUCTION

In almost all the societies, women have less power than men, have less control over resources and receive lesser wages for their work. They remain as an 'invisible' work force. Inevitably, all these affect women's capacity to open up, grow, develop, exceed and excel. It is unfortunate that because of centuries of inertia, ignorance and conservatism, the actual and potential role of women in the society has been ignored, preventing them from making their rightful contribution to social progress.

Women in India constitute about 50 per cent of the total population and comprise one third of the labour force. It is, therefore, important that when considering the economic development of this segment of the population, due attention is given to their socio-economic empowerment. India envisions a future in which Indian women are independent and self-reliant (Agarwal, 2001).

Women must be empowered by enhancing their awareness, knowledge; skills and technology use efficiency, thereby, facilitating overall development of the society. In various national policies and developmental programmes, emphasis has been given on organizing women in Self Help Groups and thus, marks the beginning of a major process of empowering women (Ashford, 1995).

Micro finance and SHG intervention have brought tremendous change in the life of women at the grass root. Unlike the other kind of micro finance, self help group have savings as a base which created a binding on the part of the women and also the financial partners, say banks, to extend credit to the hitherto unreached poor, women. It has succeeded in bringing several women to

* Assistant Professor, Department of Management Studies, Vellmamal Engineering College, Chennai.

** Professor, Department of Commerce, Annamalai University, Chidambaram.

compulsory savings and through some committed women in the group and NGOs support they have been able to avail micro credit in the form of revolving credit and economic assistance.

Entrepreneurship development and income generating activities are a feasible solution for empowering women. It generates income and also provides flexible working hours according to the needs of home makers. Economic independence is the need of the hour. Participation in income generating activities helps in the overall empowerment of women. Empowering women through education, ideas, consciousness, mobilization and participatory approach can enable them to take their own decisions, make them self-reliant and self-confident.

The emergence of women entrepreneurship in the past two decades and especially in the second half of the 1990's is not a coincidence. First of all, the entire business environment has changed. Women are being encouraged to participate in various business activities - a process that was unimaginable decades ago. Next, the rapid development of computers and information technology makes starting and operating a business easier, with less capital and a lower minimum efficient level of production. Third, the rapid expansion and specialization of the service sector have provided women with new opportunities to pursue their own business careers. Finally, new business tools, like the internet and e-commerce make flexible working hours possible and help balance women's responsibilities in workplace and the family.

Although women are taking on important positions in the business sector, they continue to face barriers to their entrepreneurial activities, compared to their male counterparts. Some barriers are general to women and men, such as administrative barriers, including the regulations of business establishments. However, others are gender-specific and have severe implications for women entrepreneurs, especially those in SMEs and micro businesses. Women still have to struggle with their traditional role in order to balance career and household responsibilities. They have to endure negative social value and cultural bias that lead to unfair perceptions about their ability to operate a business and legal constraints also limit the pursuit of economic independence by women. With this background, the present study was attempted to study the influence of growth determinants on business income of women entrepreneurs through SHGs in Tiruvallur district of Tamil Nadu.

METHODOLOGY

Among the different districts in Tamil Nadu, the Tiruvallur district has been purposively selected for the present study. Among different geographical locations in the district, Madavaram, Manali, Redhills and Tiruvallur have been again purposively selected based on the concentration of number of Self Help Groups (SHGs) and members. The data and information have been collected from the respondents by adopting random sampling technique. The district has been selected purposively followed by geographical location and the sample respondents have been selected randomly thus, multi-stage random sampling technique has been adopted for data collection. The data and information have been collected from the sample size of 500 through pre-tested, structured interview schedule through direct interview method. The primary data collected from respondents pertains to the year 2008-2009.

STATISTICAL TECHNIQUES

Descriptive Statistics and Chi-Square Test

In order to analyze the socio-demographic features, the descriptive statistics has been carried out. Besides, in order to analyze the differences among the socio-economic features, the Chi-Square test is employed and the formula is:

$$\chi^2 = \Sigma\left(\left(\frac{O-E}{E}\right)^2\right)$$

Where

O = Observed Frequency in each category

E = Expected Frequency in the corresponding category

df is the "degree of freedom" (r-1)(c-1)

Determinates of Business Income

In order to assess the influence growth determinants on income generation of women entrepreneurs, the multiple linear regression analysis by Ordinary Least Square (OLS) estimation has been applied for identified variables. The functional form of multiple liner regression model are given below:

$$Y = \alpha + \beta_i X_i + e_i$$

Where

Y = Dependent Variable (Business Income)

X_i = Independent Variable(Growth Determinants)

i = 1 to 15

α = Intercept

β_i = Partial Regression Coefficients

e_i = Random Error or Stochastic Disturbance Term

The α and β_i are the coefficients which are to be calculated through Ordinary Least Square (OLS) estimation.

RESULTS AND DISCUSSION

Socio-Demographics

The socio-demographic features of women entrepreneurs were analyzed and the results are hereunder discussed. The age distributions of women entrepreneurs were analyzed and the results are presented in Table 1. From the Table, the majority of women entrepreneurs (52.80 per cent) belonged to the age group of 30-45 years followed by less than 30 years (41.80 per cent). Only 5.40 per cent of women were in the age group of 45 and above 45 years. The chi square value was 0.01 and it was statically significant at five per cent level of significance indicating that there was a significant difference between age of the women entrepreneurs.

Table 1
Frequency Distribution of Age of Women Entrepreneurs

Age	*Frequency*	*Per cent*	*Chi Square Value*	*Sig*
< 30 Years	209	41.80	0.010	0.00
30-45 Years	264	52.80		
45 and Above	27	5.40		
Total	500	100.00		

Source: Primary & Computed Data

The educational qualifications of the women entrepreneurs are presented in Table 2. The results indicated that about half of the entrepreneurs (50.40 per cent) have school education followed by under graduation (42.80 per cent). The post graduation and professionals accounted about only 2.60 per cent while illiterates were only 4.20 per cent. The chi square value was 0.05 and it was statically significant at five per cent level of significance indicating that there was a significant difference between educational qualifications of the women entrepreneurs.

Table 2
Frequency Distribution of Qualification

Educational Qualification	*Frequency*	*Per cent*	*Chi Square Value*	*Sig*
School Education	252	50.40	0.050	0.00
Under Graduation	214	42.80		
Post Graduation and Professionals	13	2.60		
Illiterates	21	4.20		
Total	500	100.00		

Source: Primary & Computed Data

The source of income from business for women entrepreneurs are presented in Table 3. The results showed that about 48 per cent of women entrepreneurs earned income in the range of Rs. 50000-1 lakh from their business followed by less than Rs. 50000 (33.00 per cent). About 18 per cent of entrepreneurs earned the income in the range of Rs.1 lakh-150000 and only 0.4 per cent earned their income in the range of above 2.5 lakh. The chi square value was 0.02 and it was statically significant at five per cent level of significance indicating that there was a significant difference between business income for the women entrepreneurs.

Table 3
Frequency Distribution of Business Income

Business Income (Rs)	*Frequency*	*Per cent*	*Chi Square Value*	*Sig*
< 50000	165	33.00	0.02	0.01
50000-1 Lakh	240	48.00		
1 Lakh- 150000	90	18.00		
150000-2.5 Lakh	3	0.60		
> 2.5 Lakh	2	0.40		
Total	500	100.00		

Source: Primary & Computed Data

The distribution of sector wise business activity is presented in Table 4. It is clear that about 48 per cent of women entrepreneurs were involving in marketing followed by supplier (23.40 per cent). About 16.60 per cent of the women carried manufacturing activities while, only 12.00 per cent was involving in service sector activities. The chi square value was 0.01 and it was statically significant at five per cent level of significance indicating that there was a significant difference between sector of business activity of the women entrepreneurs.

Table 4
Frequency Distribution of Sector of Business Activity

Sector	*Frequency*	*Per cent*	*Chi Square Value*	*Sig*
Manufacturing	83	16.60	0.01	0.00
Marketing	240	48.00		
Supplier	117	23.40		
Service	60	12.00		
Total	500	100.00		

Source: Primary & Computed Data.

The enterprise base of the women entrepreneurs is presented in Table 5. From the table, it is apparent that the enterprise base for majority of the entrepreneurs (60.40 per cent) was semi-urban followed by urban (37.60 per cent).Only two per cent of them, used metropolitan area as their enterprise base. The chi square value was 0.02 and it was statically significant at five per cent level of significance indicating that there was a significant difference between enterprise base of the women entrepreneurs.

Table 5
Frequency Distribution of Enterprise Base

Sector	*Frequency*	*Per cent*	*Chi Square Value*	*Sig*
Semi Urban	302	60.40	0.02	0.01
Urban	188	37.60		
Metropolitan	10	2.00		
Total	500	100.00		

Source: Primary & Computed Data

Determinates of Business Income

In order to assess the influence growth determinants on income generation of women entrepreneurs, the multiple linear regression analysis by Ordinary Least Square (OLS) estimation has been applied and the results are presented in Table-6. The results of multiple linear regression analysis through OLS estimation is presented in Table 6. The results show that the coefficient of multiple determination (R^2) is 0.46 indicating the regression model is moderately fit.

Table 6
Regression Estimates of the Variable Influencing the Business Income

Growth Determinants	*Regression Coefficients*	*t-value*	*Significance*
Intercept	2.030**	11.468	.000
My status improved when I achieved better results	-.008	-.247	.805
My advisers help me in smooth conduct of business	-.008	-.251	.802
My past experience strengthens and develops network	-.021	-.720	.472
Capital planning at each stage helped me to develop	.041**	2.224	.021
Correct business location contributed to my success	-.075**	-2.508	.012
Incentives, subsidies and concessions provided by Central/State Government are great assistance to me	.072**	2.376	.018
I take measures to protect the environment as I grow	-.035	-1.038	.300
As I gain more experience I commit less mistakes	.037**	2.145	.023
Legal status of the organization led to my growth	.038**	2.227	.020
Proper pricing strategy enhanced my growth	-.014	-1.058	.291*
Orientation and training assisted me to run my business	-.045	-1.417	.157
Infrastructure facilities provided by the Government has led to development of the business	.029**	2.842	.010
Liberalization, Privatization and Globalization policy of the Government led to my present growth	-.095**	-2.623	.009
Quick and prompt decision marking helped me to grow	.038	1.105	.270
My friendly attitude towards labour led me to my success	-.017	-.572	.568
R^2	0.46		
Adjusted R^2	0.28		
F	2.304		0.004
N	500		

Note: **Significance at one per cent level
Source: Computed Data.

The independent variables of My past experience strengthens and develops network(X_4), Correct business location contributed to my success (X_6), I take measures to protect the environment as I grow (X_8), As I gain more experience I commit less mistakes (X_9) and Orientation and training assisted me to run my business (X_{12}) are statistically significant at one per cent level of significance and these variables are positively influencing the business income of the women entrepreneurs.

The factors Capital planning at each stage helped me to develop (X_5) and Infrastructure facilities provided by the Government has led to development of the business (X_{13}) are also statistically significant at one per cent of level of significance but, these factors are negatively influencing the business income of women entrepreneurs through self-help groups.

CONCLUSION

The forgoing analysis indicted that the socio-demographic features of the women entrepreneurs are significantly different in various aspects. About 52.80 per cent of women entrepreneurs belong to the age group of 30-45 years followed by less than 30 years. It was evident that about 62.42 per cent of women in the business income group of Rs. less than 50000, 55.42 per cent in the income group of Rs. 50000-1 lakh and 73.00 per cent in the income group of Rs. 1 lakh-15000 have invested less than Rs. 25 lakhs. About 48 per cent of women entrepreneurs were involving in marketing followed by supplier (23.40 per cent). About 16.60 per cent of the women carried manufacturing activities while, only 12.00 per cent was involving in service sector activities.

My past experience strengthens and develops network, Correct business location contributed to my success, I take measures to protect the environment as I grow, As I gain more experience I commit less mistakes and Orientation and training assisted me to run my business are positively influencing the business income of the women entrepreneurs.

Entrepreneurial development should not be left to chance, as is the practice now. The training programmes should include identification and selection of potential entrepreneurs, and their motivation into entrepreneurial career through provision training and other inputs necessary to set up entrepreneurial units.

The growth of women entrepreneurs should be encouraged by providing special incentives, tax concessions, reduced rat of interest, transport and fuel subsidies. For creating a healthy entrepreneurial environment, they should also be given orientation about the various tools and techniques of accounting and finance.

Lack of coordination among the institutions in providing power, water, communication and finance seriously hinder the growth of women entrepreneurship. To improve this situation, the proper coordination mechanism and monitoring system should be formulated and implemented.

References

Agrawal, S. (2003), "Technology Model for Women's Empowerment", *Kurukshetra*, May, pp. 18-28.

Ahmad, M.A. (1999), "Women Empowerment: Self Help Groups", Kurukshetra, April, pp. 13-15.

Ashford, L. (1995), 'Gender Equality and the Empowerment of Women'. *Population Bulletin,* 50 (1), pp. 17 - 22.

Batliwala, S. (1994), 'The Meaning of Women's Empowerment: New Concepts from Action'. In Sen, G., Germain, A., and Chen, L., (Eds). Population Policies Reconsidered: Health, Empowerment and Rights, Boston, Harvard University Press.

Bharat Dogra (2002), "Women Self-Help Groups Kindling Spirit of Entrepreneurship", *Kurukshetra,* 50(5), pp. 40-42.

Deepti Agarwal (2001), "Empowerment of Rural Woman in India", *Social Welfare,* 48(4), pp. 3-4.

Gain, Raji T. S. and P. Satish (1995), "A Micro Study on Group Dynamics and Group Functioning", Working Paper No. 6, Banker's Institute of Rural Development.

Huq, A. and Richardson, P. (1997), "Business Ownership as an Economic Option for Middle-Income Educated Urban Women in Bangladesh", Frontiers of Entrepreneurship Research, pp. 240-241.

Kabeer, Naila (1999), "Resources, Agency, Achievements: Reflections on the Measurement of Women's Empowerment", Development and Change, 30, pp. 435-464.

Leelamma Devasia, V., V., Devasia (1994), Empowering Women Folk Sustainable Development, Ashish Publishing House, New Delhi.

Manimekalai, M. and Rajeshwari, G. (2001), "Nature And Performance of Informal Self Help Groups–A Case From Tamil Nadu", *Indian Journal of Agricultural Economics,* 56 (3), pp. 34-46.

Morrison, A., Breen, J. and Ali, S. (2003), "Small Business Growth: Intention, Ability and Opportunity", *Journal of Small Business Management,* 41(4), pp. 417-425.

Naggayya, D. (2000), "Micro-Finance for Self Help Groups", *Kurukshetra,* 42(2), August, pp. 15-26.

Purithavarthy Pandian, S., R., Eswaran (2002), "Empowerment of Women Through Micro-Credit", *Yojana,* November, pp. 124-132.

Reserve Bank of India (2005), Report of the Internal Group to Examine Issues Relating to Rural Credit and Microfinance.

Senthil Vadivoo, K. and V. Sekar (2004), "Self Help Groups a Movement for Women Services: How the Poor in India Could be Better Served?", *Kissan World,* 31(7), pp. 13-14.

Sharma, K. C. (2001), "Micro Financing Through SHG's", *Indian Journal of Agricultural Economic,* 56 (3), pp. 76-86.

Srinivasan, R. and Sriram, M. S. (2003), "Round Table Microfinance in India: Discussion", *Management Review,* 15(2), pp. 52-86.

Tripathy K.K (2004), "Self-Help Groups-A Catalyst of Rural Development", *Kurukshetra,* 52(8) pp. 40-43.

Vijayanthi (2002), "Women's Empowerment through Self-Help Group: A Participatory Approach", *Indian Journal of Gender Studies,* pp. 263-273.

RETAIL REVOLUTION IN FMFPs (FAST MOVING FOOD PRODUCTS) TARGETING ORGANISED INDIAN–RETAIL MARKETS

*D. Ravindran**

INTRODUCTION

In last two decades the world itself facing the tremendous changes in the manufacturing and retailing consumer products. The industrial and services sector growth has direct impact on the need of the development of agriculture sector, mainly the demand for the food products. The increase in the purchasing power of the global population and the innovations in farm practices, advancement in food processing storing and organized distribution leads to the importance of food retailing concept. The market is now with variety of consumers with changing lifestyle, food habits and buying behavior caused the emergence of new format food and grocery stores, food chains and retail stores. New format stores or modern outlets are evolving with heavy investments, under global brand banners along with structured management setup. Many chain stores are coming up newly as a diversification of various business giants, as they identified the opportunity in retail trade and growing need of food and consumption related products with convenience of availability and service. Though India is ranking in top among the production of food categories in the world and also largest milk and dairy producer at lower cost of production, But it backdrop in handling, storing, processing and marketing encouraged the foreign players and retail giants to enjoy the gaps in the food retailing with huge profit and growth. The industrial and service sectors development in urban market attracts the population to get crowded in the metros due to employment and educational opportunities. The rural population is focusing on agricultural activities. The retail majors acts as an intermediary in procuring rural food products and processing, packing and promoting them in the urban market.

* Lecturer, JSN School of Management, Kanchipuram.

RETAIL HISTORY IN INDIA

Retailing is not a new concept in India, India was referred as "Nation of Shopkeepers", as it has the large number of retail enterprises in the country. In 2003 itself it accounted about 12 million retail shops among them over 78% were family-owned having family members both in management and service level. By National readership survey in 1999, averagely 6.6% of urban adults and 2% rural adults were shopkeepers. In that time organized retail was only 3% of total in terms of value, but at the same time US was 80%, West Europe 70%, Brazil and Argentina 40%, Korea and Taiwan 35%, Malaysia, Thailand and China 20%. Food beverages and tobacco contributed 71% of the retail sales.

But now the retail revolution all over world including India is tremendous with the emergence of new format stores. Co-operative retail, Supermarkets, retail chains, shopping malls, retail outlets with in the organizations, cinema theatres etc. As the business giants identified the retailing opportunities they are investing huge and huge for retail development. Some manufacturing companies are concentrating production of certain products focusing only the customer of these retails. Breaking the FDI limitations in retail sector, in India by 1997, foreign retailers made their entry by franchising agreements with local players. By 1990's itself "Chain Stores" concept evolved.

Table 1
Fastest Growing Retail Segments In India

Category	*Growth in %*
Food & Grocery	91
Clothing	55
Furniture & Fixtures	27
Pharmacy	27
Durables	18
Leather & Footwear	18
Watch & Jewellery	18

Source: KPMG in India Retail Survey 2005.

Table 2
Malls and Mall Space in 2008

Town	*Malls*	*Gross Leasable area (m.sf)*
Delhi	96	23.5
Mumbai	55	16.2
Bangalore	14	8.0
Chennai	6	2.5
Kolkatta	10	3.2
Hyderabad	12	4.2
Pune	19	5.6
Ahmedabad	7	2.7

Source: Deutsche Bank Research 2008

RETAIL COMPANIES IN INDIA

In India there exist large number of retail companies and outlets. To name a few, given as below:

Aditya Birla Retail Limited, Arvind Brands Ltd., Avenue Supermarts Pvt. Ltd., (D-Mart) Bharat Petroleum Corporation Ltd., Ebony Retail Holdings Ltd., Heritage Foods (India) Ltd., Infiniti Retail Ltd., ITC Ltd., Kirtilal Kalidas & Co., Koutons Retail India Ltd., Lakewood Malls Pvt. Ltd., (Haiko) Levi Strauss (India) Pvt. Ltd., Lifestyle International Pvt. Ltd., McDonald's India (West & South), MnM Marketing Private Ltd., NEXT Retail India Ltd., Odyssey India Ltd., Oswal Retail Pvt. Ltd. Pantaloon Retail (India) Ltd., Personality Ltd., (Weekender) Piramyd Retail Ltd., Planet M Provogue India Ltd., Reliance Petro Marketing Pvt. Ltd., RPG Retail, Sankalp Retail Value Stores Pvt. Ltd., Shoppers' Stop, Subiksha Trading Services Pvt. Ltd., Vishal Retail Ltd., Wadhawan Food Retail Pvt. Ltd., WITCO (India) Ltd. Hot Spot Retail, AIMS Retail-Mc club, Home Store, Spinac etc..

ORGANISED RETAILING TRENDS IN INDIA

In India the structure of retailing is also developing rapidly. Shopping malls are becoming increasingly common in large cities. The number of department stores is growing much faster than overall retail, at an annual rate of 24 per cent. Supermarkets have been taking an increasing share of general food and grocery. The Indian retail sector is highly fragmented with about 15 million retailers. Out of the large number of total retail outlets in the country, majority of them relate to the food items. Since 1990s, big industrial houses like Rahejas, Piramals, Tatas, etc have started entering the retail industry. Besides, several Indian and foreign companies have been franchising for establishing exclusive outlets for their brands, both within the country and overseas. For instance, 'Bharati Group' had entered into a joint venture with the world's largest retail chain the 'Wal-Mart'. As a result, the Indian retail sector has been undergoing a rapid transformation in the past few years. The traditional formats of kirana stores, hawkers, grocers, etc are being gradually taken over by the modern formats of department stores, discount stores, malls, supermarkets, convenience stores, fast food outlets, specialty stores, warehouse retailers, hypermarkets, etc. For example, Pantaloon started the 'Big Bazaar' discount stores in 2002; Reliance opened its first supermarket named 'Reliance Fresh' outlet in Hyderabad and has since fanned out to several States; Subhiksha outlets have been fast spreading across the nation; etc. Thus, the current face of Indian retail comprising the unorganised small and medium retailers is slowly changing into a more organised form of retailing.

As per the available estimates, of the Rs.1,330,000 crore retail market, food and grocery retail is the single largest block estimated to be worth Rs.7,92,000 crore (with 59.5 per cent share), but the share of organised sector in this is miniscule. Clothing, textiles and fashion accessories constitute the second largest block with a 9.9 per cent share at Rs. 1,31,300 crore. But the largest segments as far as organised retailing is concerned are the time wear (48.9 per cent share) and footwear (48.4 per cent share) sectors. In 2007, the share of organised retail was estimated to be 5.9 per cent, which was Rs. 78,300 crore. This retail is expected to touch Rs. 2,30,000 crore (at constant prices) by 2010, constituting roughly 13 per cent of the total retail market. However, the modern retail segment grew at the rate of 42.4 per cent in 2007 and is expected to maintain a faster growth rate, especially in view of the fact that major global players and Indian corporate houses are entering into the market in a big way. This growth in modern retailing is linked to several factors particularly, the increasing purchasing power; rapid global interaction and integration as well as the changing consumer needs, lifestyle and attitude. Further, shopping centre business alone is estimated to become Rs. 40,000 crore business by 2010-11.

RURAL RETAILING IN INDIA

The higher income group in rural India is growing at a phenomenal rate, and the concept of brands and quality are very much prevalent. These current consumption trends provide compelling opportunities for marketers to capitalize on the increasing mass market in India for almost all product categories. Both corporations and entrepreneurs are exploring the rural retailing. ITC's Choupal Sagar, HLL's project Shakthi and Mahamaza are some of the models that are being tried out. Many more such concepts are likely to be tested in the future. The case for Indian retailers to explore rural markets is strong. Given the size of the rural population and the agricultural income growth in rural India, the rural market is definitely an opportunity for retailers with an innovative retail proposition.

Table 3
Share of Urban and Rural markets

Category	*Rural*	*Urban*
Food	64 %	36 %
Clothing & Footwear	61 %	39 %
Misc. Consumer Goods	57 %	43 %
Durables	50 %	50 5
Consumer Services	44 %	56 %
Entertainment	33 %	67 %

Source: NSSO- 5th Round KPMG in India analysis 2005.

Food Retailing

In India average spending of the population in food and grocery items is around 70% of total purchase. Food retail sales in India are around 60% of total retail sale. But the sales of fresh and packaged food through organized retailers are not even 5%. But the same thing is raying from 30–50% in Latin America, China, and Southern Asia etc. This clearly shows the opportunities in food retailing. Nowadays we can see the vegetables, fruits, poultry, meat, dairy products both in fresh and processed manner in the organized retail showrooms with reasonable price in sophisticated environment for buying.

Table 4
Few Food Retailers in India

Name	*Type*
Big Bazaar	Hyper Market
Giant	Hyper Market
Food world	Food Supermarket
Nilgiris	Food Supermarket
Margin Free Markets	Discount Grocery
Subiksha	Discount Grocery
More	Hyper Market
Spencer	Food Supermarket
Reliance Fresh	Food Supermarket
Food Bazaar	Food Supermarket
McDonald's	Food Supermarket
Pizza Corner	Pizza Point
Dominas	Pizza Point
Café-Coffee Day	Refreshment
Barista Coffee	Refreshment
Trinethra	Food Market
Apua Bazaar	Hyper Market
Namdhari's Fresh	Fresh Fruit & Vegetable Market
Hopcoms	Fresh Fruit & Vegetable Market

Table 5
Food Products Available in Food Retail

Type	*Products*
Commodity	Tea, Coffee, Rice, Wheat etc
Pices	Cardamom, Black Pepper, White Pepper, Ginger, Turmeric, Vanilla, Mustard, Tamarind, Clove, Cinnamon, Chilli etc
Fruits	Mango, Banana, Pine apple, Grapes, Passion fruit, Cashewnut, Walnut etc.
Vegetables	Brinjal, Onion, Tomato, Potato, Cabbage etc.
Oils	Sesame, Castor, Sunflower, Dalda etc.
Pulses	Red Gram, Black Gram etc.

Table 6
Top 10 Food Retailers in the World

Company	*Head quarter*
Wal-Mart	USA
Carrefour	France
Tesco	UK
Metro Group	Germany
Kroger	USA
Ahold	Netherlands
Costco	USA
Rewe	Germany
Schwarz Group	Germany
Aldi	Germany

Source: www.supermarketnews.com

RPG GROUP

Rama Prasad Goenka group which ahs more than 20 companies in seven different industries like power, tyres, retail etc was one of the early entrants in to the organized retail sector in India. "Food World" was launched by RPG in 1999 had 90 Food World stores. Food World has Joint venture with Spencers & company and Dairy farm foundation of US. It was growing at 30% CAGR (Compounded annual Growth Rate). It has operation in 12 cities.

It stocks about 5000 items (fresh vegetables, fruits, cereals, pulses). An outlet geneses ranges from 3000 to 3500 safe in size. Handle 600 customers. It operates on "Hub and Spokes" model (i.e. a large stores as the control point hug) for servicing a smaller stores (spokes) Scattered geographically.

"Food World" sells some products in their own with pricing other 10-15%. Lower than brand leaders, and services of "No Questions Asked Replacement Guarantees." These own branded contributes to 22%. Of total business RPG also owns Spencer's Hypermarket, a chain of retail hypermarket providing all product Categories.

PANTALOON RETAIL INDIA LIMITED (PRIL)

The mega retail outlet in India exists in varies forms Pantaloon, Big Bazaar, Food Bazaar, Gold Bazaar, and Central Mall. It was incorporated in October 1987 as' Manz Wear Private Ltd.', and become public limited company in September 1991. PRIL in 2005 extended its business with 16 Pantaloon department stores, 21 Big Bazaar, 33 Food Bazaar, 3 Central Malls, Among this Food Bazaar mainly focused towards selling food items and groceries. It has over 50,000 Stock Keeping Units (SKU) that covered a range of products like cereals, Pulses, Sugar, Rice, Juices, milk products and FMCG products besides Vegetables and Fruits, The products are sold at discounts ranging from 2-20% the " In house brands" (Made by themselves) are marketed under the name of 'Premium Harvest', for pulses, rice, flour etc. While , 'ready to cook or eat ' products are sold under 'Tasty Treat' brand.

Table 7
Six Hot Shops in Food Bazaar

Shop Name	*Purpose*
Farm Fresh	Selling Good quality fresh fruits and Vegetables at lower price...
Chill station	Selling Dairy products, Aerated drinks, Juices and Frozen Foods...
Golden Harvest	Selling varieties of rice, wheat, pulses, cereals, flour, oils, tea, spices both in loose and packed forms...
Chef Zone	Selling instant cooked foods like soups, gravy mix, sausages...
Hungry Kay!	Selling ready to eat food items like biscuits, chocolates, chips...
Head-to-Toe	Selling personal care items like Shampoos, Cosmetics, Talcum powders...

FOOD SAFETY AND PRICING ISSUES

To ensure a strong presence in global markets, India needs to meet international standards in food safety. The increase in world food trade and the advent of the Sanitary and Phytosanitary (SPS) Agreement under the World Trade Organization (WTO) have also raised interest in food safety requirements. The Government has put more stringent food safety and public health measures on manufacturing, storing and packaging of foodstuffs. The Codex, HACCP (The Hazard Analysis Critical Control Point) and food-hygiene standards have been adopted by the Bureau of Indian Standards, the national standards body in India. Food processing units are being encouraged to adopt these systems on a voluntary basis. There are extensive controls on packaging, labeling and certification. The Bureau of Indian Standards (BIS) maintains a list of over 17,000 product standards of which only around 3,700 are in line with international norms. BIS health and safety certification marks are obligatory for certain food products. Price controls have been progressively liberalized since 1992, but a small number of items covered by the Essential Commodities Act 1955 remain fully controlled, including coal and petroleum products. Sugar and some foods such as cereals are partly controlled; prices of kerosene and liquid petroleum gas are subsidized by central government. Most packaged goods and all imported goods must carry maximum price tags. In general, prices not controlled by central government can only be limited to a maximum price; minimum price maintenance is not permitted.

LESSONS TO BE LEARNED BY FOOD RETAILERS

Domestic operator Subhiksha is one of the retailers that expanded rapidly, growing from some 50 stores in 2006 to a store network of over 1,500 outlets today. While its aggressive approach to growth is typical of India's expansionary local players, unlike many of its more cautious peers, Subhiksha has expanded almost entirely through debt. The company's inability to re-service its mounting debts resulted in a sustained failure to pay both suppliers and employees. In February around 600 Subhiksha retail outlets and warehousing facilities were vandalised when the normally-guarded units were left unstaffed after the company's repeated non-payment of security service bills, according to a report in the Financial Times. Subhiksha is now in talks with investors about raising an estimated INR3bn (US $61.8mn) to get it back on track in the short term, while it is also examining ways of restructuring its heavy debts. With neither measure likely to have an immediate resolution, it is expected to be forced to close a large number of its stores. Similarly, Foodland Fresh, a company that pursued expansion via the introduction of innovative, high-end retail offerings, announced in February that it will close most of its Mumbai store network, shutting down operations at 39 of its 42 stores across the city. Meanwhile, Reliance Retail, a leading conglomerate often linked with the possible entry of grocery multinationals, has revealed that it is considering scrapping its wholesale ambitions, in addition to closing a number of Reliance Fresh supermarkets, in order to control costs. Thus even if the "Food retailing industry" is having huge potential, the companies should have clear strategies and investment plan to avoid losses due misunderstanding of the market and wrong investment.

CONCLUSION

With vast population base, growing middle class and strong macroeconomic environment, the "Food retailing" has emerged as the one of the fastest growing segments in the Indian retail industry. Rapid lifestyle transformation, particularly among those living in urban areas, has resulted into a dramatic increase in the demand for processed or health food, packaged and ready-to-eat food products. Arrival of food multinationals and proliferation of fast food outlets have further added to the growth.

Reference

———(October 2004), "Changing Trends in Retailing and FMC Industry in India", ICFAI University Press.

———(March 2005), "Food Retailing-Emerging Trends in India," Effective Executive, 13-18.

———(June 2005), "Retailing of Organic Products-Challenges and Opportunities", Effective Executive, 20-25.

———(March 2006), "Food Marketing in India", Effective Executive, 37-39

N. Viswanadham (October 2006), "Food & Retail Chains in India", Institute of South Asian Studies.

Jeff Imlet (April 2007), "Organised Retail Industry in India", Case Study in Retail Management, ICFAI 39-62.

Websites

www.business.gov.in

www.citeHr.com

www.imageretail.com

www.rpggroup.com

POLICY PLANNING FOR QUALITY IMPROVEMENT IN TECHNICAL EDUCATION – A SYSTEM DYNAMIC APPROACH

Sanjay Soni, Prakash Verma** & Alok Choubey****

INTRODUCTION

India is flooded with technical institution imparting Engineering/Management courses. There is exponential growth in the number of technical institutions in almost all states except few and hopefully in coming years the remaining states will also be able to establish number of the technical Institutes. But it is accepted and unfortunate facts that accept few premiere Institutes rest are substandard. Irony is that all premier Institutes get the creamy layer of intakes. Meritorious students getting admission in pioneer Institutes are natural professional. Unfortunately substandard Institutes get non creamy layer of intakes of are just producing Technical graduates having certificate but not required skills because of non quality practices. There is a need to find out the factors which affect the quality of the Technical education system.

India has the world's second largest education system and provides one of largest pools of skilled manpower. In the recent years, the problem of quality among professional graduates is a cause of concern. Substandard Institutes are producing mere graduates instead of true professional, who cannot meet the expectations of Industries. There is immediate need to take few corrective measures otherwise India will face an explosion of unemployed technical graduates. Academia will have to understand the nerve of Industries and require producing true professional instead of mere graduate. Kapu and Mehta argue that higher education in India is being de facto privatized on a massive scale. But this privatization is not a result of changing ideological commitments but, a result from a breakdown of the state system and an exit of Indian elites

* Lecturer, Department of Industrial & Production Engineering, Jabalpur Engineering College, Jabalpur, (*Soni563@yahoo.com*)

** Head of Department, Industrial &Production Engineering, Jabalpur Engineering College, Jabalpur, (*pvjbp@yahoo.com*)

*** Dy. Registrar, R. G. P. V. Bhopal

from public institutions, to both private sector institutions within the country as well as abroad. Private philanthropy in higher education, which was supportive of public institutions in the past, is also increasingly withdrawing its support. Consequently the ideological and institutional underpinnings of this form of privatization remain exceedingly weak (Kapu and Mehta, 2004). In this context of increase in the demand and supply of technical education and increasing role of private institutions as well as individuals quality assurance becomes more and more critical for the success of technical education in the country. External audit mechanisms including accreditation agencies such as All India Council for Technical Education (AICTE), the National Board of Accreditation were established in 1994. Also, international quality certifications ISO have enhanced the status of many organizations including educational institutions as quality performers. At the same time, a more informal assessment of "good performance" results when prospective students arrive at their judgments with regard to the "quality" of the institution under consideration for purposes of admission. While the certification by the external agencies such as AICTE and NAAC (National Assessment and Accreditation Council) is an official endorsement, the perception of potential students with respect to the quality of the programmes offered by these technical institutions plays an important role in their success. Such perceptions are in a sense self perpetuating. As students start perceiving a particular institution to be better, high quality students will get attracted to the institution. Consequently, the academic performance of the student body as a whole will improve which will result in better placement for the students as well as improvement in the reputation of the institution. This will naturally attract still better students for the next set of admissions. The same self-perpetuating cycle could also work in the reverse direction in the sense that if there is a drop in the perceived quality of the institution, the slide could continue to push the reputation downwards.

Thus, it is important to create a positive perception in the minds of the students as well as other stakeholders of the institution. There are many factors that contribute to the perceptions as well as the delivery of high quality education to the students. This paper attempts to identify the factors that promote high quality technical education and how they are affecting the technical education system.

OBJECTIVES

The following are the specific objectives of the study;

1. To identify factors contributing to quality of technical education system.
2. To identify there close interactions with technical education system.
3. To Prepare a model which can measure the effect of change in these factors on Quality of technical system.

A Brief Literature Review

Education in general and higher education in particular represents too-process-oriented, intangible and multiple-stakeholder situations. Most of the performance measurement systems of higher educational institutions do not reflect the full range of interested stakeholders and are not closely linked to the strategic management. Therefore, Cullen *et al.* (2003) propose the use of a balanced scorecard approach in order to reinforce the importance of managing rather than just monitoring performance. Garretson (2004) confirms the importance of the expectation of key stakeholders in the educational process while exploring the meaning of quality through students' evaluation of an MBA programme using a combination of qualitative and quantitative approaches. Temponi (2005) analyses the main elements of continuous improvement in higher education that address the concerns of academia's stakeholders during the process of its implementation. Lomas (2004) emphasizes the selection of a particular quality management model such as European Forum for Quality Management (EFQM) and Total Quality Management (TQM) for promoting continuous improvement of quality in education. In addition, a few studies highlight the method of pedagogy and selection of institutes of higher learning (Felix, 2001; Poonikom *et al.*, 2004).

Views on Quality and its Measurement

Education quality is a multi-dimensional concept (Eriksen, 1995). It can be viewed as the combination of the quality of input, process, and output of the education system. Many opinions can be observed in the literature about the factors influencing the quality in engineering education. Some of them are teaching process (Eriksen, 2003), University – Industry collaboration (Natarajan ,2003), role of management (Gopalan, 2003), student intelligence & interest (Mouly, 2003), excellence of teachers (Shrivastava, 2003), accreditation standards (Vrat, 2003), e-education (Maji, 2003) and proper documentation of activities (Jagdeesh, 2001). For some of the academicians, quality is synonymous with the continuous improvement (Bhat, 2000), selected for identifying the barriers to the quality improvement of engineering education in India.

System Approach

The origin and development of the system approach can be traced to cybernetics, biological sciences and industrial management. Romiszowaski (1994) contends that the term system approach grew out of general system theory and cybernetics as a creative and heuristic approach to the understanding and improvement of probabilistic system. It was recognized that the complexity involved in social systems could not be controlled or manoeuvred easily as can be done in simple mechanical processes. Hence, a systems approach is characterized by careful analysis of interrelationships and interdependence of constituent units and sub-systems and interpretation of these interactions in terms of predicting what may happen in outer parts of the system if certain changes are made in a particular part (Neil, 1979). From the perspective of managing change, a system may be defined as being an organized assembly of components, which are related in such a way that the behavior of any individual component will influence the overall status of the system. All system, physical or soft must have predetermined objective that the interrelated components strive to achieve (Paton and McCalman, 2000). Page and Thomas (1977) defined the systems approach to education, in The International Dictionary of education, as: Conscious use of systems analysis and systems design techniques is an endeavor to identify and solve complex problems in learning and instructional systems. The components of the approach include the establishment of a systems boundary, the identification of all actual or possible inputs and outputs to the system and examination of their interaction. The few important concepts that emerge out of the definition by page and Thomâs and other areas is anticipated and recognized.

Problem solving: The purpose of the system approach is to solve complex problems. Hence, the systems approach is not about fancy intellectual gymnastics but about practical tools for problem solving. The main contention in the system approach is to solve a problem in the context of interrelationships so that the impact-adverse or otherwise-of the action in other areas is anticipated and recognized.

System boundary: The digestive system is a system. It is sub-system of the human body as a system. The human body is a sub- system of the human being as the system. This illustrates the case for defining the systems boundary so that one may restrict the analysis and action for problem solving to a meaningful limit.

Input: The word input is self-explanatory.it includes all that is invested to create a product. In industrial terms, input includes raw material, infrastructure and human resources.

Process: The term process implies, largely, the activities that go on to convert the input into a product or an output. Whatever a goldsmith, for example, does to convert gold into ornaments is the process.

Output: The output is the product that comes out of a system. It is the input converted through processes.

Environment: The environment is the setting in which a system works. It is an extremely important concept, particularly in social systems, for not only a system influence the environment but also vice-versa. Despite having equivalent inputs, rural schools generally perform lower than their urban counterparts; the rural environment is an important determinant of the system efficiency.

Feedback: Set in an environment with a well-defined boundary, the input, the process and the output are in a linear sequence. Since there are causal relationships, it is believed that feedback has the potential to improve system performance in the quality and quantity of products through adjustment of inputs and processes and sometimes by adjusting system goals.

The Educational Institution as a System

An educational institution as a system has inputs such as students, infrastructure, financial resources and instructional resources. The processes are admission, instruction, evaluation, etc. While the outputs are the graduates and their behavioral, academic and physical qualities. An institution has a well-defined boundary and an environment in which it is set. Another they are interlinked and interdependent in systemic framework.

Sub-Systems of Technical Education System

A system obviously comprises several sub-systems. The basic approach of systemDynamic is identifying the sub-systems and understanding their interrelationships and interdependence and to study there dynamic behavior. The various sub- systems of Technical education system are faculty module, student's module, academic module, and administrative module. (Narula, 1992)

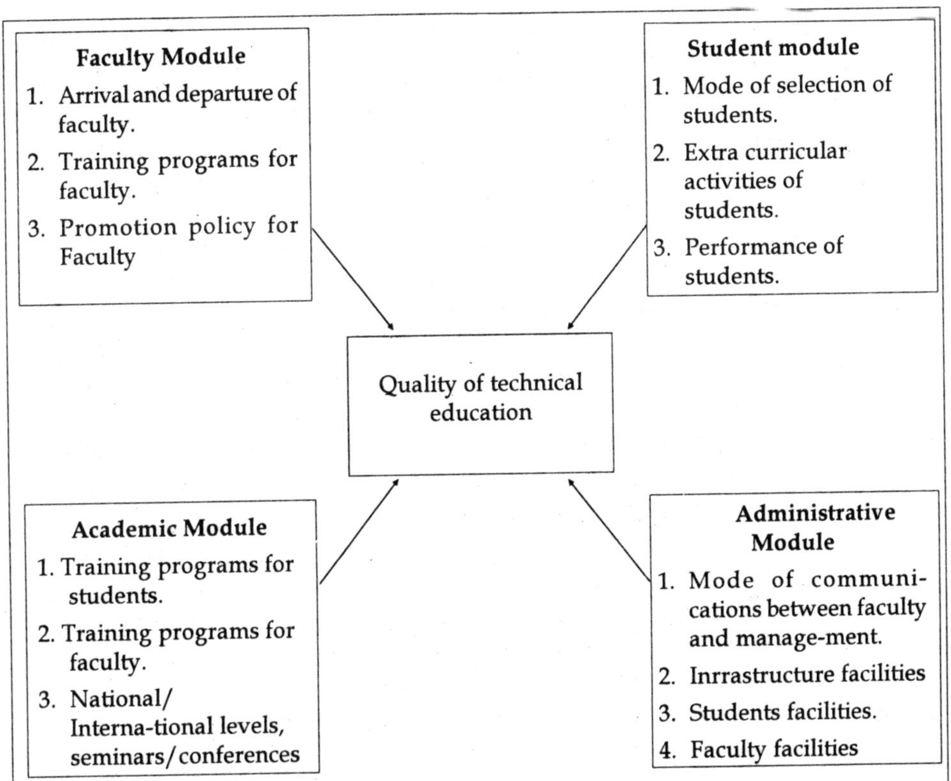

Figure 1: Sub-Systems of Technical Education System

CLOSEDLOOP INTERACTIONS

The interrelationship in the sub-systems can be studied with the help of causal loop diagrams of various modules and there impact on quality can be studied. The loop clearly depicts the causal explanations.

FACULTY MODULE LOOP (R1, R2)

The loop shown below is depicting the impact of faculty over Quality of technical education. Quality of technical education is enhanced by arrival of trained qualified teachers activity which in turn enhances the academic excellence (University teaching plan is fulfilled) as a result of which new admission are attracted which promotes the fund availability of institute and enhances the research and development activity in the institute as a result of which PhD enrollment increases which enhances the quality of technical education. The balancing loop R2 is articulates that an increase in the quality of technical education increases the placement of students in industry as a result of which availability of students for higher studies reduces which results as less number of post graduates for technical education system which reduces the quality of technical education.

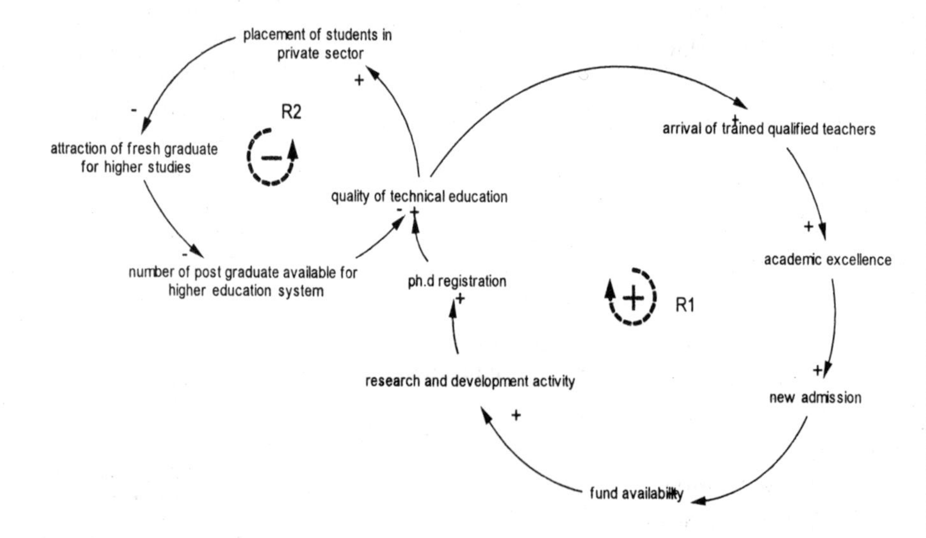

Figure 2: Faculty Module Loop

STUDENT MODULE (R3, R4, R5)

The loop shown in Figure 2. Depicts the causal explanations of students module loop R3. Show that as the quality of technical education is increased the performance of students increases in the semester exams as a result of which new admissions are attracted which ultimately increases the available funds. An increase in available funds increases the training programs for teachers which increases the academic performance of teachers which in turn enhances the quality of technical education. Loop R4 is balancing loop which show as the attraction for new admissions is increased the demand for new colleges increases which results in the shortage of qualified and experienced teachers the impact of this results in poor performance of students in the new established colleges which in turn decreases the quality of technical education. Loop R5 is a balancing loop which articulates as the performance of teachers is increased in the institute new research projects are attracted in the institute but market conditions have direct relationship with the research projects which in turn increases the total funding as a result of which the training programs of teachers are increased which impacts by increasing academic performance of teachers which enhances the quality of technical education.

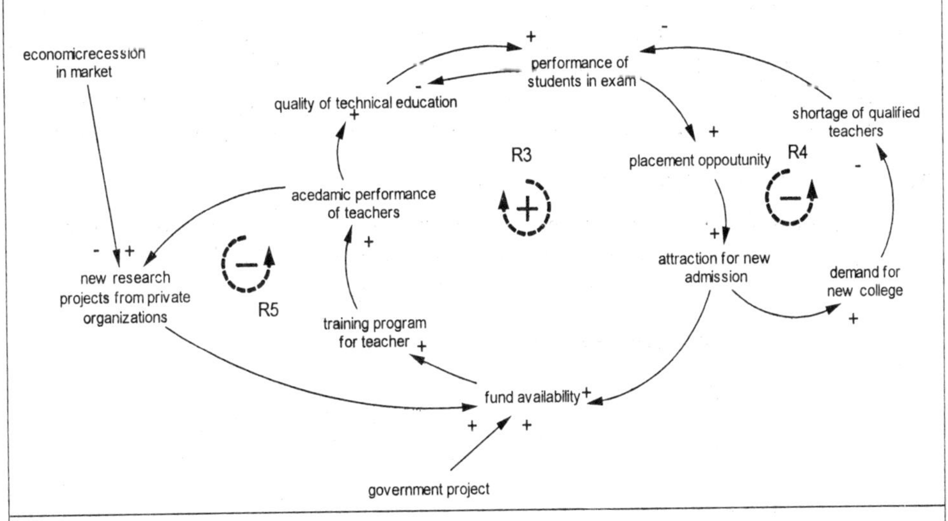

Figure 3: Student Module

ADMISTRATIVE MODULE (R6)

The loop R6 show the causal relationship of admistrative module which articulates as the quality of technical education increases the student teacher interactions increases as a result of which teaching enhances which promotes the performance of students in semester exams as a impact of which the placements are increased which attracts new admission which ultimately increases the available funds which in turn are utilized for the development of infrastructure of the institute (library, internet, etc.) which results in the increase in the quality of technical education system.

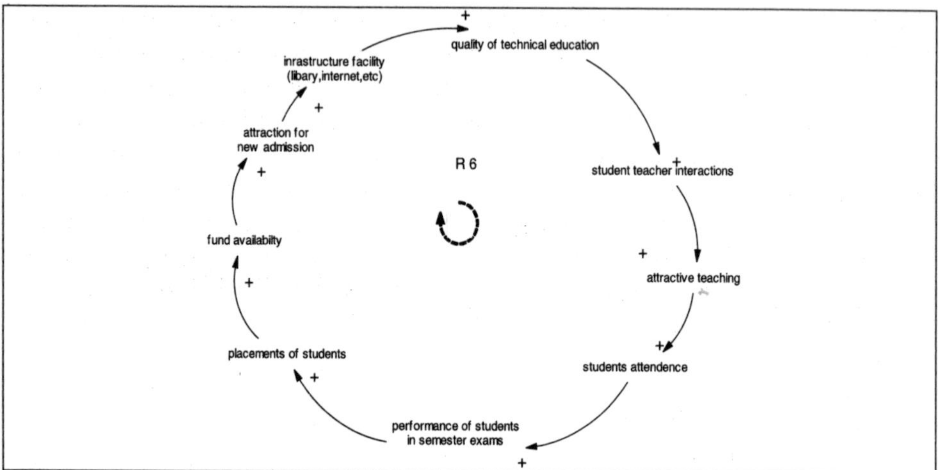

Figure 4: Admistrative Module

THE MODEL

Taking causal loop diagrams as a base a system dynamic model is constructed in which quality of technical education system is a level variable which is linked with teachers arrival rate and teacher quitting rate.quality of technical system is also linked with number of passout students and placements of students in industries.

RESULT AND DISCUSSION

By putting data the effect of various parameters can studied over a long run. The graph plotted shows the simulation of the model with the data provided. The model can be further extended by adding more variables.

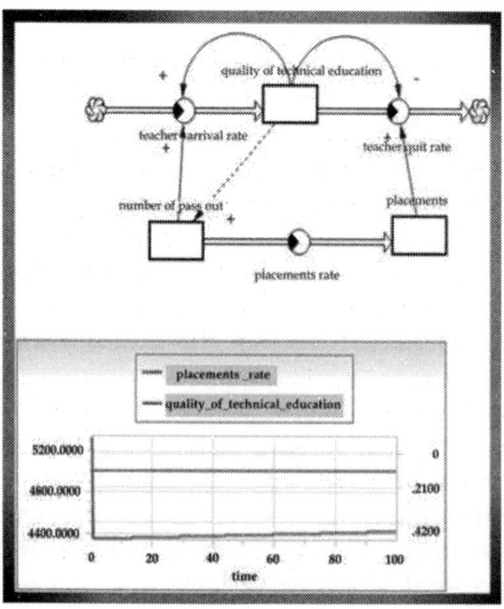

CONCLUSION

From the above study we reveal that the quality of higher education is not independent but has causal relationships with other parameters of technical education system sy While discussing the quality issues of technical education the feedback of these parameters on quality of technical education cannot be ignored. The model constructed by taking the base of causal loop diagram of various sectors of technical education system helps in predicting the effect of these parameters on long run. The model can be used as the base for planning policy for quality in technical education.

References

The Report of the Board of Planning of Technical Education. Re-engineering of Engineering Education, AICTE, New Delhi, 2003.

K. H. Mok, K.H. Wat (1998), Merging of the Public and Private Boundary: Education and the Market Place in China, *Int. J. Educational Development,* Vol. 18, No. 3.

K. A. Padmanabhan (1999), Dr. Daya Swarup Memorial Lecture, 14 November, IIT, Kanpur, India.

S. D. Eriksen (1995), TQM and the Transformation from an élite to a Mass System of Higher Education in the UK, Quality Assurance in Education, Vol. 3, No. 1.

D.H. Eriksen (2003), A Case of Compulsory Teaching Accreditation of Engineering Faculty, Guest Editorial, IEEE Transactionson Education, Vol. 46, No. 4.

R. Natarajan (2003), The Role of Social and Societal Responsibility as a Core Value of the University and Corporate Sectors, *The Indian Journal of Technical Education,* Vol. 26, No.1, pp. 1-21

M. N. Gopalan (2003), QualityAssurance in Technical Education, *The India Journal of Technical Education,* Vol. 26, No. 2, pp. 72-78.

C.M.C. Mouly, M. Padmaja (2003), Quality in Technical Education: A Critical Analysis of the Governing Factors, *The Indian Journal of Technical Education,* Vol. 26, No. 2, pp. 50-54.

J. P. Shrivastava (2003), Shortage of Qualified Teachers and Remedies for Quality Assurance in Technical Education, *The Indian Journal of Technical Education,* Vol. 26, No. 2, pp26-30.

P. Vrat (2003), Quality Assurance in Technical Education: Recent Trends and Challenges Ahead, *The Indian Journal of Technical Education,* Vol. 26, No. 2, pp. 12-14.

S. Maji (2003), Quality Assurance in Technical Education: Possibilities through E-Learning in Distance Education, *The Indian Journal of Technical Education,* Vol. 26, No. 2, pp. 19-25.

R. Jagdeesh (2001), Improvement of Quality of Higher Education in Engineering Sciences with an Emphasis on International Aspects, *The Indian Journal of Technical Education,* Vol. 24, No. 2, pp. 50-55.

I. K. Bhat (2000), Quality Education in Technical Institutions, *The Indian Journal of Technical Education,* Vol. 23, No. 2, pp. 1-7.

D. P. Tiwari (2000), Total Quality Management in Technical Institutions, *The Indian Journal of Technical Education,* Vol. 23, No. 2, pp. 67-69.

S. P. Pai, K. S. Bhat (2003), "From ISO 9000 to Total Quality Management in a Technical Institution: A Journey Towards Continuous Improvement", *The Indian Journal of Technical Education,* Vol. 27, No.1, pp. 49-55.

S. Sahney, D. K. Banwet, S. Karunes (2004), Changing Trends in Education: The Relevance of Total Quality Management, *The IndianJournal of Technical Education,* Vol. 27, No. 3, pp. 101-109.

V. P. Gosavi (2001), Application of TQM in Engineering Education, *The Indian Journal ofTechnical Education,* Vol. 24, No. 2, pp. 28-32.

DEBIT CARDS VIS-A-VIS CREDIT CARDS IN INDIA– A CRITICAL APPROACH

*Ch. Satyanarayana Reddy**, *Ch. Srikanth Verma*** & *V. Ranaprathap****

INTRODUCTION

Payment card covers a range of different cards, which can be used by a cardholder to make payments. These cards offer more security, convenience and control than any other payment method. The payment card was first introduced India in the early 1980s. Payment cards replace cash and cheque payment with an electronic form of payments and this has far reaching implications - especially for India. Firstly, it will help us align with the global financial services industry by making our systems more efficient and cost effective. It will also help us in addressing the special challenges facing India - the large unbanked population, the unregulated cash economy and lack of financial transparency. Payment cards yield many more benefits than merely replacing cash and cheques. They provide wider benefits for the economy as a whole through lower transaction costs, increased operational efficiency and improved financial infrastructure. They also provide an opportunity for the fast growing Indian economy to globalise further.

NEED FOR THE STUDY

Indian consumer is treading cautiously in purchasing on credit. He generally displays credit-averse behavior. This can be seen from the steep rise in spending through debit cards vis-a-vis the rise in spending in through credit cards in India. The 'pay now' feature of debit card discourages dependency on credit. It also helps in better financial planning and control of purchases by consumers. A credit card encourages the customers to "purchase now and pay later", which

* Associate Professor and Head, Department of Commerce, Lal Bahadur College, S. P. Road, Warangal.

** Lecturer, Department of Business Management, P. G. Center, Lal Bahadur College, S. P. Road, Warangal, (*e-mail: vermasricherala@gmail.com*)

*** Lecturer, Department of Business Management, P. G. Center, Lal Bahadur College, S. P. Road, Warangal.

is still not inculcated in Indian culture. Indians are still lacking behind the western countries in making use of credit cards. In this back drop, it is felt necessary to assess the growth of debit cards vis -a- vis credit cards in Indian financial industry. This paper adopts a critical approach to analyze the usage of both cards by Indians.

Objectives of the study: This paper has the following specific objectives pertaining to the study.

(1) To analyze the market penetration of both debit and credit cards in India.

(2) To examine the usage patterns of both debit and credit cards by Indian customers.

(3) To indentify the reasons for low proliferation of credit cards in India vis-a-vis debit cards.

(4) To suggest remedial measures to popularize credit cards in India.

SOURCES OF DATA

The study is based on the data collected from secondary source which is gathered from the Annual Reports of different banks, published materials in the form of books, articles from journals, websites and reports relevant to the study. The study of debit cards and credit cards covers a period of 05- financial years, commencing from 1st April, 2004 to 31St March, 2009.

DEBIT AND CREDIT CARDS MARKET IN INDIA

In India, two varieties of payment cards are available namely credit and debit cards. A credit card entitles its holder to buy goods and services based on the holder's promise to pay for these goods and services. The issuer of the card grants a line of credit to the consumer (or the user) from which the user can borrow money for payment to a merchant or to draw a cash in advance to meet the requirements of the user. A debit card (also known as a bank card or check card) provides an alternative payment method to paying in cash in purchases. It is also used for instant withdrawal of cash at Automated Teller Machines (ATMs). Debit cards also eliminate the risk of carrying cash.

The growth rate of credit cards for the past 5 years has been relatively less when compared to that of debit cards. An analysis is done by examining the number of cards, both debit and credit issued by various banks over the past 5 years. The growth rates of both cards are tabulated and presented in Table 1.

Table 1 reveals that the credit card issuers have been facing a crunch in their business, as the number of credit cards in India during the financial year ended March 2009 declined to 246.99 lakh from the previous year base of 275.47 lakh, registering a negative growth rate of 10.34%. With the increasing delinquency rate in the country, banks and card issuers are likely to remain hesitant in issuing new credit cards. Many banks have been closing inactive

Table 1
Number of Cards Issued by Banks in India

Payment Cards \ Financial Years	(Number of cards in Lakh)				
	Mar–05	*Mar–06*	*Mar–07*	*Mar–08*	*Mar–09*
Credit Cards	141.05	173.27	231.23	275.47	246.99
Growth Rate %	40	23	33	19	-10
Debit Cards	355.01	497.63	749.76	1024.37	1374.31
Growth Rate %	96	40	51	37	34

Source: RBI Annual Reports-2010.

and unproductive accounts from their credit card portfolio. But, India has seen remarkable growth in its debit card market over the past few years. The number of debit cards issued by banks grew by 34% in financial year 2009, compared to the fall of over 10% for credit cards in the same year. At present, there are around 1,374 lakh debit cards and 247 lakh credit cards in India.

USAGE PATTERN OF BOTH DEBIT AND CREDIT CARDS

More Indians are now using payment cards for purchasing goods and service at merchant establishments. The relevant data pertains to the last five years are analyzed and presented in Table 2.

Table 2
Total Spending of Debit & Credit Cards at Merchant POS Terminals

Years	*Value of Transactions (Rs. Cr)*	*Growth Rate %*
2004–05	31,047	18
2005–06	39,784	28
2006–07	49,533	25
2007–08	70,506	42
2008–09	83,903	19

Source: RBI Annual Reports- 2009.

Table 2 shown that total spending at merchant POS through Credit and Debit cards has registered a growth of 19% in 2008-09 on year on year basis. The total spending has increased to 83,903 crores in financial year 2009 from 70,506 crores in financial year 2008. But this growth rate is very much lower than the 42% recorded in 2007-08. This fall in growth rate can be attributed to the negative impact of financial meltdown, increasing consciousness among the customers, and reduction of credit limit by some banks.

Now-a-days, paying through cards, both credit and debit, has become one of the preferred modes of payment by Indian cardholders. Though cards have been present for more than 2 decades, the payment through them has gained wide acceptance of late. In this regard, it is felt necessary to assess the growth of payment transactions by both cards, for the last 5 years. The relevant data are presented in Table 3.

Table 3
Card-Based Payment Transactions

Financial Years / *Payment Cards*	*Amounts (Rupees crore)*				
	Mar-05	*Mar-06*	*Mar-07*	*Mar-08*	*Mar-09*
Credit Cards	25,686.36	33,886.47	41,361.31	57,984.73	65,355.80
Growth Rate %	45	32	22	40	13
Debit Cards	5,361.04	5,897.14	8,171.63	12,521.22	18,547.14
Growth Rate %	10	10	38	53	48

Source: RBI Annual Reports-2009.

Table 3 reveals that the credit card spending is increased by 13% to Rs. 65,356 crore from 57,984.73 crore during the year 2008-09. However, the growth is lower than the 40% recorded in 2007-08. The debit card spending at merchant POS terminals increased significantly by 48% to Rs. 18,547 crore during the year 2009 from Rs. 12, 521 crore during the previous year. There is a considerable rise in spending through debit cards. This shows that consumer is exhibiting credit averse behaviour. Debit card serve as a substitute for cash which discourages dependency on credit cards. Besides, benefits like reward points and discounts by merchants as well as bankers can also be attributed to the growth of debit card usage in India.

SPENDING IN DIFFERENT SEGMENTS BY CREDIT CARD:

In spite of decrease in the credit card base, the credit card spending has increased during the year 2009. It shows that more Indians are using credit cards for purchasing essentials as well as luxury goods. Other major drivers caused this spurt that are growth in e-commerce transactions, increase in travel service, leisure industry. Around 70% of credit card purchases come from jewellery, dining and traveling etc. Indian Credit Card Industry is still at a nascent stage, when compared to those in West countries. From among Indian credit card holders, 73% spend less than $35 on average per month. Around 25% spend between $35 and $300 every month. Only 25% credit card holders spend more than $300 per month. It indicates that credit card usage is still very less in India. According to a survey by TOI- New Delhi, 73% Indian credit card holders use it only for 1-2 times in a month. Another 23% use it for 3-5 times, the remaining 5% use it for more than 5 times a month. It shows that volume and frequency of credit card transactions are less in India.

An analysis is done to examine the distribution of credit card spending by Indians on different segments. The relevant data are presented in Table 4.

The data in Table 4 shows that, from among all the transactions made by Indian credit card holders, 44% were made on clothing. Shopping in the supermarkets/Grocery stores accounted for 14% Hotels accounted for another 9%., Restaurants constitute around 06% of total transactions. Other various transactions comprised that remaining 27%. It is observed that Indians mostly use credit cards for purchasing clothing and Grocery etc.

Table 4
Credit Cards Spending Segments in India

Categories	*Spending Segment*
Clothing's	44%
Supermarket/Grocery Shopping	14%
Hotels	09%
Restaurants	06%
Others	27%
Total	100%

Source: The TOI, New Delhi - March, 2009.

REASONS FOR LOW PROLIFERATION OF CREDIT CARDS IN INDIA VIS-A-VIS DEBIT CARDS

Now-a-days Indian consumers easily spend most of their money with plastic cards than they do with cash. This has been the case since 2003, when the number of credit and debit card purchases surpassed the number of cash and check transactions. There are a couple of obvious reasons why we prefer plastic. First, internet shopping has skyrocketed, and you simply can't spend cash and checks online. Second, people have learned the convenience of paying with a piece of plastic rather than cash. It's easy, instantaneous, and safer than carrying a huge wad of cash in your wallet.

With the convenience of plastic, however, comes risks (at least as far as credit cards are concerned). Credit card spending has gotten out of control in recent years. Our consumer debt loads have grown too steep, and played a major part in bringing about the current credit crunch. Debit cards are linked directly to your bank account. You can use them to buy goods or withdraw cash and the amount is taken from your account right away. You can also use debit cards to get 'cash-back' from shops when you buy goods and also ask for money back from the cashier, although not all shops offer this. The total amount is deducted from your account right away. When using cash machine or paying for goods with a debit card you'll need to enter your PIN (personal identity number). When buying goods you usually enter it into an electronic hand held device, but in some cases you may have to sign. Most bank accounts offer debit cards. Most debit cards double up as 'cheque guarantee cards', guaranteeing that your cheque will be honoured by your bank up to a stated amount.

Bankers expect debit card usage to surpass credit card usage mainly on account of convenience, which is a primary driver for the adoption of plastic money. Moreover, unlike credit cards, debit cards do not involve any borrowings/loan from the bank, and typically do not need a credit review before they are issued, making them ideally suited to a larger population of the banked public. In the current scenario, there is an increased risk of credit cards defaults due to the financial crisis that is affecting the consumers. Certain banks have now started adopting stringent measures such as debiting savings accounts of card holders for non-payment of card dues. Banks are also going slow on credit card issuance and have been promoting spending through debit cards by offering various incentives to the consumers such as loyalty rewards, discounts by selected retailers and cash-back options. As against credit cards, ATM cum debit cards offers a ready consumer base in the bankable population of India. The increasing acceptance of debit cards at both physical and online merchants is also driving spends through debit cards.

A credit card is a form of borrowing. Firms lending money to customers must be licensed by the Office of Fair Trading (OFT) under The Consumer Credit Act 1974. The Act requires certain credit and hires agreements to be set out in a particular way and to contain relevant information for the person borrowing. Credit cards allow you to 'buy goods now and pay later'-called 'buying on credit'. They aren't linked to your bank account. Like debit cards, they can be used to buy goods in shops over the telephone and internet, with the same details being required. You can also get a 'cash advance' by drawing money at bank cash machines. Your bank may offer you a credit card, or you can apply for one to any institution offering one. The credit card provider will normally run checks to see if you've had problems repaying debts before offering you one (called a 'credit check').

There are some cases where debit cards can be useful as opposed to credit cards. Sometimes debit cards have good offers on select purchases or at select shops. Always keep track of any offers on your credit and debit cards, and use whatever gives you maximum benefit for that specific purchase. Also, some shops charge a fee (say 2%) if you pay through credit cards, but none if you pay through debit cards. Some shops may only accept debit cards. And most certainly, never ever withdraw money from an ATM using a credit card! Always use a debit card. If you don't have cash in your account but have some time, then go in for a personal loan that will have an interest rate of around 14% per annum. Credit cards charge an interest of around 3% per month, which adds up to 36% per annum! This is nothing but daylight robbery! Do it only if you need money urgently and have no time to even go and borrow it from a friend.

REMEDIAL MEASURES

Banks in India traditionally lent money against collateral and after satisfying themselves that there was a need. Trouble arose when such 'conservative' practices were replaced in a milieu where meeting targets became the main goal. Pointing out several deficiencies the Reserve Bank of India (RBI) has asked banks to initiate the following remedial measures.

(1) Issuing unsolicited cards: As a rule nobody who does not seek one should be given a card. In case such cards are issued, activated and billed without the customer's consent, banks should not only reverse the entries but pay a fine amounting to twice the value of such outstanding.

(2) There have been instances of new cards being intercepted and misused by unscrupulous elements before they reach customers. The issuing banks will be responsible for such monetary loss. As a rule there should be safeguards against misuse. The RBI suggests one or other of fraud-minimizing devices such as photo identity cards, embossing a PIN and signature lamination.

(3) Wherever cards have been packaged with an insurance element - commonly accident insurance—details such as the nature and extent of insurance, other conditions if any, should be explicitly stated. Also, the person in the insurance company who can be contacted by the customer should be mentioned.

(4) Reasons for rejecting a card application should be communicated to the applicants.

(5) Banks should get explicit permission from customers for sharing information about them.

(6) Customer education should receive top priority and cover the entire gamut of credit card operations. Illustrative examples should be used. Call centre employees should be suitably trained.

(7) Closure and blocking of lost cards should be given top priority.

It is difficult to imagine why these basic rules, by no means unique to credit cards, are being given a go by so extensively prompting another RBI warning. But then some banks adopt the most illogical practices when it comes to card issues. One such practice ought to be familiar to all who have tried to return the cards issued to them. They would have found that while it is the easiest thing to get a card – sometimes even without asking for them – returning them can be a daunting task. Many banks do not give their full postal address but only a box number.

Finally, one gets an uneasy feeling that the government owned banks are not adept at leveraging their strengths whenever they venture into businesses such as credit cards. They are sitting over a gold mine of information. No foreign or new private bank has that advantage. Their numerous savings bank account holders alone would constitute a very valuable source of information for those marketing a credit card or any other product. Often, these banks part with the data for a song and on occasions without even being aware of it. SBI's joint venture was a fiasco. But many customers of SBI continue to receive unwanted calls from agents of sundry banks offering financial products including credits. Information has a price. It is also confidential. Equally pertinent, did SBI get anything in return for passing on information of its large clientele?

CONCLUSION

The number of credit cards in India during the financial year ended March 2009 declined to 246.99 lakh from the previous year base of 275.47 lakh, registering a negative growth rate of 10.34%. With the increasing delinquency rate in the country, banks and card issuers are likely to remain hesitant in issuing new credit cards. Many banks have been closing inactive and unproductive accounts from their credit card portfolio. But, India has seen remarkable growth in its debit card market over the past few years. The number of debit cards issued by banks grew by 34% in financial year 2009, compared to the fall of over 10% for credit cards in the same year. At present, there are around 1,374 lakh debit cards and 247 lakh credit cards in India.

Both cards have their advantages, but in the last two years, there is a slump in credit card market. Indian credit card industry was growing at an annual rate of 25 percent to 30 percent but in the wake of the financial crisis, credit card transactions declined, it is because debit card usage is considered safer and requires no credit to be extended to the user.

If one wants to keep mostly free of monthly bills then one should go for a debit card since it allows payments directly from bank account. A credit card is safer than a debit card because a debit card is directly linked to bank account. An unauthorized user may be able to clean out the account very quickly. If one can manage ones' expenses, then owning a credit card is better as it gives an option to pay after 20 to 50 days without any extra charges, it is also safe as its misuse can be tackled a lot better than that of a debit card.

References

Books

A. V. Ranganadha Chary, K. Anjaneyulu, and K. Lalitha, "Banking and Financial System", (Revised Edition-2008), Kalyani Publishers, Ludhiana-141 008.

D. M. Mithani, E. Gordon (2008), "Banking and Financial Systems", (Eighth Revised & Updated Edition: 2008), Himalaya Publishing House, Mumbai-400 004.

Kapoor V. K. (1983), "Banking Services", (Edition-1983), Himalaya Publishing House, Mumbai-400 004.

Articles

Amit Singhal, Bikram Duggal (2005), in their study "Extending Banking to the Poor in India", Law and Economics Working Paper No. 049, The University of Texas School of Law, April 2005.

David Cracknell (2004), in his study "Electronic Banking for the Poor - Panacea, Potential and Pitfalls", Banking Systems Specialist at MicroSave, Electronic Banking for the Poor, 2004. Small Enterprise Development Vol. 15, No. 4.

Mohammad Nazmul Huq and Ishrat Jahan Tania (2005), in their Study "Measurement of Consumer Satisfaction of Credit Card Users", Economic Growth Centre, Division of Economics, School of Humanities and Social Sciences, Singapore-639798, Working Paper No. 2005/13,

Patsy Everett (2005), in their Study "Smart Card News", *Sprott Letter,Working Paper,* Sprott School of Business, Carleton University, SL 2007-035, Ottawa, Canada. November, 2007.

Ronald J. Mann (2006), in his Study "Global Credit Card Use and Debt: Policy Issues And Regulatory Responses", Law and Economics Working Paper No. 049, The University of Texas School of Law, April 2005.

Statistics Canada (2005), A Feasibility Report on Improving the Measurement of Fraud in Canada. Canadian Centre for Justice Statistics. Catalogue no. 85-569-XIE. ISBN 0-662- 42984-2.

Web sites

Annual Reports of Reserve Bank of India (2008), Reserve Bank of India, Department of Payment & Settlement Systems, March 31st, 2009. *www.rbi.org.in*

Indian Payment Card Industry Annual Reports- March 31st, 2006, 2007, 2008, 2009. *www.ipaci.com*

Reserve Bank of India Report (2006 - 2007), "Review of Payment & Settlement Systems in India", Reserve Bank of India, Department of Payment & Settlement Systems, This review for the year ended March 31, 2007. *www.rbi.pss.org.in*

Payment Card Survey Reports–2006, 2007, 2008, 2009, 2010. *www.vertureinfok.com*

The free encyclopedia that anyone can edit. *www.wikipedia.org*

A STUDY ON QUALITY OF SERVICE AS A TOOL FOR ENHANCEMENT OF CUSTOMER SATISFACTION IN BANKS

P. UDHAYANAN* & A. NIRMAL RAJ**

INTRODUCTION

"If you cannot measure it, you cannot improve it." - Lord William Thomson Kelvin (1824-1907).

The working of the customer's mind is a mystery; that is difficult to solve and to understand the nuances of customer satisfaction is a challenging task. These applications in the context of the banking industry will give us an insight into the parameters of customer satisfaction and their measurement. This vital information will help to build satisfaction amongst the customers and customer loyalty in the long run, which is an integral part for any business. The customer's requirements must be translated and quantified into measurable targets. This provides an easy way to monitor improvements, and deciding upon the attributes that need to be concentrated in order to improve customer satisfaction and the organizations can recognize where they need to make changes to create improvements and determine if these changes, after implemented, have led to increased customer satisfaction.

Satisfied customers are central to optimal performance and financial returns. In many places in the world, business organizations have been elevating the role of the customer to that of a key stakeholder over the past twenty years. Customers are viewed as a group whose satisfaction with the enterprise must be incorporated in strategic planning efforts. Forward-looking companies are finding value in directly measuring and tracking customer satisfaction (CS) as an important strategic success indicator. Evidence is mounting that placing a high priority on CS is critical to improved organizational performance in a global marketplace.

With better understanding of customers' perceptions, companies can determine the actions required to meet the customers' needs. They can identify

* Senior Lecturer, DOMS, Easwari Engineering College, Chennai, (*e-mail: udhayananp@gmail.com*)

** Senior Lecturer, DOMS, *Velammal* Engineering College, Chennai, (*e-mail: nirmalraaj75@gmail.com*) their own strengths and weaknesses, where they stand in comparison to their competitors, chart out paths for future progress and improvement. Customer satisfaction measurement helps to promote an increased focus on customer outcomes and stimulate improvements in the work practices and processes used within the company.

THE RESEARCH CONTEXT

Banks—assaulted by the pressures of globalization, competition from non-banking financial institutions, and volatile market dynamics—are constantly seeking new ways to add value to their services. The question "What drives performance?" is at the top of the minds of managers and policy makers alike, as the first step is delivering quality of service to the customers that can be achieved by bridging the gap between customers' service perceptions or expectations and experiences.

LITERATURE REVIEW

During the past few decades, service quality has become a major area of attention to practitioners, managers and researchers owing to its strong impact on business performance, customer satisfaction, customer loyalty and profitability. Parasuraman, Zeithaml, and Berry (1985) viewed quality as "the degree and direction of discrepancy between customers' service perception and expectations." According to this approach, services are different from goods because they are intangible and heterogeneous and are simultaneously produced and consumed. Ramaswamy (1996) described service as "the business transactions that take place between a donor (service provider) and receiver (customer) in order to produce an outcome that satisfies the customer"(p. 3). Zeithaml and Bitner (1996) defined service as "deeds, processes, and performances" (p. 5). Tignieh Mersha and Veen Adlakha (1992) examined the attributes of service quality the customer's perspective. The authors have used Delphi process and identified 12 attributes of service quality. Accordingly, the top rated attributes of service quality are classified in to attributes of good service quality and attributes of poor service quality. The attributes of good service quality are knowledge of service, accuracy, consistency, reasonable cost, and willingness to correct errors and prompt service. The attributes of poor service quality: lack of knowledge about the service, employee indifference on "I don't care"attitude, reluctance to correct errors, service inconsistency, sloppiness and high cost. Wayne Kwan and Tan Jing Hee (1994) measured service quality in Singapore retail banking they concluded that gap analysis indicates that perceived service performance generally falls short of expectations. Dabholkar, Thorpe, and Tentz (1996) proposed a hierarchical model of service quality that describes service quality as a level, multidimensional construct. The construct included (a) overall consumer perception of service quality; (b) a dimension level that consists of physical aspects, reliability, personal interaction, problem solving, and policy; and (c) a subdimension level that recognizes the multifaceted nature of the service-quality dimensions. Dabholkar and colleagues found that quality of service is directly influenced by perceptions of performance levels. In addition, customers' personal characteristics are important in assessing value, but not in assessing quality. Stafford *et al* (1998) attempted to examine the determinants of service quality and satisfaction in the auto causality claims process in United States. The study found auto insurance providers should provide superior levels of service to the customers. In case of auto insurance industry, reliability, empathy and assurance are the influencers of the service quality. Ahmad Jamal and Kmala Naser (2002) examined the key antecedents of customer satisfaction in retail banking. A sample of 167 respondents from Abu Dhabi Commercial bank took part in the study. The finding indicated that both core and relational dimensions of service quality appear to be linked to customer satisfaction. Caruana (2002) examined Service loyalty: the effect of service quality and the mediating role of satisfaction. Results indicated that customer satisfaction does play a mediating role in the effect of service quality and service loyalty. The findings also indicated that the identified measures of service loyalty, customer satisfaction and service quality exhibited acceptable psychometric properties in terms of reliability and validity. Their results confirmed the relationship that the service quality is found to act on service loyalty via customer satisfaction. The results also showed that education and age also played a major role in determining the perception of customer about the construct. Using empirical data derived from the Greek Banking, Gounaris *et al.*, (2003) attempted to model the influence of bank specific and customer specific parameters on the customer perception of service quality. Service quality as measured with employee competence, the bank reliability, and branch network. The findings of the study suggest all the antecedents examined do not influence the various dimensions of the quality of service offered by bank. Moreover, the perception of the various dimensions of quality was also found to vary considerably, with certain dimensions being more influenced by the same parameter than others. Prabakaran and Satya (2003) examined the various service attributes in the banking sector and the study pointed out that the borrowers are not only satisfied with the money they get as loan they also keen about how they get it. Quality Service alone will act as winning edge in the highly competitive environment where there is not much of product differential. Quality service was exhibited in the study through the dimensions namely reliability, tangibility, responsiveness, assurance and empathy. Hussein A. Hassan Al-Tamini (2003) analyzed service quality in the UAE Islamic banks and compared between the Dubai Islamic Bank and Abu Dhabi Bank. Linear Regression indicated that there was a positive and significant relationship between overall service quality and SERVQUAL dimensions in the UAE Islamic Bank. ANOVA results also indicated that there was no significant difference in the level of service quality in the UAE Islamic banks based on Customer gender and nationality. Liang and Wang (2004) developed and empirically tested model examining the relation among attributes, benefits, customer satisfaction, trust and Customer behavioral loyalty in a financial service industry in Taiwan. The result showed that there are symbolic benefits has positive influence on customer satisfaction. As a part of relationship quality and behavioral loyalty, the path coefficient is not only significant but also of high value. The finding of their study suggests that customer by dissimilar financial products with different benefit, with different attributes, hence the difference in the level of customer satisfaction and behavioral consequence. Mushtaq A. Bhat (2005) made attempt to study service quality in banks and its variation across demographic variables. The findings of the study: Service quality in banks is comparatively better among higher age groups where as reverse is the case among lower age groups. The Service quality of banks was relatively better as perceived by respective bank customers in Delhi and Mariana, where as quite reverse is the case in J&K State. The Study also brought in light that banks provide comparatively better service quality to business group customers in comparison to service group customers, as they are comparatively high level of income as against service group customers. Different education levels, however do not exhibit greater variation in service quality. Zillur Rahman (2005) in his study dealt with the measurement of service quality of banks in India. It investigates the discrepancy between customers' expectations and perceptions towards the quality of services. The study was conducted using the SERVQUAL instrument. The results indicated that the sample population had perpetual problems with their banking service experiences. Findings from this study provide initial direction in determining the optimum service quality attributes to focus on in promoting banking services. The largest discrepancies were found along the reliability dimension. This is alarming, since it was identified as the most important dimension in their overall perceptions. This indicates that the sample population appears not to be getting what they expect from their banking service experience. If the industry persists in measuring and monitoring the perceptual aspects of banking service quality, the complementary aspects of basic outcome must be tracked as well to ensure an appropriate and satisfactory customer experience. It is important that service quality be reassessed on a regular basis. The assessment provides a baseline for comparison with the future assessments.

The perception of service quality depends on the nature of difference between the actual service and the perceived service by the customer. When the actual service is quarter than the perceived service the customers tend to achieve higher satisfaction. When the actual service equals the perceived service, service quality is satisfactory. Service quality thus can be operationalised on performance minus expectation. Many researchers have recommended the use of measured confirmation, where customers are asked to mentally estimate 'performance' against 'expectation'. According to Zeithaml and Bitner (1996), customer hold two types of expectations desired defined as the wished for level of performance, which is a blend of what customer believes can be and should be and the lower level expectations termed adequate i.e. the level of service the customers will accept in the light of certain controllable and uncontrollable resource constraints. It also indicates that adequate service level is always lower than the desired service level because desires service is less subject to change as it is shaped by factors like needs and service philosophies. In the view of the study broadly intends to find answers for the following questions:

- What is the level of quality of Service being offered by the banks to its customers?
- What factors mitigate in minimizing the service delivery gap?
- What effective role does the frontline employee have in delivering quality of service to the customers?

Service Quality Dimensions

Rust & Oliver (1994) and Parasuraman, Zeithaml and Berry (1988) contributions to service quality led to the conceptualizations of the five dimensions: Tangibles (T), Reliability (R) Responsiveness (R) Assurance (A) and Empathy (E) that eventually led to the development of SERVQUAL. Their definitions are:

Tangibles: Physical facilities, equipments and appearance of personnel.

Reliability: Ability to perform the promised service dependably and accurately.

Responsiveness: Willingness to help customers and prompt service

Assurance: Knowledge and courtesy of employees and their ability to inspire trust and confidence

Empathy: Caring, individualized attention the firm provides its customers.

METHODOLOGY

A total of 350 customers from two banks (182 and 168 customers respectively) that included the current account holders, saving account holders, depositors, borrowers and pensioners formed the samples for this study. The data for study was obtained through a non-designed structured questionnaire consisting of five dimensions, the tangible measures, the reliability measures, the responsiveness measure, the assurance factors and empathy factor with respect to banking sector. Factors namely parking facilities in the bank; lighting; ventilation; provision of drinking water; convenience of bank working hours; location of ATM (Automated Teller Machines) and availability of adequate stationeries: challans, forms etc were categorized as tangibles.

Factors such as ease of systems and procedures in the bank and knowledge and skill level possessed by the employees were treated as reliability dimension. Factors such as the attitude level of the employees and professionalism of the employees constituted the assurance dimensions. Knack of customer handling and the employee availability formed the responsiveness dimensions. Factors that were related to the bank and its process such as the time and process involved in processing cheques; cash; deposits; loans and other services were treated as empathy as it really involves the interaction of both the customers and the employees and all these tasks requires the employees to be empathetic. Total of seventeen statements measuring all the above factors constituting major five dimensions measuring the customers banking experience formed the questionnaire. A five point likert scale ranging from strongly agree to strongly disagree was adopted as the scale for the statements in the questionnaire and method of data collection was through personal (one- to one) mode. Convenience sampling was adopted and data were collected during the period October 2009 to December 2010 spanning three months period. Demographics and psychographics variable were not considered for the study as it was not the main focus of the study. Descriptive measures namely mean; percentage and statistical method t-test was applied for analysis of the data.

ANALYSIS

The data collected was analysed for the gaps under the major five headings, namely tangibles, reliability, responsiveness and assurance. Table 1 details the overall summary of the customers' perception of the services provided by their banks on all the dimensions. This table includes the opinion of both the banks' customer rating. Overall it can be inferred that approximately 75 per cent of the customers have provided higher ratings, which implies that predominantly the customers are satisfied on the various performance dimensions. At the same time it can also be studied that there exists a huge scope to improvise on the performance dimensions.

GAP ANALYSIS

The raw data obtained on the expectations of the costumers on all the five dimensions of the quality, viz, tangibles, reliability, responsiveness, assurance, empathy was used to calculate the 'gap' that exists. This gap analysis was done for all the dimensions. Their levels were assessed purely on the basis of their mean values comparing with a reference mean value of '5' which was considered to be the maximum and that any organization should like to achieve for excelling. The gaps i.e., the difference between the costumer score and the reference mean value is the 'service gap'. Table 2 details the service gap on all five dimensions of services.

Table 1
Overall Statistics for Two Banks on the Performance Dimensions

	Overall Statistics (350 Samples)				
	Lowest Rating				*Highest Rating*
Factors	1	2	3	4	5
TANGIBLES					
Parking facilities	8.6% (30)	20.3% (71)	14.9% (52)	43.4% (152)	12.9% (45)
Lighting	_	1.1% (4)	7.7% (27)	67.4% (236)	23.7% (83)
Ventilation	0.3% (1)	3.7% (13)	6% (21)	66% (231)	24% (84)
Drinking Water	1.4% (5)	2.6% (9)	8% (28)	65.1% (228)	_
ATM location	4.6% (16)	11.4% (40)	24.3% (85)	53.4% (187)	6.3% (22)
Convenience of Banking Hours	0.3% (1)	2.9% (10)	5.7% (20)	56% (196)	35.1% (123)
Availability of Challans & forms	0 %	2.3% (8)	3.4% (12)	15.1% (53)	79.1% (277)
RELIABILITY					
Understanding of Systems & Procedures	0.6% (2)	4.6% (16)	8% (28)	68.6% (240)	18.3% (64)
Knowledge & Skill Level	0.3% (1)	2.6% (9)	11.7% (41)	60.3% (211)	25.1% (88)
ASSURANCE					
Attitude level	0.6% (2)	2.6% (9)	14.3% (50)	54.9% (192)	27.7% (97)
Professional Approach	0.3% (1)	3.7% (13)	10.6% (37)	58.9% (206)	26.6% (93)
RESPONSIVENESS					
Handling & Response to Customer Complaints	0.9% (3)	5.1% (18)	15.7% (55)	58.6% (205)	19.7% (69)
Man power availability	_	3.4% (12)	10.6% (37)	59.7% (209)	26.3% (92)
EMPATHY					
Processing of Cheques	1.4% (5)	9.1% (32)	17.7% (62)	48.9% (171)	22.9% (80)
Cash Deposit	0.9% (3)	10.6% (37)	16% (56)	50.6% (177)	22.0% (77)
Processing of Loan	1.3% (5)	11% (38)	18.9% (66)	49.7% (174)	19,2% (67)
Processing of other services	0.6% (2)	10.2% (36)	19.8% (69)	50.5% (177)	18.9% (66)
Overall Experience	1.1% (4)	8% (28)	16% (56)	59.2% (207)	15.7% (55)

Source: Primary data
Note: Numbers in parenthesis denotes the number of customers and should be read the number of customers who had rated on the various levels.

A service gap of greater than '1' was considered to be highly critical area for the improvement of the performance dimensions. A service gap of less than 0.50 was treated as less significant and a difference of 0.5 to 1 was considered as critical and further needs for improvements. It has been found that in tangibility, it is the parking facility (1.68) that should be considered critical. Followed by the parking facility is the location of ATM, drinking water facility, ventilation and lighting facilities that are to be given consideration. The customers are satisfied with the stationeries available in the banks a service gap of (0.29 less than 0.50). On the whole its found that a critical service gap exists in the reliability, responsiveness, assurance and empathy dimensions, as it can be seen from that Table 2 that all those factors in the above listed dimension have a service gap of greater than '0.50' and or greater than '1' which ought to be considered critical and improvement of services on those factors are required.

Table 2
Gap Analysis for the Performance Dimensions Gap Analysis for Tangibles

Dimensions	*Expected mean score*	*Experienced mean score*	*S.D*	*Service gap*
Parking	5	3.32	1.182	1.68
Lighting	5	4.14	0.585	0.86
Ventilation	5	4.1	0.683	0.9
Drinking Water	5	4.05	0.734	0.95
Stationeries	5	4.71	0.642	0.29
Convenience of banking hour	5	4.23	0.711	0.77
ATM location	5	3.80	0.68	1.20
GAP ANALYSIS FOR RELIABILITY				
Knowledge & Skill Level of Employees	5	4.07	0.702	0.93
Understanding of Systems & Procedure	5	3.99	0.706	1.01
GAP ANALYSIS FOR RESPONSIVENESS				
Handling & Response to customer Complaints	5	3.92	0.794	1.08
Employee Availability	5	4.09	0.707	0.91
GAP ANALYSIS FOR ASSURANCE				
Attitude of Employees	5	4.07	0.756	0.93
Professional Approach	5	4.08	0.736	0.92
GAP ANALYSIS FOR EMPATHY				
Processing of Cheques	5	3.90	1.01	1.10
Cash Deposit	5	4.21	0.78	0.79
Processing of Loan	5	3.86	0.65	1.14
Processing of other services	5	4.05	0.90	0.95

t- Test Analysis

Independent samples t-test was used to find any existence of difference between the perceptions of the two set of customers towards their banks on the various performance dimensions. Table 3 shows the results of the t-test performed.

Table 3
t-Test for the Performance Dimensions

	Mean		*Standard deviation*		
Dimensions	*Bank 1*	*Bank 2*	*Bank 1*	*Bank 2*	*t-value*
Tangibles	4.15	3.95	1.10	1.24	1.05 (ns)
Reliability	3.72	3.49	1.12	1.02	0.32 (ns)
Assurance	4.20	3.90	1.01	0.98	1.25 (ns)
Responsiveness	3.99	4.25	1.23	0.80	1.08 (ns)
Empathy	4.21	4.01	0.97	1.32	0.86 (ns)

Note: ns - not significant.

The t-test results revealed that there is no significant difference between the perceptions of the two sets of customers on all the five performance dimensions with respect to their banks.

IMPLICATIONS

The five dimensions service quality (SQ) framework enjoys considerable support in the service quality literature. It is a well-accepted dimension in both academic and corporate. But the consideration is how to deploy the resources for these dimensions for the benefits of customers and increases customer satisfactions. Identification of the relative importance of the service quality dimensions given by the customers and the less valued services by the customers should be the right point to start. In this study to find out the least valued (perceived) dimensions by the customers and the frequency rating was used and to find out the service gaps in the various dimensions, gap analysis was applied as a tool. The study revealed that majority of the customers has least valued (perceived) the tangibles. Among the factors, the parking facility, ATM locations were rated the least by the customers followed by drinking water facilities and ventilation in the banks. Similar to the tangibles, on the assurance dimensions, customer rated least on the services provided by the banks. On the assurance dimension the customers were not happy with the process and the way in which loans were distributed. The same trend could also be found in the responsiveness dimension. The customers were not happy on the delivery of the services provided by the employees. On the whole the banks seemed to have performed better in care of 'Responsiveness' 'Reliability' and 'Empathy' than in other dimensions. Poor scores on tangibles and assurance clearly depict how unimportance had the bank attributed to the infrastructure of the bank and its department. Low scores in assurance imply the need for employers on the skill enhancement else it shall lead to a poor performance and create a sense of insecurity among customers. The gap analysis revealed critical distance on parking, ventilation, drinking water facility, more waiting time of customers, less awareness of the new services launched, customer handling techniques and the professional approach and the employees' attitude. Analysis of the results on the grounds of 'service context' revealed that the tangible was perceived least and improvements are required at vast level. The systems and procedure adopted by the bank was dominating and all the other factors on the five service dimensions need to be improved for better quality perception. The results here conclude that the performance delivery with respect to the banks has to be enhanced to leverage and improvise the level of service quality dimensions.

DIRECTIONS FOR FUTURE RESEARCH

The importance of technology is rapidly increasing in the banking sector. Though customer acceptance of technology is still a budding phenomenon, it is a huge determinant in the performance of the bank and thus shall prove dominant in the service quality dimensions with respect to bank and hence more importance and focus can be given in identifying the real potential factors of technology in appraising service performance. Second the analysis of SQ based on the demographics can reveal unexplored areas such that the bankers can leverage on the explored facts and finally a comparative study of services can be done for better understanding on the customers' perceptions and expectations on the various service sectors and thus it can lead to differentiate the perceptions of customers based on the sectors.

CONCLUSION

In this Study, service quality and its model of gaps were studied by taking the service offered by the banks in to account. Gap analysis was used as an analytical approach for evaluating the difference between customers' expectations and the experience of quality. In conclusion, though the satisfaction level of service being offered is at a acceptable level, the organization has to keep abreast in an ever changing environment to be competent and bridging the gap between the customers experience and expectations is the only means of making a mark. By identifying strengths and weaknesses pertaining to the dimensions of service quality, organizations can better allocate resources to provide better service.

References

Ahmad Jamal and Kmala Naser (2002), Customer Satisfaction and Retail Banking: An Assessment of Some of the Key Antecedents of Customer Satisfaction in Retail Banking, *International Journal of Bank Marketing,* Vol. 20 (4), pp. 146-160.

Berry, L. L., Parasuraman, A. & Zeithaml, V. A. (1988), The Service-quality Puzzle. *Business Horizon,* 31(5), 35-43.

Caruana, A. (2002), Service Loyalty: The Effect of Service Quality and the Mediating Role of Satisfaction. *European Journal of Marketing,* Vol. 36(7/8), pp. 811-826.

Correlates of Service Quality in Banks: An Empirical Investigation.

Mushtaq A. Bhat (2005), Correlates of Service Quality in Banks: An Empirical Investigation, *Journal of Services Marketing,* Volume 5 (1) (April-September 2005).

Dabholkar, P., Thorpe, D. I. & Rentz, J. Q. (1996), A measure of Service Quality for Retail Stores. *Journal of the Academy of Marketing Science.* 24(Winter), 3-16.

Gounaris, S. P., Stathakopoulos., Athanassopoulos, A. D. (2003), Antecedents to Perceived Service Quality: An Exploratory Study in the Banking Industry. *Inernational Journal of Bank Marketing,* Vol. 24(4), pp. 168-190.

Hussein A. Al-Tamimi (2003), "Measuring Perceived Service Quality at UAE Commercial Banks", *International Journal of Quality and Reliability Management,* Vol. 20(2). pp. 119-132.

Liang, C. J. and Wang, W. H. (2004), "Attributes, Benefits, Customer Satisfaction and Behavioral Loyalty—An Integrative Research of Financial Services Industry in Taiwan," *Journal of Services Research,* Vol. 4, No. 1, pp. 57–91.

Parasuraman, A., Zeithaml, V. A. & Berry, L. L. (1985), A Conceptual Model of Service Quality and its Implications for Future Research, *Journal of Marketing*, 49(Fall), 41-50.

Parasuraman, A., Zeithaml, V. A., and Berry, L. L. (1988), SERVQUAL: A Multiple-Item Scale for Measuring Consumer Perceptions of Service Quality. *Journal of Retailing*. 64(1), 12-40.

Parasuraman, A., Zeithaml, V. A., and Berry, L. L. (1985), A Conceptual Model of Service Quality and its Implications for Future Research. *Journal of Marketing*. 49(Fall), 41-50.

Prabhakaran, S. & Satya, S. (2003), An Insight in to Service Attributes In Banking Sector, *Journal of Services Researches*, April 2003.

Ramaswamy, R. (1996). Design and Management of Service Processes: Keeping Customers for Life. Reading, MA: Addison-Wesley Publishing Co.

Rust, Roland T. and Richard L. Oliver (1994), "Service Quality: Insights and Managerial Implications from the Frontier," in Roland T. Rust and Richard L. Oliver, Eds., Service Quality: New Directions in Theory and Practice. Thousand Oaks, CA: Sage Publications, 1-19.

Spiros P. Gounaris, Vlassis Stathakopoulos, Antreas D. Athanassopoulos (2003), Antecedents to Perceived Service Quality: An Exploratory Study in the Banking Industry, *International Journal of Bank Marketing*, Vol. 21, (4), pp.168-190.

Stafford, M., Stafford, T. F., and Wells, B. P. (1998), Determinants of Customer Satisfaction in the Auto Casualty Claims Process. *The Journal of Services Marketing*. 12(6), 426-60.

Tan Jing Hee. & Wayne Kwan (1994), Measuring Service Quality in Singapore Retail Banking: A Gap Analysis & Segmentation Approach, Singapore Management Review; Jul 94, Vol. 16 Issue 2, pp. 1-25.

Tignieh Mersha and Veen Adlakha (1992), Measuring Service Quality in Singapore Retail Banking: A Gap Analysis & Segmentation Approach. Singapore Management Review; Jul 94, Vol. 16 (2), pp 1-25.

Zeithaml, V. A. & Binter, M. J. (1996), Service Marketing. New York. NY: The McGraw-Hill Companies, INC.

Zeithaml,Valarie A. and Bitner, Mary Joe (1996), Customer Expectations of Services, Services Marketing, New Delhi, McGrawhill.

THE JOURNEY OF VENTURE CAPITAL AND PRIVATE EQUITY IN INDIA

T. SATYANARAYANA CHARY*

INTRODUCTION

Entrepreneurship is the dynamic process of creating incremental wealth. Individuals who assume the major risks in terms of equity, time, and/or career commitment or provide value for some product or service create the wealth. The product or service may or may not be new or unique but value must somehow be infused by the entrepreneur by receiving and locating the necessary skills and resources.

As evidenced by the many different definitions, the term entrepreneurship means different things to different people and can be viewed from different conceptual perspectives. However, in spite of the differences, there are common aspects: risk taking, creativity, independence and rewards. These commonalities will continue to be the driving force behind the notion of entrepreneurship in the future. One thing is clear - the future for entrepreneurship appears to be bright.

The role of entrepreneurship in economic development involves more than just increasing per capita output and income; it involves initiating and constituting change in the structure of business and society. This change is accompanied by growth and increased output, which allows more to be divided by the various participants. What in an area facilitates the needed change and development? One theory of economic growth depicts innovation as the key not only in developing new products or services for the market but also in stimulating investment interest in the new ventures being created. This new investment works on both the demand and the supply sides of the growth equation: the new capital created expands the capacity for growth (supply side) and the resultant new spending utilizes the new capacity and output (demand side).

* Associate Professor and Chairman Board of Studies, Department of Commerce, Telangana University, Nizamabad, Andhra Pradesh, India, (*e-mail: tsnchary@gmail.com*)

In spite of the importance of investment and innovation in the economic development of an area, an adequate understanding of the product-evolution process is still lacking. This is the process through which innovation develops and commercializes through entrepreneurial activity, which in turn stimulates economic growth.

Although the entrepreneurial spirit was so considerable in global countries, specifically in India, the major problem that can be considered as a challenge for entrepreneur is finance. As it is true that the economic development of a country directly depends on the contributions of entrepreneurs through their innovative ideas generate from their creative abilities. Hence, most of the entrepreneurs were deterring starting on their enterprises due to lack of financial assistance. Not only that, the complex behavior of traditional investors away from new and innovative businesses due to high degree of risk and uncertainty. However, there was a big gap in financing the entrepreneur's ventures.

While suffering a lot in getting finance the entrepreneurs started looking at a new solution that can help them very highly in surmounting the problems of financing their ventures. Fortunately, in this direction a new financial instrument as well as a service emerged in the name of venture capital to cater to the needs of technocrats and budding entrepreneurs. Hence, after a decade due to the changing paradigms of venture capital from the perspective of its risk concept, it has started to converse it self slowly in to a different form namely known as private equity.

THE CONCEPT OF VENTURE CAPITAL

Venture capital is a new financial service, the emergence of which went towards developing strategies to help a new class of new entrepreneurs to translate their business ideas into realities. As the name suggests it implies capital provided to start a new venture, it is known as venture capital. This new financial intermediary emerged in eighties. The term venture capitalist denotes institutional investors that provide equity financing to projects and play an active role in advising the managements. Venture capital is an important source of funds for technology-based industries, which contribute significantly to growth process. It helps entrepreneurs to actualize scientific ideas and inventions. Hence, Venture capital is a potential source for augmenting the supply of good securities with track record of performance to the stock market, which faces shortage of good securities to absorb the savings of the investors. However, Venture capital is quite distinguishable to traditional bank and institutional finance as the feature of the Venture Capital is different from the traditional one.

Venture capital is one of the least-understood areas in entrepreneurship. Some think that venture capitalists do the early-stage financing of relatively small, rapidly growing technology companies. While true, this is a narrow definition; it is better to view venture capital more broadly as a professionally managed pool of equity capital. Frequently, the equity pool is formed from the resources of wealthy limited partners. Other principal investors in venture-capital limited partnerships are pension funds, endowment funds, and other institutions, including foreign investors. The pool is managed by a general partner - the venture-capital firm - in exchange for a percentage of the gain realized on the investment and a fee. The investments are in early stage deals as well as second- and third-stage deals and leveraged buyouts. In fact, venture capital can best be characterized as a long-term investment discipline, usually over a five-year period , in the creation of early-stage companies, the expansion and revitalization of existing businesses, and the financing of leveraged buyouts of existing divisions of major corporations or privately owned businesses. In each investment, the venture capitalist takes and equity participation through stock, warrants, and/or convertible securities and has an active involvement in the monitoring of each portfolio company bringing investment, financing planning, and business skills to the firm.

HOW VENTURE CAPITAL WORKS?

A promoter comes forward either with a new business as yet an untried product or process. He/she needs a financial backer to help him/her to set up his/her plans or buy out a part or the whole of an existing enterprise. He/she may not be able to go to the regular bank or conventional financial institutions for one of the two reasons; the predict may be untried and there may be teething problem to overcome in its design and marketing. Alternatively, their promoter may have no previous track record as investor. In such cases, the financier (a venture capitalist) may come forward and lend him the money in the understanding that, if the enterprise proves successful, it will go public, i.e., it will make an initial public offer (IPO) of its share. The more successful venture ensures the higher profit to both the promoter and financier through sale of shares. So it is intended that the venture capital assistance should go mainly to the schemes with the objectives of encourage the indigenous technology and its commercial application, adopt and modify the applications of imported technology in such a manner that it will be appropriate to the Indian environment. The assistance is generally being provided for the purpose of Setting up of pilot projects, for technological innovations and modernization, for developing appropriate technology, and for meeting the cost of marking surveys and market promotion programmes.

THE CONCEPT OF PRIVATE EQUITY

Private equity is the ownership of shares or other equity or equity-like interests in companies that do not trade publicly on a stock exchange, or over-the-counter, among investment dealers. As there is no instantaneous market for trading, these investments are appropriate only for patient investors with a long-term view. Because the investments often involve the acquisition of a controlling interest or significant influence costing several millions of dollars, private equity opportunities are generally more appropriate for large institutional investors with the time and resources to evaluate the potential risks and returns, and the patience to wait 10 years or longer to maximize investment returns.

Private equity is essential to fuel the economy and nurture the budding entrepreneurs/technocrats. Not only that, even private equity can work very well in making the country to excel in the total entrepreneurship of the country that can contribute a lot for the nation. Hence, the main reasons for the need of private equity are as follows:

1. Private equity firms often work in conjunction with other providers of finance and may be able to help to put a total funding package together for the business.
2. Private equity firms also bring in required expertise in multiple functions.
3. The placement with reputed investor will further enhance the brand image of the company.
4. Private equity helps achieve ambitions of a company and provide a stable base for strategic decision-making.
5. Private equity firms will seek to increase a company's value to its owners, without taking day-to-day management control.
6. Private equity firms usually provide higher valuations in normal Stock Market conditions and lower valuations when Stock Market is booming.
7. Investors can also help company in improving and developing its business and strategies.

HOW PRIVATE EQUITY WORKS?

Private equity fund managers raise money from investors with the aim of investing for long term in a portfolio of potentially high growth private companies. The criterion for choosing Investee Company depends upon the factors as (1) A superior business or idea, (2) Quality and depth of management, (3) Modern and robust corporate governance, (4) An appropriate way to invest in the company, and (5) A strategy for exiting the investment. Private equity strategies vary widely with a focus on its maturity as it is not so fancy proposition for promoters for various reasons, they are: Fear of losing the confidentiality and control over the company, private equity is a high cost option, and Participation of outsiders to stick the nose in the business.

STEPS IN THE PROCESS OF PRIVATE EQUITY

There are so many steps that involve in the private equity process, they are:

1. Screening of the Company.
2. Short-listing of possible investors to be targeted.

3. Preparation of preliminary information memorandum that is an executive outline covers Promoters, Management and key managerial personnel, industry scenario, existing business of the company, financial performance, ratio analysis, SWOT analysis, project details financial projections, investment details and Returns and exit routes.
4. Data room setup that refers to compilation of authenticated statutory and other records of the company to facilitate detailed due diligence by the advisor and investor for setting up of the quantitative valuation.
5. Preparation of the Valuation Report.
6. Presentations and one to one meeting with investors.
7. Preparation of Confidential information memorandum.
8. Investor Negotiations.
9. Closure of the Transaction.

EXIT ROUTES FOR VENTURE CAPITAL AND PRIVATE EQUITY

The critical aspect either in venture capital or private equity is exit route. Because, the exit route can decide the fate of both the investee and investor. There are different exit routes namely known as listing of shares, offer for sale, and sale to strategic investors, etc. In the following lines the different types of exit routes are discussed.

1. *Listing of Shares:* The listing of shares subsequently after public offer, is a well-linked route for exiting, as it enable freely transfer of securities in open market.

2. *Offer for Sale:* The private equity investor may get out off the transition by offering their holding to any other interested investor.

3. *Sale to Strategic Investors:* The private equity holder, if not restricted by the covenants of the agreement, may sell their stake to any acquirer, who is interested in taking over the management of the company.

4. *Tag Along Rights:* A contractual obligation used to protect minority shareholders. Basically, if a majority shareholder sells their stake, then the minority shareholder has the right to join the transaction and sell their minority stake in the company.

5. *Management Buy-out:* When the mangers and / or executives of a company purchase controlling interest in a company from existing shareholders.

6. *Auction of Shares:* The private equity investor may sell their stake in an open market transaction by way of auction.

7. *Buy Back by Promoters:* The holding of outsider investor is being purchased by promoters through buy back complying with the provisions of the Companies Act, 1956.

8. *Merger with Listed Companies:* The most popular way of exiting is merger or amalgamation of Investee Company with any other listed company, enabling the shareholders to freely transfer the shares in open market.

REVIEW OF THE LITERATURE

Venture capital is a financial innovation of the twentieth century became known after the famous legend of Apple Computers, which started out in U.S. in 1977 with the Capital firm, Arthur Rock and Co. it bas become the major topic of discussion and is attracting more attention at present than ever before due to globalization. There has been a plethora of literature on venture capital finance and private equity that helps the practitioner's viz., venture capital finance and private equity companies and fund managers and academicians for better understanding the role of venture capital and private equity in economic development.

There are number of studies on Venture Capital and activities of Venture capitalists in developed countries, Clark, 1987; Bygrave and Timmons, 1985 and 1992; Fried and Hisrich, 1988 and 1994; Macmillan *et al,* 1985 and 1987; Tyebjee and burno, 1984, Wan, 1991; Wilson, 1993 concentrated on the venture investment process and evaluation criteria.

There are few studies in the context of Asian countries: Ray 1991; Rayand Turynin, 1993; Pandey, 1995, they view that in the developing countries venture capital industry is at take-off it needs policy and other measures like developed countries to boost necessary development.

Those who have been most influential are the Americans like Bostern, James W., Gill. D, Green, Nilford, Henderson J.W., Klug, Jhon R, Lorens, Tony, Mc Graty, T.P., Oerez, Robert, Rogers E. M., J. K. Harsen, Gampers, Raul, Mull, Frederick. H and Neher, Darwin V is of the view that, venture capital finance is a capital investment in a business enterprise that carries elements of high risk that is very significant to the development of new business.

Pratt and Pratt (Guide on Venture Capital, 1983 USA) views that venture capital is "the earkt stage financing of new and young enterprises seeking to grow rapidly'.

Dean, B. V. and Bakou, S. K. 1990, (Co-operations management in a venture capital fund: In Strategic Management-Methods and Studies); Glad Stone, D. 1988 (Venture Capital Hand Book); Henderson, J. W. 1988 (Obtaining Venture Financing; Principles and Practices); Lorens, Tony, 1988 (Venture Capital Today); Mc Garthy, T.P 1989 (Business plams that win Venture Capital); Mc Naughton, Rod B. 1991 (Venture Capital–The developing literature) emphasized on Principles , Practices and How to get Venture Capital.

Venture Capital is the respinse of the market forces to fill the void between sources of fund for innovations and traditional lower cost sources of capital available to ongoing projects, BobZider, 1998 (How Venture Capital Works-Harvard Business Review).

Gompers, Paus, 1993 (Harward University); Mull Frederick, H.1990 (University of Geotfia) and Neher, Darwin, V. 1994 (Prinston University) concentrated in their Ph.D., thesis on the theory, structure and performance of Venture Capital.

Kucchal, S.C 1990, Verma, J.C view that the venture capital can promote well the Indian industry if the problems pertaining to venture capital industry are solved.

Guptha , O.Pm Verma, J.C, Pandey, I.M, Srivasthava, Hemanth patwsrdhan, Ganeshan, Nhattacharya, Pandya Mukul, Machi Raju and Prasenna Chandra, view that the venture capital captivity has just begun in India. It can play amore innovative and developmental role in a developing country like India by combining risk financing with management and marketing assistance. It can foster the development of entrepreneurship and transfer of technology. Moreover this venture capital is right solution to the industrial sickness and up gradation of technology in small-scale industries.

Venture Capital - withering and dying - Amy Cortege, 25th October 2001, The Hindu explains about the future of venture capital industry and the reduction of investment and closing or shutting-down of offices by new comers.

Venture Capital comes of Age - Sandhya Prakash - Indian Management capital in the developing country like India.

Sethi, Sudhir, 24th February 1999, Venture Capital and entrepreneurship, The Economic Times (Pg. 8) discusses about the entrepreneurship through venture capital.

D. Mukhopadhayay - November 1995 - Venture Capital Fund - A Perspective - Management Accountant explains about the history, operation and management of venture capital funds and indicates a set of policy measures required for their effective functioning in India.

Venture capital niche exists because it addresses the problems and imperfections like asymmetry of information, adverse selection and agency problem in the capital market a unique and distinct manner, William 1990, NeherDarwin 1994, Sankir 1994, Hellman, 1993, Gompess and Paul, 1993, Jacob 1993, Hagan John Terry 1999, Hober 1990.

The road to success is not smooth. Getting venture capital is tough. Only ten in hundred get beyond pre-evaluation stage and only one gets funded. Getting money out of another person's pocket was never easy; what is really required is confidence in one's abilities and perseverance, Bikrmjeet S. Guram, Venture Forth, 2nd June 2001, The Economic Times.

Dotcoms may have brought down the credibility of venture capitalists but the future especially of the technology companies depends entirely on this form of funding, at ate Nagendra V. Chowdary and Dr. G.Ramakrishna Reddy, Venture Capital - A Beleagured Past and a Promising Future?, Indian Management, March 2001.

Venture Capital can play a more innovative and developmental role in a developing country like India. It could help the rehabilitation of sick units through people with ideas and turnaround management skills. Not only that, it can also play a significant role in service sector including tourism, publishing, health care and financial services etc of developing countries, Dr.T.Sathyanarayana Chary, Venture Capital Industry - Issues and Measures for Development, Pratibimba, 2nd August 2001.

Aspects of Venture Capital industry especially financing value addition and disinvestments mechanism may have far reaching implications for the development of the whole venture capital industry, Vishnu Varshney, Productivity, 3rd October - December 1999.

I .M. Panday's Venture Capital: Indian experience, deals with evaluation and experience of venture capital in India and various countries of the world well that covered problems and prospects of venture capital in India with comparison of developed counties. Measures needed to boost the venture capital industry are also discussed.

T. Satyanarayana Chary in his research work on private equity has mentioned that is essential to fuel the economy and nurture the budding entrepreneurs/ technocrats. Not only that, even private equity can work very well making the country to excel the total entrepreneurship of the country that can contribute a lot for the nation.

NEED FOR THE STUDY

Venture capital and private equity new financial instruments emerged in the 19th century to promote new and innovative business proposals that can lead the high economic growth. The role of venture capital finance and private equity is quite different and distinguishable to traditional type of finance, as venture capitalists and private equity participate not only in the capital but also in the management. So, there is a need to study the role play of typical venture capital organizations and private equity firms in development and promotion of business ventures of various entrepreneurs come from the first generation and technocrats having sound knowledge and creativity.

OBJECTIVES OF THE STUDY

The main objective of the study is to analyze the state of venture capital and private equity industry and their role in promotion of entrepreneurism in India. Hence, the other specific objectives of the study are:

1. To study the concept of Venture Capital & Private Equity.
2. To review the state of Venture Capital and Private Equity industry in India.

3. To analyze practices, problems and prospects of Venture Capital and Private Equity financing through selected case studies.

SCOPE AND LIMITATIONS OF THE STUDY

The study covers a rigorous analysis over the concept of Venture Capital and Private Equity with specific objectives. Analysis was made with regard to evaluation and growth of Venture Capital and Private Equity as well as role of Venture Capital and Private Equity in promoting entrepreneurs in India. Though the study is a very comprehensive one with case analysis it is subjected to certain limitations, they are:

- The findings of case analysis cannot be generalized to other Venture Capital funds, and
- Impact of Venture Capital is not studied form the perspective of various macro parameters.

DATA SOURCES AND METHODOLOGY

The present study used secondary data only collected from various sources, namely, literature of Venture Capital and Private Equity, annual reports of Indian Venture Capital association, and APIDC Venture Capital Ltd and India Direct fund Data, thus, collected with regard to growth of Venture Capital, industry wise finance, sources of finance, methods of finance, investment by stages, investment by region and states in India as well as list of venture capital undertakings, financial performance, Funds flow and investment portfolio of APIDC Venture Capital Ltd, as well as private equity growth in India and role play of the India Direct Fund is processed, analyzed and presented in a systematic way through various statistical tools, namely, Percentages, Pie-diagrams, Column charts and Bar charts.

THE GROWTH OF VENTURE CAPITAL IN INDIA

The Government of India felt the need of venture capital funds in India in the context of structural development and growth of small-scale business enterprises. Because small-scale industries form the major constituents of the backbone of Indian Economy and economic prosperity and development of the state is rather impossible without adequate economic support of the small-scale industrial sector. 1986-87 is an eventful year for the venture capital industry in the country. A 5 per cent cent was levied on all know-how payments to create a venture capital fund by IDBI. ICICI also started to become a partner of the venture capital industry in the same year. 'Necessity is the mother of invention' was apathy applicable to the industrial thought of the promoters of Indian venture capital funds in those days when the new and young entrepreneurs were facing difficulties to raise equity capital from the conventional market during 1988-89. Under the circumstances, the scheme to launch venture capital funds was formulated.

Initially, a fund under the nomenclature of venture capital fund (VCF) was required to be established with certain corpus for being invested in the new and young firms with high potential of returns. Government decided to allow them concessional treatment of capital gains arising out of liquidation of equity holding in the assisted firms. At present, several venture capital firms are incorporated in India and they are promoted either by all India Financial Institutions like IDBI, ICICI, IFCI, State level financial institutions, Public Sector Banks, or promoted by Foreign Banks/Private sector of financial institutions like Indus Venture Capital Fund, Credit Capital Venture Fund etc.

In Table 1 an attempt has been made to analyze the growth of venture capital in India. It has moved from $ 20 million in 1996 to $ 14,234 million in 2007. But when we look at the growth over the period from 1996 to 2007, there is a considerable decline in the growth except in the year 2000, 2006 and 2007. It is because the apprehension of the failures of the ventures, slow-down of the economy, lack of creativity in the entrepreneurs and the poor venture capital culture in India.

Table 1
Growth of Venture Capital in India

Year	*US Dollars (in Million)*
1996	20
1997	80
1998	250
1999	500
2000	1160
2001	937
2002	591
2003	470
2004	1650
2005	2200
2006	7500
2007	14234

Source: IVCA Reports

THE GROWTH OF PRIVATE EQUITY IN INDIA

Although private equity is a relatively young business—the first of today's large private equity firms, Warburg Pincus, was founded in the late 1960s - now there are more than 2,700 such companies worldwide. In addition to Warburg, other large players include the Blackstone Group, Texas Pacific Group and the Carlyle Group.

Leading investment banks such as Goldman Sachs, Lehman Brothers and JPMorgan Chase also have private equity units that are now huge players in the industry. Private equity firms raise money for funds from entities such as pension funds, endowments, corporations and wealthy individuals.

Funds are typically set up as limited partnership, thus the LP at the end of most of their names, as in JPMorgan Partners Global investors, LP. Investors in the funds act as limited partners, a private equity firm as general partner. A private equity firm will first spend time raising money for a fund. Once it hits a certain amount, it will then announce a first "closing" and begin looking for deals. It could take several years to invest all the money in a fund, and a private equity firm might raise more money in a fund after the first closing. Only when a firm announces a fund's final closing is it no longer open to new investors.

The Indian private equity market has been getting more active by the day. During the last years or so, almost all the major global VC and PE firms have either established an on-ground presence in India or raised significant India-dedicated funds. In 2007 PE investments levels increased by more than 200% to almost $14.234 billion from $7.5 billion in 2006. This quantum leap was not the result of a low base, but the Indian GDP growth coming within striking range of double-digits. Annual growth rates of 7-9% are unheard of in mature western economics. And global investors want high returns. Furthermore, several key sectors of the Indian economy, viz, IT, BPO, Telecom, Pharma/ Healthcare, Financial Services, Retail and Automotive Components that are investment targets and experiencing even higher growth than the said levels of growth rate. The other reasons for the same is well positioned economy that can mine the opportunities of globalization, an increased appetite for innovation and entrepreneurship, well regulated and fully functional capital markets and a spurt in consumerism powered by the young demographic profile (see Table 2 and 3 to aware about the growth of private equity and the top 10 private equity companies in India). It can be asserted based on the data from the tables that the future of PE is so high in the days to come as it is moving at a considerable growth rate.

Table 2
The Growth of Private Equity

Year	*No. of Deals*	*Value of Deals (Rs. $ Millions)*
2000	280	1160
2001	110	937
2002	78	591
2003	56	470
2004	71	1650
2005	146	2200
2006	299	7500
2007	387	14234
2008	312	10,590

Source: Various issues of Business World.

Private Equity firms invested a record $7,460 million over 299 deals in India during 2006, according to a study by Venture Intelligence a research service focused on Private Equity and Venture Capital. The latest quarter ended December 2006 witnessed PE firms investing $2,559 million across 67 deals, that. do not include investments in Real Estate. Total investments by the amount invested during 2006 was well over three times that during the previous year, which itself was a record one Mega deals like Idea Cellular's pre-IPO placement and the KKR-Flextronics Software buyout contributed significantly to the total. The year witnessed several large global PE firms - with appetite for large deals-making their first investments in India. There were 26 deals involving investments of over $50 million during 2006 compared to just nine such deals in the previous year.

Private Equity firms are boldly creating innovative partnerships with entrepreneurs to take corporate India to new levels. Information Technology and IT-Enabled Services (IT & ITES) continued to remain the favorite industry among PE investors during 2006 accounting for $1,470 million across 87 investments. The manufacturing industry followed attracting 55 investments worth $962 million. Other industries that attracted significant PE investor attention during the year included BFSI (Banking, Financial Services and Insurance), Healthcare & Life Sciences and Engineering & Construction. Late-stage investments accounted for 36% of all deals while PIPEs (PE investments in listed companies) accounted for 22% of the deals. Early-stage investments accounted for about 20% of deals during the 2006, the Venture Intelligence study showed.

Private Equity firms invested about US$2,085 million across 76 deals during the quarter ended June 2006. The amount invested during the latest quarter was five times higher than that during the same period last year (which witnessed 40 deals totaling $407 million) and 1.5 times that during the January-March 2006 quarter (which had witnessed 69 investments worth $1,384 million). Total investments by Private Equity investors during the first six months of 2006 has touched $3.5 billion - 1.6 times the $2.2 billion invested in the entire of 2005, with 17 deals worth about $200 million, Manufacturing overtook the Information Technology & IT-Enabled Services (IT & ITES) as the favorite industry among PE investors during the latest quarter. Engineering & Construction companies emerged as the third most favorite industry attracting $372 million across thirteen deals."While PE interest in Manufacturing was growing rapidly right through 2005, this is the first quarter in which investments in this industry has actually overtaken the number of deals in IT, Other industries that witnessed significant interest from PE investors during the quarter included Banking & Financial Services and Food & Beverages. Like in the past several quarters, the latest quarter too witnessed a strong focus on investments in late stage and listed companies. These two categories together accounted for a 60% of all PE deals in the latest quarter compared to the 49% in the immediate previous quarter However, the number of Late Stage (including pre-IPO) deals overtook the number of "PIPE" (Private Investment in Public Enterprises) deals during the latest quarter. Early and Growth Stage companies accounted for 30% of PE deals (in volume terms) during the period.

Given that the main competition to PE in India over the last 18 months have been the public markets-something which caused several deals to fall through due to mismatch in valuation expectations - the correction of this likely to encourage some PE investors, who chose to not to participate in the highly competitive late-stage segment over the last few months, to become more active now. Hence the sheer size of the funds lined up specifically for India will ensure that the momentum in the PE segment continues uninterrupted.

Despite the vicious meltdown leveling stock valuations, the n umber and value of PE deals recorded actually fell in 2008. According to Grant Thornton India, the total number of private equity deals announced in 2008 was lower, at 312 with the total announced value at $10.59 billion, compared to the 405 deals with an announced value of $19.03 billion in 2007.

CASE ANALYSIS OF VENTURE CAPITAL AND PRIVATE EQUITY

APIDC - Venture Capital Limited

Andhra Pradesh Industrial Development Corporation (APIDC) promoted APIDC-Venture Capital Limited (VCL) on 29th August 1989. The approval of the Government of India to commence operations was accorded in April 1990. APIDC-VCL was privatized in 1994 and Dynam ventures (East) Pvt. Ltd, has been awarded control of APIDC-VCL after a competitive selection process. Thus it has become a subsidiary of Dynam Venture (East) Pvt. Ltd., a firm promoted by professionals with a wealth of experience in entrepreneur ship, consulting, equity investments, technology development, etc.

The company acts as manager and trustee to the APIDC Venture Capital Fund (VCF), 1990. It is the first state level Venture Capital Fund in India to be managed by owner-managers with strong entrepreneurial skills. The fund manager's strength is their understanding of what conceiving and building a business or enterprise is all about, having gone through the process themselves.

Initially it was incorporated with an authorized capital of Rs. 2 million, out of which Rs. 0.2755 million was paid-up capital in 1989. The paid up capital was raised to the level of authorized capital of Rs. 2 million during 1991-92.

The company managers the venture fund of Rs. 135 million. The authorized corpus capital of the fund is Rs. 135 million out of which Rs. 41.35 million is paid-up, which forms the corpus of the fund known as ' APIDC Venture Capital Fund - 1990'. The fund resources come from the World Bank, the Industrial Development Bank of India (IDBI), the Andhra Pradesh Industrial Development Corporation (APIDC), Small Industrial Development Bank of India (SIDBI), Andhra Bank, Indian Overseas Bank (IOB) and NRIs etc.

APIDC-VCL is the first of series of venture capital funds that will invest in companies in Southern & Western India, with a focus on the state of Andhra Pradesh. It will invest across several business sectors, with projections that seek to exploit key differentials (in market potential, technology, operations, and return on capital) between India and industrialized world. Generally it will invest in start-up as well as expansion type of projects.

APIDC-VCL will invest in companies with the ability to builds unique competitive advantages that others will find difficult to emulate. It will add value to portfolio companies through support in activities external to the company, being a responsive facilitator of the entrepreneurial process.

The new Equity Policy of the company proposes to give a special impetus to Industrial Development. The company has identified the following for special focus for investment.

1. Food & Agro processing except traditional industries.
2. Petroleum and Petro-chemicals.
3. Chemicals & Fertilizers.
4. Engineering & Automotives.
5. Minerals based industries.
6. Information Technology.
7. 100% Export Oriented Units.
8. Biotechnology.
9. Renewable sources of Energy.
10. Energy Saving Devices, Appliances, etc.
11. Energy Efficient and Waste Reduction Technologies and Processes.
12. Pollution Control Equipment and Devices.
13. Waste Utilization and Recycling.

Biotech Investment

APIDC-Venture capital has put investments of $1.62 million (Rs. 8.1crore) in three US-Indian biotech companies. In the first batch of funding from its recent Biotech Venture Fund, it has put in $5,40,000 each in Bioserve Biotechnologies, Gnomic Design Pharma and Silicon Insights. The investment through the APIDC-Venture Capital has attracted tremendous response from several banks and insurance companies. So, it planned with a corpus of Rs. 150crore, and has closed commitments for Rs. 40 crore, including contributions from GIC, LIC,

Table 3
VC Undertakings Assisted by APIDC-VCL

Name of the company	*Amount Sanctioned (Rs.lakhs)*	*Business*	*Competitive Strength*
Suyog Chemicals Pvt. Ltd., Nagpur	60.00	Specialty chemicals with applications in mining, paper, sugar, effluent treatment etc. Xanthates, acrylic polymers, Phthalates and other chemicals	1. Indigenous developed continuous process technology for Xanthates competitive batch process, giving rise to better yields and lower cost of production. 2. Innovative management team.
Kakatiya Electronics Pvt. Ltd., Hyderabad	5.90	Provide innovative products based on Infrared sensors in Automotive industry.	Indigeneously developed Auto dippers for LCVs & Cars for the first time in the country.
Gland Pharma Limited, Hyderabad.	150.00	Pharma company with focus on small volume parenterals (injectibles). Moving from a contract manufacturing company to direct marketing capitalizing its strengths in institutional sales and SVPs.	Collaboration from Vetters Injekt, Germany, one of the best contract manufacturing companies in the World, for prefilled syringes for the first time in the country.
Srinisons Cables Limited, Chennai	50.00	Providing wiring harnesses for automotive and white goods industry.	One of the two integrated wiring harness manufacturers in the country and only Indian company.
Trendex Retail Informatics Pvt. Ltd., Hyderabad	9.04	Providing information data base to FMCG sector.	Development of 100 % reliable data base of retail outlets for various cities.
Ocean Sparkle Ltd., Hyderabad.	250.05	Providing OEM services for ports, ship to shore cargo transport, etc.	Excellent management team with hands on shipping experience. Established virtual monopoly in managing private sector corporate ports and moving into Govt. managed ports like Goa, Ennore, etc.

Contd...

Name of the company	*Amount Sanctioned (Rs.lakhs)*	*Business*	*Competitive Strength*
Nucon Zander (India) Pvt. Ltd., Hyderabad	48.48	Manufacture of high efficiency, air/ gas filters and dryers	German collaboration for Manufacture of high pressure filter elements in the pneumatic applications. One of the top two companies in the country.
Dodla Dairy Ltd., Nellore	170.40	Procuting and processing milk, and manufacture of value added products.	Collaboration with IMAC USA, one of the top three dairy technology companies in the US, for milk processing and value added products. Developed cultures that increase the shelf life of the milk at room temperature.
Viprah Technologies Ltd., Nellore	100.00	Acoustic enclosures for DG sets and other heavy equipment to reduce noise pollution.	Product continues to have good potential in industrial and commercial applications with PCB's taking tough stance on noise pollution.
Creative Wares Limited, Kolkata & Hyderabad	120.00	Manufacturer of thermoformed polypropylene and polystyrene disposable containers for food & cosmetic applications	
E. P. Indl. & Agro Products Pvt. Ltd., Hyderabad.	100.00	Manufacture of Cellulose based products for wide range of applications.	Indigeneously developed technology for the manufacture of polyanionic cellulose for the first time in the country for applications in oil drilling industry.
Moschip Semiconductor Technology Ltd., Hyderabad.	324.00	Design, development and marketing of semiconductors, chips for applications in data communications and Input/ Output.	First fabless chip design company in the country to sell chip under its own brand name Moschip. Excellent management team of relevant experience.
Taruni Techno vision Pvt. Ltd., Hyderabad.	156.81	Development and providing cutting edge and state of the art technologies in the wireless sector.	Data Communications through Wireless Application protocol. It is the first company in India to provide two way SMS messaging services to cellular phone users. Also it is one of the first companies in the world to develop a superior middle are platform products.

Contd...

Name of the company	*Amount Sanctioned (Rs.lakhs)*	*Business*	*Competitive Strength*
N-Logue Communications Pvt. Ltd., Hyderabad.	100.00	Providing telecom services (both voice telephony and Internet) in rural areas and small towns based on WILL technology.	Rural telecommunication system (WLL) through indigenously developed Cordect technology facilitating usage of internet and telephony on the same line at the same time.
CxK Networks, Hyderabad.	50.00	Providing researched content to corporate sector.	Excellent management team.
Indus Technology Pvt. Ltd., Chennai & Singapore	100.00	A Computer Machine Vision Solutions company, providing high-end machine vision solutions to customers in the manufacturing industry.	Collaboration with IIT, Madras & TeNet group and has sound domain knowledge and expertise in the technology and business of machine vision. It has delivered a variety of solutions to several leading companies in the field of semiconductor manufacturing, both in the front-end and the back-end areas of operation.
Triad Fleetcontrol India Pvt. Ltd., Singapore.	50.00	Providing automated Fuel and Fleet Management System (FMS) (CRM technology tool) to fleet managers of large fleet transport organizations.	Technical collaboration with Rose man Engg., one of the world leaders for automated fuel and fleet management systems.
Vibromech Engineers & Services Ltd., Chennai.	125.00	Manufacture of Vibration Dampers, Lube Oil Pumps and Air Cylinders Assemblies.	Company has significant advantages in technology; cost of manufacture and cost of design, over the developed market vendors, who are the only current competitors for the large auto majors around the world.
Foursoft Ltd.	100.00	Logistics	

Source: Annual report of APIDC-VCL

Andhra Bank and the AP Government. The fund has picked start-up and early-stage businesses such as healthcare, drug discovery, agriculture, dairy etc. The portfolio of investments made by APIDC Venture Capital Ltd. is clearly demonstrated in table.

The India Direct Fund

The India Direct Fund (IDF) was among the first private equity funds set up in 1996 for investment in India. International Equity Partners, Washington (IEP) is the fund. Manager and IDEA is the Advisor to the fund. Housing Development Finance Corporation Ltd, (HDFC) is the strategic advisor to the fund. The IDF is an India dedicated $34 million Private Equity fund and invests in companies in India centric business plans. The fund has made 10 investments and is now fully invested.

The objective of the Fund is to provide mezzanine to high-growth companies in India. IFC (Washington), GIC) (Singapore), Mitsui & Co. (Japan), and Nomura Jafco (Japan) are among the Principal subscribers to this fund. Since its inception, the IDF has committed investment aggregating $28 million in ten companies. IDEA's representation in the IDF Investment committee enables IDF to contribute with its knowledge of Indian industry.

While six of the initial investments are in old economy companies, the last 4 investments have been in the technology sectors. The Company started disinvestment of its portfolio and have already returned over 30% of the fund to the investors. Hence, the initial returns of this fund have been good.

Investment, Deal Flow and Due Dilligence

IDF & IEP have the ability to effectively tap a series of industry experts both in India and the US to form a part of the investment committee, which vets the investment decisions. Given the networking enjoyed by its team and its presence in the Indian Private Equity scenario, IDF has the ability to attract good quality deals on a preferential basis. Given the investment experience of its team and the expensive networking enjoyed by it, IDF offers skill set for conducting due diligence on the proposed investment determining the credibility of management etc.

Portfolio of IDF

The India Direct Fund (IDF) which was set up in 1996, has focused principally on investments in unlisted companies. It has also invested in listed securities in special situations through negotiated transactions. The IDF has bough substantial minority stakes in companies (up to 47%) and has in all cases maintained, either on its own or through co-investments with like-minded financial partners, a greater than 25% share of the voting securities of each of its portfolio companies. Investment amounts in each company ranged from $1 million to $3.6 million (for details see Table 4).

Table 4
India Direct Fund-Portfolio Status

Particulars	*Industry*	*Investment Merits*	*Amount (USD MN)*
Alok Textile IndustriesLimited	Textiles – Weaving	Growth oriented venture Extensive supplies to Garment exporters	3.81
Brain GEM LLC	Software Development and maintenance services for e-businesses	e-services company based in Boston with a back end in India	1.13
Delta innovative Enterprises Ltd.	Communication Services	Pioneer in two –way messaging facility Establishing VSAT network across the country early market entry advantage	1.04
Drish Shoes Limited	Leather footwear	Export oriented operations strong presence in Germany revenues and local outlays	3.46
Ecoboard industries limited	Building products –Particle Boards	Environment – friendly non-wood based particle boards	3.51
New World Application	Application Services Provider	Provides Internet delivery platforms tailored to customer requirements	2.40
Secure Meters Limited	Electronic Meters	Over 60% Market share In-house technology development unit in the UK (PRI)	1.72
Sun-Earth Ceramics Limited	Ceramic Wall and Floor Tiles	Third Largest Indian tile manufacturer existing dividend paying and listed company excellent growth and profitability record	4.03
Time Packaging Limited	Plastic Packaging – Industrial	Over 62% market share in high growth industry Technical collaboration with Mauser Werke GMBH, the world leadr in Plastic drums	1.82
United studios Limited/ UTV	Media & Entertainment	Promoted by UTI- one of the largest in post – production facilities and 2-D animation in India	3.36
		Total	26.28

CONCLUSSION

Venture Capital funds in India are working with greater objectives and passion, but they couldn't achieve so far the objectives for which they are working, it does mean that still they are yet take-off stage. It is due to the traditional behavior of venture capitalists in India. Hence, to surmount all the problems, both operational and financial the venture capitalists, government and the regulator agencies should play their role very cagily. Such a way if the boost is given adequately to the venture capital industry, it is beyond doubt that the venture capital industry can take-off very shortly.

Private equity is known as investing in securities through a negotiated process. The majority of private equity investments are in unquoted companies. Private equity investment is typically a transformational, value- added, active investment strategy. It calls for a specialized skill set that is a key due diligence area for investors' assessment of a manager. Private equity investing is often divided into the categories that have subcategories and dynamics provides a useful basis for portfolio construction. Hence, the private equity has become the means of financing the new and innovative projects and to boost the entrepreneurial spirit over the world. So there is a need to focus and initiate on the same to ensure the greater level of entrepreneur development in India through which the country can get hold of the development status.

References

Jaffrey Zygmont (2000), The VC Way - Investment Secrets from the Wizards of Venture Capital.

Mahim Bist (1999), Venture Capital: Concept, Project Evaluation & the Indian Scenario, Productivity, Vol. 40, No. 3, October-December.

Pandey, I.M. (1996), Venture Capital: The Indian Experience, Prentice Hal of India Pv.t Ltd. New Delhi.

Sandhya Prakash (2000), Venture Capital Comes of Age, Indian Management, pp. 15-21 (April, 2000).

Shashank Rajurkar (1999), Issues Facing the Indian Venture Capital Industry, Productivity, Vol. 40, No. 3, October-December.

T. Satyanarayana Chary (2000), Venture Capital in India–An Overview, Management Researcher, Tiruvananthapuram.

T. Satyanarayana Chary (2001), Venture Capital Industry–Issues and Measures for Development, Pratibimba.

T. Satyanarayana Chary (2001), Venture Capital Industry, JIMS 8 M, Nov.-December.

T. Satyanarayana Chary (2003), Venture Capital Industry in India – An Overview, Published in Prabandh, Augst, 2003 Jaipur.

T. Satyanarayana Chary (2004), VC Funding – Nothing Ventured, Nothing Gained, *Business Line*, Tuesday March 30, 2004.

T. Satyanarayana Chary (2005), Mission of Venture Capital in Promotion of New Enterprises - A Study, Udyoga Prgati, Jan.-March, 2005, *The Journal of Practicing Management,* NITIE, Mumbai.

T. Satyanaryana Chary (2005), Venture Capital: Concepts & Applications Macmillan India Limited.

T. Satyanarayana Chary (2008), Venture Financing for Biotechnology Concept Publications, New Delhi.

T. Satyanarayana Chary, Private Equity in India

Zider & Bob (1998), How Venture Capital Works? *Harvard Business Review,* (November December, 1998), pp. 131-139.

A STUDY ON FINANCIAL AWARENESS ON INVESTORS (WITH SPECIFIC REFERENCE TO INITIAL PUBLIC OFFER)

P. Shalini* & S. Sudha*#

INTRODUCTION

Finance is the life of business. Every organization needs money to carry out its commercial activities. Normally an organization collects its money keeping in mind its long term activities of the business. Hence it prefers to collect the money in the form of equity capital, debentures, bank loans etc. When it collects money the company can go for an Initial Public Offer. In this case the public are said to be its investors who are said to be the future shareholders of the company.

When the company goes for an Initial Public Offer it is necessary that the organization takes sufficient measures in reaching the public, so the offer can be fully subscribed. The company needs to know if it is going for the first time for an IPO then it should be placed in the primary markets. If the IPO is for the second time then the company goes to the primary market for its FPO. Whether it is primary or secondary markets how the investors or the general public will know that this particular company is going for an IPO?

Meaning of Investors awareness: Investor Awareness is a term used in investor relations, by public companies and similar bodies, to describe how well their investors, and the investment market in general, know about their business, what is happening in the business, how well the market is progressing, how their funds doing? Etc. Investor awareness is knowledge the investment community has of a company. One such investor's awareness program has been carried by Securities and Exchange Board of India (SEBI). It is very important to know SEBI plays a vital role in safeguarding the interests of the investors. They not only determine the level of activity in the securities market but also the level of activity in the economy. However, many investors may not possess adequate expertise/knowledge to take informed investment

* Asst. Professors, MBA Department, VIBA, Vels University Chennai, (*e-mail: *shalini_at@yahoo.com, #narasimhan.sudha@gmail.com*)

decisions. Some of them may not be aware of the complete risk-return profile of the different investment options. Some investors may not be fully aware of the precautions they should take while dealing with market intermediaries and dealing in different securities. They may not be familiar with the market mechanism and the practices as well as their rights and obligations. That is why SEBI has launched a campaign called *"Securities Market Awareness Campaign" (SMAC)*. The motto of the campaign is – *'An Educated Investor is a Protected Investor.'* Another basic motto of the campaign is *"Invest with Knowledge"*. This has been launched in 12 states throughout India.

The campaign has been carried on mostly in the form of work shops, educative materials, advertisements, All India Radio, TV etc.

ABOUT SEBI

An Act to provide for the establishment of a Board to protect the interests of investors in securities and to promote the development of, and to regulate, the securities market and for matters connected therewith or incidental thereto.

The Board shall be a body corporate by the name aforesaid, having perpetual succession and a common seal, with power subject to the provisions of this Act, to acquire, hold and dispose of property, both movable and immovable, and to contract, and shall, by the said name, sue or be sued.

The main powers of the board are:

1. to protect the interests of investors in securities and to promote the development of, and to regulate the securities market, by such measures as it thinks fit.
2. regulating the business in stock exchanges and any other securities markets;
3. registering and regulating the working of stock brokers, sub-brokers, share transfer agents, bankers to an issue, trustees of trust deeds, registrars to an issue, merchant bankers, underwriters, portfolio managers, investment advisers, foreign institutional investors and such other intermediaries who may be associated with securities markets in any manner;
4. registering and regulating the working of venture capitalists;
5. Promoting and regulating self-regulatory organizations;
   - (a) Prohibiting fraudulent and unfair trade practices relating to securities markets;
   - (b) Promoting investors' education and training of intermediaries of securities markets;
   - (c) Prohibiting insider trading in securities;
   - (d) Regulating substantial acquisition of shares and take-over of companies;

(e) Calling for information from, undertaking inspection, conducting inquiries and audits

6. conducting research etc.

Objective: The main purpose of the paper is to know 1. To study on the financial awareness among the investing community.

Scope of the study: The main aim of this research is to know about the investors' awareness in IPO and the study has been carried out in the area of IPO only and secondly the research has been carried out only in Chennai city.

Limitation of the study: The limitations are:

1. Time factor is the main constraint,
2. Secondly the research has been carried out among limited investors only.

Data Collection: The primary data has been collected in the form of questionnaire from 30 respondents. The respondents have been identified as investors who have been into investing and possess the knowledge about the stock market for a long period of time.

REVIEW OF LITERATURE

Zvi Singer "Discretionary Financial Reporting: Items Manipulated By IPO Firms, and Investors' Increased Awareness" (2008). The article examines on discretionary financial reporting of three major accounting items, earnings, sales, and research and development expense, unawareness of the investors for a sample of 2,975 initial public offering (IPO) firms in the period 1988-2000. The article concluded that companies do not change their practices either because of unawareness of investor learning or because the cost of discretionary reporting is too small to cause behavioral change.

Zhen Liu "Fair Disclosure and Investor Asymmetric Awareness in Stock Markets" (2009). The paper examines on The U.S. Security and Exchange Commission implemented Regulation Fair Disclosure in 2000. The regulator aims to reduce information asymmetry among investors, and expects public forums to subsume the forbidden information channel of selective forums. The paper concludes that the regulator's consideration on investor awareness.

Shuangge Wen "Institutional investor activism on socially responsible investment: effects and expectations" (2009). The article examines on significance that has emerged is institutional investors' growing awareness and practice of socially responsible investment (SRI). The article concludes that significance that has emerged is institutional investors' growing awareness and practice of socially responsible investment (SRI).

Laura Albareda Vivo, Maria Rosario Alaguer Franch "The Challenges of Socially Responsible Investment among Institutional Investors: Exploring the Links between Corporate Pension Funds and Corporate Governance" (2009).

The paper examines on there is a growing tendency among different institutional investors to take into account non financial aspects—social, environmental, and ethical values—of company management. The paper concludes with some proposals to encourage wider SRI acceptance and practice in Spain.

Takaya Seki "Legal Reform and Shareholder Activism by Institutional Investors in Japan" (2005). The article examines on Corporate Governance has become a widely discussed topic in Japan among academics and practitioners. But companies, protected under a tight system of cross-shareholding, seem slow to adopt new models accepted outside Japan. This article discusses the changes in the composition of shareholding, which together with legal changes are leading to greater awareness among Japanese companies of corporate governance as well as greater shareholder activism.

Honghui Chen , Gregory Noronha, Vijay Singal "Investor Awareness and Market Segmentation: Evidence from S&P 500 Index Changes" (2002). The article examines on Several studies have found that stock price changes resulting from firms added to the S&P 500 index can be best explained by a downward sloping demand curve. In this paper, we study price effects around both additions and deletions and find that the price effect of index changes is consistent with Merton's (1987) investor-awareness and market segmentation hypothesis. The paper concludes that find that the reduction in shadow cost of incomplete diversification that follows additions is correlated with abnormal returns accruing to the added stocks. It is also found that the asymmetric price effects of additions and deletions that have not been explained by empirical studies thus far are consistent with market segmentation.

INTERPRETATION

Frequencies

There are various investment avenues available for the investors. It is essential to find out which type of security is preferred by most of the investors. The above table shows the percentage of investors in each type of security. In this study, it is found that 42.1% of the investors invest in stocks, which is the most preferred security among the all others. The second most preferred security is the Bond, which is preferred by 33.3% of the investors. Some investors prefer more than one type of security. 12.3% of the investors prefer the certificate of

Investments in Securities

	Frequency	*Per cent*	*Valid Percent*	*Rank*
Stocks	24	42.1	42.1	1
Bonds	19	33.3	33.3	2
Mutual Funds	2	3.5	3.5	5
Commercial Funds	1	1.8	1.8	6
Certificate of Deposit	7	12.3	12.3	3
FD	4	7.0	7.0	4
Total	57	100.0	100.0	

deposit. The fixed deposit is preferred by 7% of the investors and it is followed by the mutual funds with 3.5%. The least preferred investment avenue is the commercial fund, which gets 1.8% of preference. These variations in the preference on the investment can be easily understood in the following pie chart.

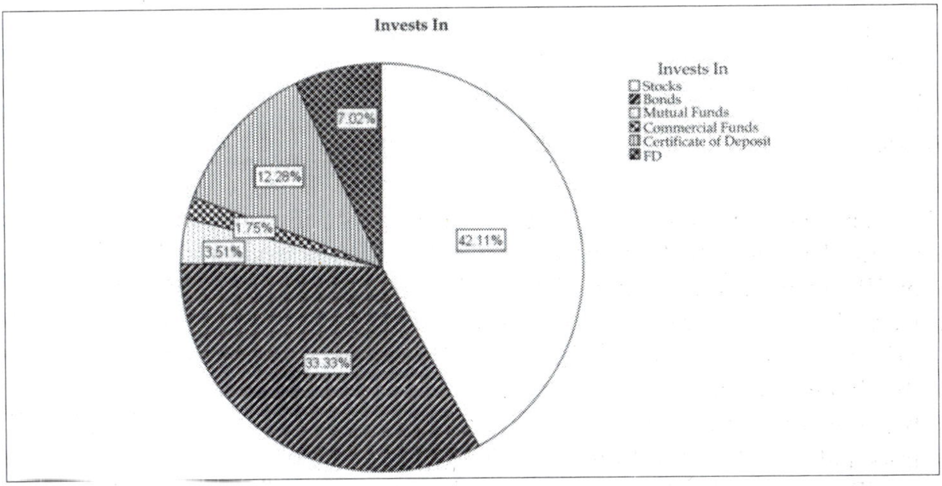

Investment in IPO

	Frequency	*Percent*	*Valid Per cent*	*Cumulative Per cent*
Yes	22	73.3	73.3	73.3
No	8	26.7	26.7	100
Total	30	100	100	

The above table shows the percentage of the IPO investors in the sample. Out of 30 investors, 22 investors invest in IPO's, which is 73.3% of the sample. It can be seen in the following pie chart. The dotted area indicates the IPO investors.

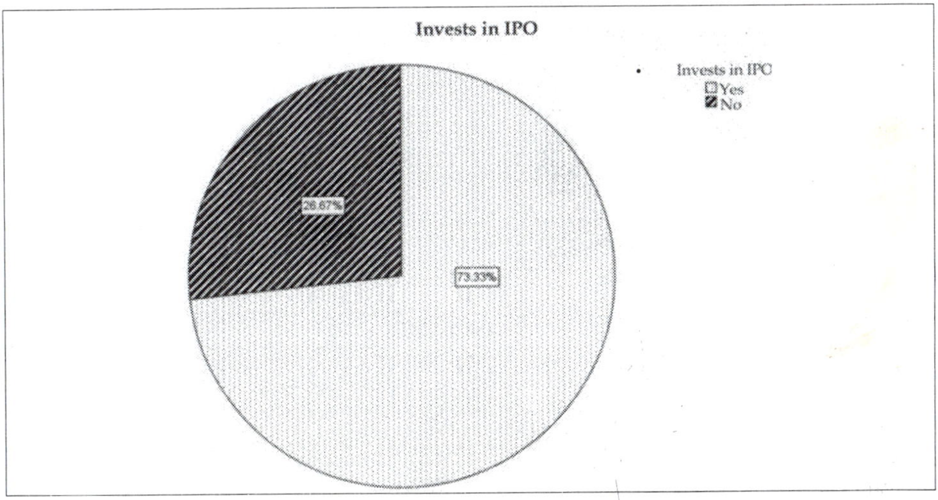

IPO Information

	Frequency	*Percent*	*Valid Percent*	*Cumulative Percent*
Newspaper	18	50	50	50
TV	2	5.6	5.6	55.6
Articles	4	11.1	11.1	66.7
Stock Brokers	3	8.3	8.3	75
Stock Broking Company	3	8.3	8.3	83.3
Friends	6	16.7	16.7	100
Total	36	100	100	

The IPO information is made available to the investors through various media. The above table shows the percentage of people getting the information on IPO from various sources. 50% of the respondents get the IPO information from the advertisements in the newspapers. 16.7% of the investors get the information on IPO through friends. The articles in the newspapers provide the IPO information to 11.1% of the investors. The stock brokers and the stock broking companies have the equal percentage of 8.3 % in providing the IPO information to the investors. The television gets only the last place in providing the IPO information to the investors with 5.6%. The following pie chart shows the percentage of investors getting the IPO information through various media.

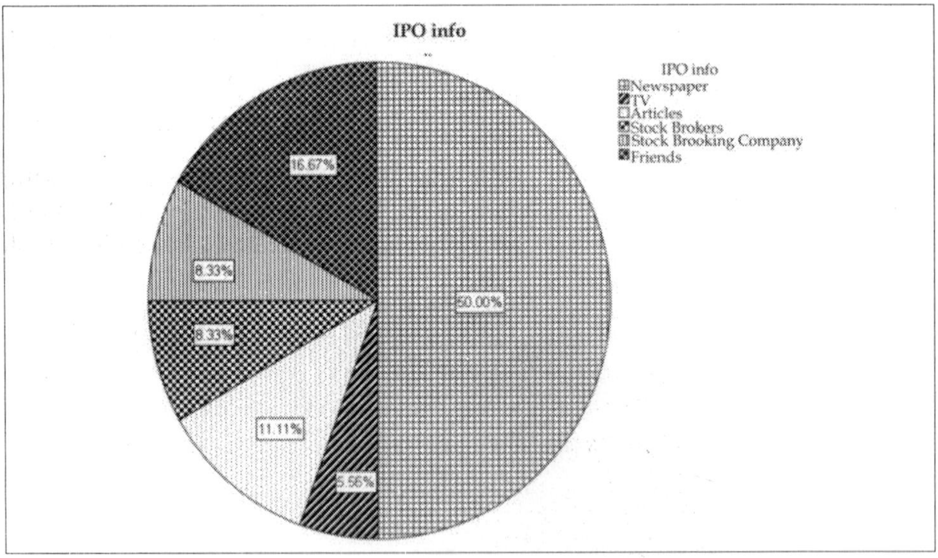

Reads IPO

	Frequency	*Percent*	*Valid Per cent*	*Cumulative Per cent*
Yes	25	83.3	83.3	83.3
No	5	16.7	16.7	100.0
Total	30	100.0	100.0	

The above table shows the percentage of investors reading the IPO regularly. Here, 83.3% of investors read the IPO and 16.7% of the investors do not read the IPO. It is represented in the following pie chart.

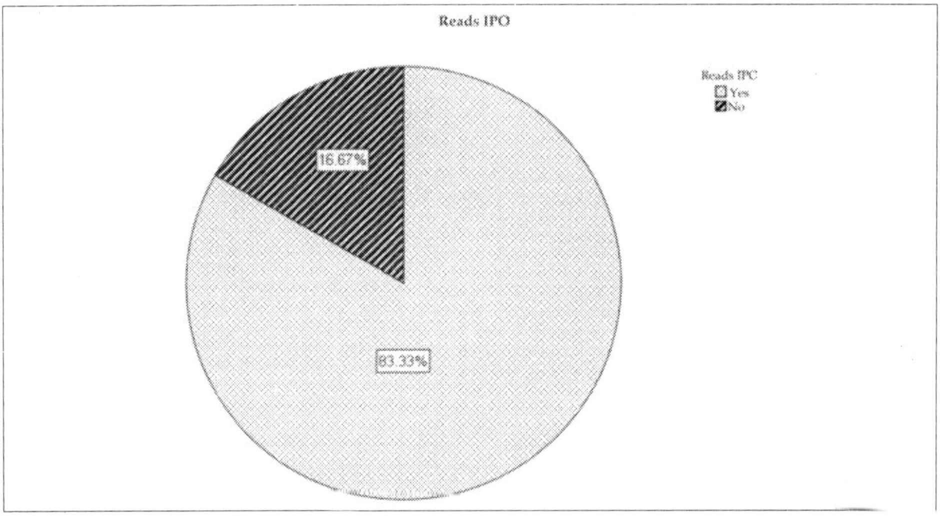

News Papers

	Frequency	*Percent*	*Valid Per cent*	*Cumulative Per cent*
Business Line	15	41.7	41.7	41.7
Economic Times	18	50.0	50.0	91.7
Financial Express	3	8.3	8.3	100.0
Total	36	100.0	100.0	

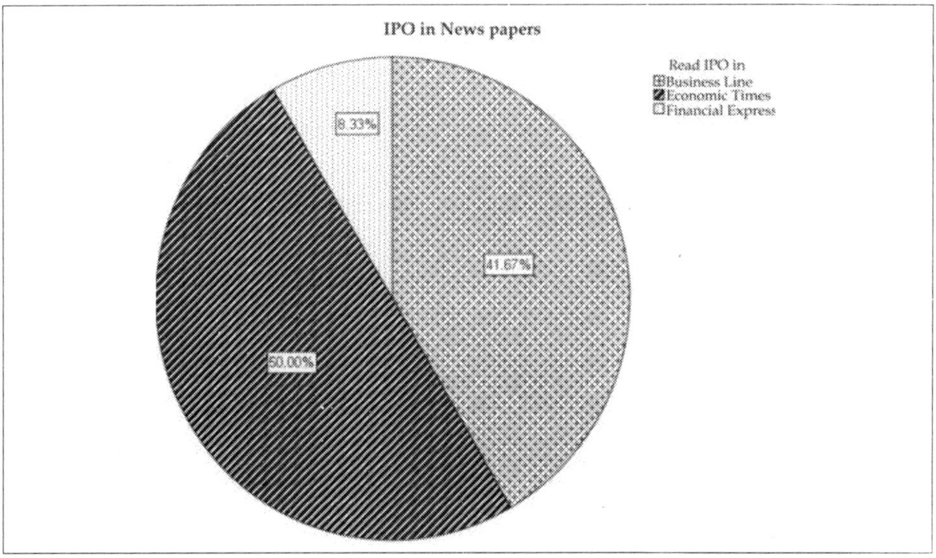

Earlier, it was found that 50 % of the investors get the IPO information through the newspapers. The above table shows the financial newspapers read by the investors frequently. 50 % of the investors read the Economic Times, 41.7 % of the investors read the Business Line and 8.3 % of people read the Financial Express. From the table, it is clear that some investors read more than one financial newspapers. The following pie chart clearly shows this information. Thus, it is found from this study that The Economic Times is preferred by most of the investors.

Visits NSE/BSE Website

	Frequency	*Per cent*	*Valid Per cent*	*Cumulative Per cent*
Yes	21	70.0	70.0	70.0
No	9	30.0	30.0	100.0
Total	30	100.0	100.0	

The market watch is the most important activity for any investors. Thus, it is essential for the investors to watch the market movements regularly. However, some investors may not be able to do so. The above table shows that 70 % of the investors visit the NSE/BSE websites regularly and update themselves. In the following bar diagram, it could be seen that out of 30 investors, 21 visit the NSE/BSE website regularly.

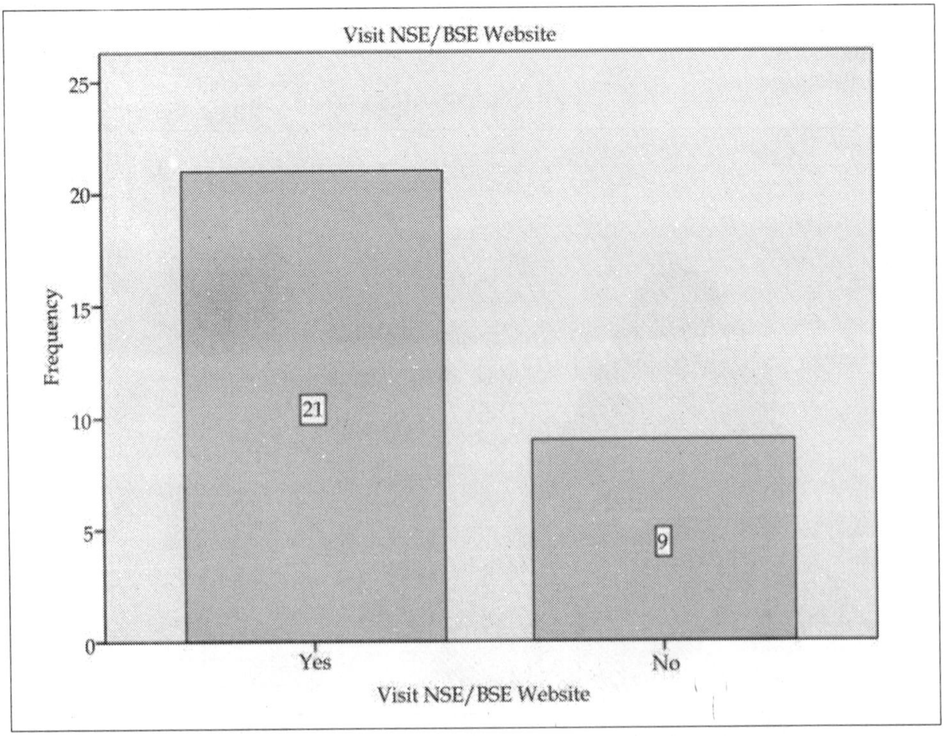

Trading

	Frequency	*Per cent*	*Valid Per cent*	*Cumulative Per cent*
Online	15	50.0	50.0	50.0
Over Phone	15	50.0	50.0	100.0
Total	30	100.0	100.0	

The trading system has faced some significant changes in recent decades. The above table shows that the online trading and the trading over phone are equally carried out by the investors.

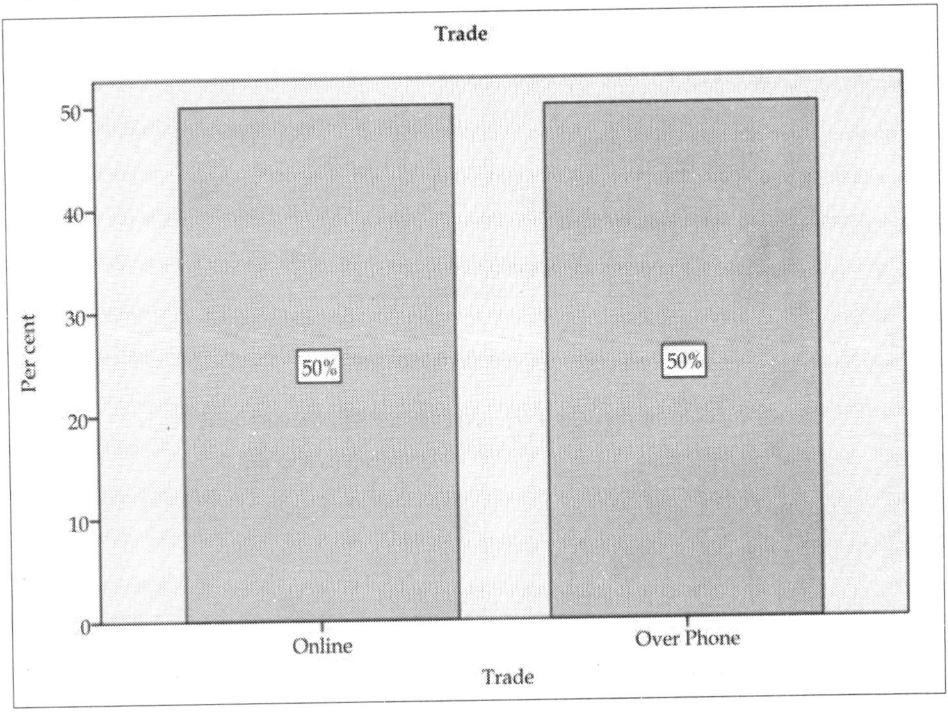

Short-term/Long-term

	Frequency	*Per cent*	*Valid Per cent*	*Cumulative Per cent*
Short-term Investor	19	63.3	63.3	63.3
Long-term Investor	11	36.7	36.7	100.0
Total	30	100.0	100.0	

The short-term investments are those which are made for less than one year and the long-term investments are those which are made for more than one year. Generally, the short-term investors aim at making the profit out of the market price fluctuations. The long-term investors aim at regular income and growth of the investment. In a broad view, short-term investments are speculative in nature. In the above table, it can be seen that 63.3% of the investors are short-term investors and 36.7% of the investors are long-term investors. This means that most of the investor s aim at getting immediate returns.

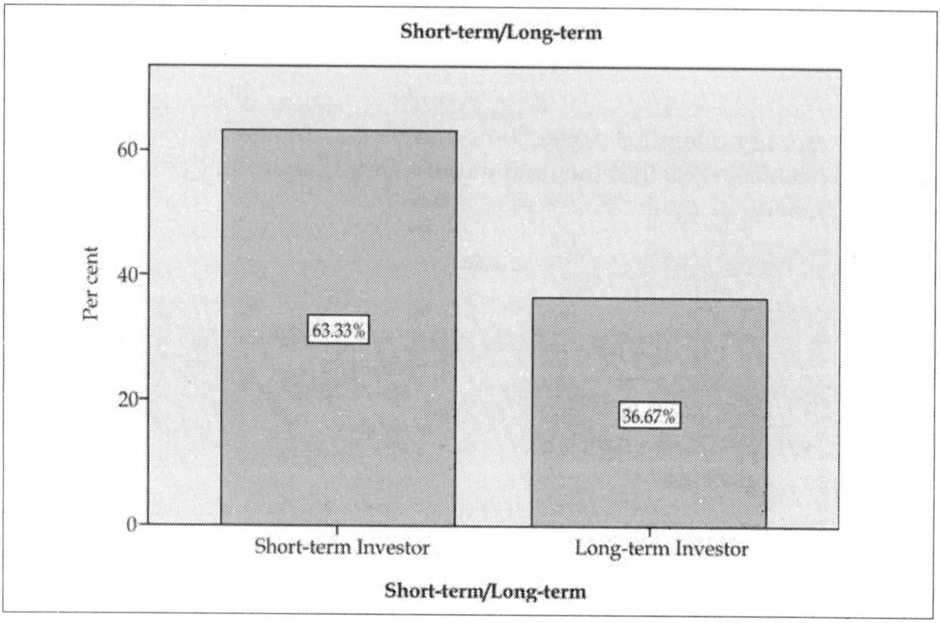

Cross Tabulation between Visiting NSE/BSE Website and Trade

		Visits NSE/BSE Website		
		Yes	*No*	*Total*
Trade	Yes	19	8	27
	No	2	1	3
	Total	21	9	30

In the above table, it is shown that out of 30 investors, 27 are traders. In these 27 traders, 19 are regularly visiting the NSE/BSE websites and 8 are not doing so. Further, 2 non traders visit the NSE/BSE websites regularly. Thus, it is essential to find out whether there is any association between the number of traders and the number of investors visiting the NSE/BSE website.

The hypotheses are as follows:

H_0: Trading does not influence the traders to visit the BSE/NSE website.

H_1: Trading influences the traders to visit the BSE/NSE website.

	Value	*df*	*Asymp. Sig. (2-sided)*
Pearson Chi-Square	.018[a]	1	.894
Continuity Correction	.000	1	1.000
Likelihood Ratio	.017	1	.895
Linear-by-Linear Association	.017	1	.896
N of Valid Cases	30		

The above table shows the results of Chi-square analysis for the hypothesis mentioned above. Here, the Pearson Chi-square significance value is 0.894. Hence, the null hypothesis has to be accepted. Thus, trading does not influence the traders to visit the BSE/NSE website. This means that being the trader is not a main reason for the investors to visit the BSE/NSE website.

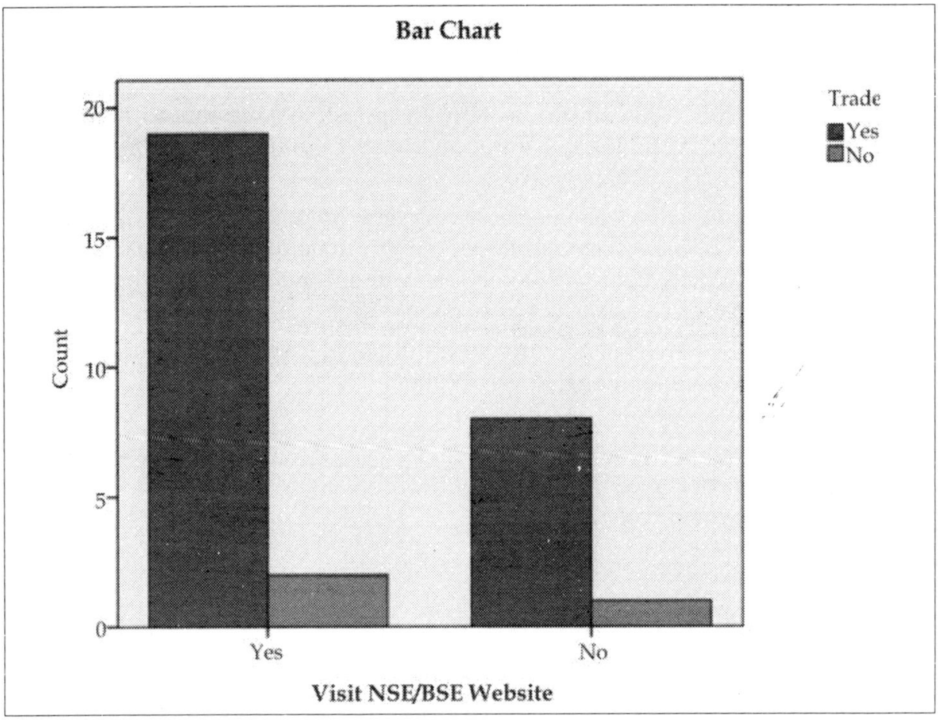

FINDINGS FROM THE RESEARCH

1. It is found that 42.1 % of the investors invest in stocks, which is the most preferred security among the all others.
2. It is found that 73.3% of the investors invest in IPO.
3. It is also found that 50 % of the respondents get the IPO information from the advertisements in the newspapers.
4. From the above research we can also conclude that 70% of the investors visit the NSE/BSE websites regularly and update themselves.
5. From the above interpretation we also come to know that the online trading and the trading over phone are equally carried out by the investors.
6. It can also be seen that 63.3% of the investors are short-term investors.

SUGGESTIONS

It can concluded that investments made by the public do play a vital role and serves as the back of the economy and the money has been utilized for various activities of the business. Hence it is important that more and more awareness among the public regarding IPO and risk factors need to be created.

References

Zvi Singer (2008), "Discretionary Financial Reporting: Items Manipulated By IPO Firms, and Investors' Increased Awareness". *(CAAA) 2008 Annual Conference Paper.*

Zhen Liu (2009), "Fair Disclosure and Investor Asymmetric Awareness in Stock Markets", Working paper series.

Institutional Investor Activism on Socially Responsible Investment: Effects and Expectations Business Ethics: A European Review Volume 18, Issue 3, Date: July 2009, Pages 308-333, Shuangge Wen.

The Challenges of Socially Responsible Investment Among Institutional Investors: Exploring the Links Between Corporate Pension Funds and Corporate Governance Business and Society Review Volume 114, Issue 1, Date: March 2009, Pages 31-57 LAURA ALBAREDA VIVÓ, MARÍA ROSARIO BALAGUER FRANCH

Legal Reform and Shareholder Activism by Institutional Investors in Japan Corporate Governance: An International Review Volume 13, Issue 3, Date: May 2005, Pages 377-385, Takaya Seki.

Honghui Chen, Gregory Noronha, Vijay Singal, "Investor Awareness and Market Segmentation: Evidence from S&P 500 Index Changes", (2002) EFA 2002 Berlin Meetings Presented Paper.

NSE Website

The Economic Times

A STUDY ON BRAND PREFERENCES OF 'B' SEGMENT CARS
(WITH REFERENCE TO MARUTI CARS)

P. NATARAJAN* & U. THIRIPURASUNDARI**

INTRODUCTION

Aristotle professed, "We are what we repeatedly do. Excellence then is not an act, but a habit." Attaining and sustaining preference is an important step on the road to gaining brand loyalty. The ability to generate more revenue, gain greater market share and beat off the competition is the reward. Branding plays a vital role in productive industry because strong brands quality increase trust in intangible products enabling customers to better visualize and understand them. Brand preference is one of the important concepts in business, practice as well as in academic research. This is become successful brands can allow marketers to gain competitive advantage including for successful extensions, resilience against competitors' promotional pressures and the ability to create barriers to competitive entry. Also a high level of brand preference increases customer satisfaction, repurching intent and high level of loyalty.

FACTORS INFLUENCING BRAND PREFERENCE

Generally customers have lot of factors to influence to prefer the brand, considering customer evaluations of sales satisfaction, product quality, vehicle performance and design, after sales service, brand image, and cost-of-ownership. The main factor influencing to prefer the Brand "Maruti" as price, quality, brand image, fuel effiency, low maintence, best sales services, excellent customer service, comfortable etc.,

INDIANS STILL LOVE MARUTI CARS

After the economic liberalization policies of the Indian government in the early 1990s, foreign car makers came running to the emerging and highly potential

* Professor of Commerce, School of Management, Pondicherry University, Puducherry.

** Doctoral Research Scholar in Commerce, School of Management, Pondicherry University, Puducherry.

Indian car market. It was a great opportunity for those companies to get access to the Indian market, especially after markets in the developed countries had largely saturated. Of late Indian consumers have seen a huge number of both small and luxury cars coming to the country. Car companies have come up with cars loaded with advanced technology and efficient engines. With the rising spending power of the Indian middle class and growing economy, car sales have risen steadily. Even luxury cars have seen constant demand among the upwardly mobile people.

Maruti Suzuki has been the market leader for long. In spite of all the competition from new car companies like Honda, Hyundai, Chevrolet, Fiat, etc, it has maintained its lead over rivals. New car makers have come up with highly successful models like Honda City, Chevrolet Spark and Hyundai Santro. Hyundai particularly has tasted success and has become No. 2 passenger Car Company in the country after Maruti. However, all this competition has failed to displace Maruti from its leadership position. Competition has pushed Maruti to come up with better products. The company has responded well to the challenge by launching new and improved Maruti cars. The maker of the best seller Maruti Alto, has recently come up with A-Star.

TAKING ON THE CHALLENGES

Building and maintaining a truly global brand is not an easy proposition. There are a lot of smart, knowledgeable people around the world looking to identify the best opportunities to expand flagship products and services, and the competition is getting keener. Bombarded with a confusing array of competing offerings and marketing messages, consumers and business customers will come to rely even more on brands to guide their buying choices.

Everywhere when you are conducting strategic planning for any company both offline and online it is mandatory to complete an analysis that takes into account not only your own business, but your competitors' activities and current industry happenings as well.

OBJECTIVES OF THE STUDY

1. To examine the various factors influencing the Brand Image on Maruti 'B' Segment Car.
2. To evaluate Brand preferences of the customers.
3. To analyze the Brand efficient in future.

METHODOLOGY OF THE STUDY

Survey method has been adopted to elicit the views of Maruti 'B' Segment car owners. The Brand Preference towards Maruti B Segment cars is studied by administering structured interview schedule to150 customers in Puducherry city.

Primary data has been collected with the help of a well a structured interview schedule from among 150 respondents Puducherry City. The researcher has adopted cluster sampling techniques for choosing sample respondents. Secondary data has been collected from published records of the company, Official Websites, Standard Text-books, Articles, Reviews, Researches and Newspapers etc.,

RESULTS AND DISCUSSION

Regarding personal profile of the consumer, the Table 1 shows that 60% respondents are between the age of 30-50 year, 70% respondents are male, around 70% respondents are married, nearly 33% respondents are business people and 50% respondents are earning above Rs. 5, 00, 000 per annum.

Table 1
General Profile of the Car Owners

Factors	*Classification*	*No. of Respondents*	*Percentage*
Age	Below 30 year	30	20
	30–50 year	**90**	**60**
	Above 50 year	30	20
Sex	**Male**	**105**	**70**
	Female	45	30
Marital status	**Married**	**105**	**70**
	Single	45	30
Occupation	Profession	40	27
	Govt. employee	30	30
	Own business	**50**	**33**
	Private concern	30	20
Income Status	Below Rs. 3,00,000	30	20
	Rs. 3,00,000-5,00,000	45	30
	Above Rs. 5,00,000	**75**	**50**

Source: Primary Data

Table 2
Ownership of Maruti 'B' Segment Cars

Car Model	*No. of respondents*	*Percentage*
Alto	90	60
Wagon R	40	27
Zen	20	13
Total	150	100

Source: Primary Data.

The observation of the Table 2 reveals that 60% of the respondents own Alto, 27% of the respondents own Wagon R, and 13% of the respondents own a Zen car. In view of the above, it is observed that the 'B' segment cars of Maruti have high percentage of Alto because of its innovative model and is comforts.

Table 3
Source of Informations to Buy a Car

Source of Information's	*No. of respondents*	*Percentage*
Self	45	30
colleagues	12	8
Friends	15	10
Relatives	24	18
Family	36	22
Neighbours	18	12
Total	150	100

Source: Primary Data.

The observation of the Table 3 reveals that 30% of the respondents are motivated on their own, 8% of the respondents are motivated by colleagues, 10% of the respondents are motivated by friends, 18% of the respondents are motivated by relatives, and 22% of the respondents are motivated by neighbours. Besides the influence from the family and relatives is also substantial (40%).

Table 4
Media Effort on Purchase

Particulars	*No. of respondents*	*Percentage*
Newspaper	18	12
Television	60	40
Magazines	50	33
Friends	22	15
Total	150	100

Source: Primary Data.

The Table reveals 4 majority of respondents are influenced by the Television and Magazines. The advertisement in Television and Magazines are more catching and effective. Colourful pictures of models of car that attracts the general public to buy Maruti Cars. Maruti models should be designed in such a way that it has attractive look, attractive shape and sparkling colours.

Indian consumers have become world-class consumers. They now look for world-class quality and service. Maruti, the car brand, has had a very strong brand repeats growth rate because of its service quality. They communicate the service quality in terms of its easy and widespread availability, as well as its performance.

An excellent combination of service quality land product quality is shown in two TV commercials of the Maruti Car campaign.

In the first one, a young Sikh lad plays with a toy car right through the day. Late in the evening, he is still at it, this time vrooming-vrooming it over his reclining father's stomach. On being reprimanded by his father for' driving his car' non-stop through the day, the child says. 'What can I do, the petrol just won't finish?', thereby implying that he would continue playing, and in the bargain reinforcing the fuel efficiency of the vehicle. This reflects the brand's good product quality performance.

In another campaign, run almost parallel, the easy accessibility of Maruti's services is highlighted.

A couple of youngsters driving their Maruti on an isolated mountain range enquire of a local child about facilities like a hotel and a restaurant. On being told that neither is available, they ask without much hope there is Maruti service station. Much to their surprise this is answered in the affirmative. With this the brand quietly underlined its vast service network which allows a Maruti vehicle owner to rest assured about maintenance and have peace of mind. This is an excellent example of product quality and service quality being used to enhance brand repeats growth.

Table 5
Reasons for Buying Maruti Cars

Particulars	*No. of Respondents*	*Percentage*
Brand name	90	60
Comparatively cheap	30	20
Easy accessibility	30	20
Total	150	100

Source: Primary Data.

The observation of the Table 5 reveals that 60% of owners of Maruti cars simply buy a Maruti Car just because of its brand name, while 20% to buy a Maruti Car for its comparative cheapness and 20% of respondents buy a Maruti Car for easy accessibility to sales services. 60% buyers purchase on the basis of brand name that shows the Brand loyalty of Maruti cars. The Maruti has to capitalize the brand image for its growth and it is an unshakable fact that efforts should be made to maintain the brand image in the face of fierce competition in the automotive market with better facility, grand link, and attractive colours. This table observation clearly shows that many Maruti customers have very strong brand influence, its very large credit to the company have strong Brand preference in mind set up of the Loyal customer of Maruti. In the modern days Maruti have very high position to satisfy their customer in terms of after sales services to retain the customer as long run to pave the way for its strong development of the concern at the long period.

The observation of the Table 6 show that 84% of the respondents have already indicated their preference of attributes towards price while buying a Maruti 'B' Segment Car. When it comes to second priority, 90% of them felt brand image is also an important factor in the decision to purchase Maruti Car, while 87% of the respondents have claimed that mileage is also one of the major features while buying a Maruti 'B' Segment cars.

Table 6
Ranking of the Various Attributes While Purchasing a Maruti Car

Ranks/Attributes	*Price*	*Mileage*	*Brand Image*	*After sales*	*Safety*
Rank 1	84	18	36	6	6
Rank 2	27	9	90	12	12
Rank 3	9	87	6	24	24
Rank 4	15	21	9	15	90
Rank 5	15	15	9	93	18
Total	150	150	150	150	150

Source: Primary Data

Table 7
Preference of Colours

Colours	*No. of respondents*	*Percentage*
White	60	40
Red	40	27
Blue	25	16
Grey	15	10
Others	10	7
Total	150	100

Source: Primary Data.

The observation of the Table 7 reveals that 40% prefer White, 27% prefer Red, 16% prefer Blue, 10% of the respondents prefer Grey and 7% prefer other colours like Pink, Yellow etc. From this, we can conclude that many of the maruti car buyers prefer the white colour cars because of its elegant appearance.

Table 8
Feel About the Car

Particulars	*No. of respondents*	*Percentage*
Good	90	60
Satisfactory	60	40
Total	150	100

Source: Primary Data.

The observation of the Table 8 reveals that most of the respondents have a very good opinion about the mileage offered by Maruti 'B' Segment Cars, since 60% of them have a high opinion on the mileage factor and 40% of the respondents feel satisfied with the mileage factors.

The observation of the Table 9 shows that almost 64% of the respondents feel that maintenance cost of Maruti cars is at moderate level. Whereas 6% of them still have the feeling that the maintenance cost of Maruti cars are high when compared with other-brand cars.

Table 9
Level of Maintenance

Maintenance	*No. of respondents*	*Percentage*
High level	10	6
Moderate level	95	64
Low level	45	30
Total	150	100

Source: Primary Data.

The observation of the Table 10 shows that 80% of the respondents' maintenance expenses are less than Rs. 5,000. 20% of the respondents require more than Rs. 5, 000. From the analysis, we can conclude that the Maruti cars have less maintenance expenses that bring comfort and happiness to the owners of Maruti.

Table 10
Maintenance Cost of Maruti 'B' Segment Car

Amount	*No. of respondents*	*Percentage*
Less than Rs. 5,000	120	80
Above Rs. 5,000	30	20
Total	150	100

Source: Primary Data.

Table 11
Features Considered Over the Competitors of Maruti Cars

Features	*No. of Respondents*	*Percentage*
Resale value	33	22
Price	82	55
Mileage	18	12
Height of the car	9	6
Comfort level	8	5
Total	150	100

The observation of the Table 11 reveals that 55% of the respondents buy Maruti Cars because of its price factor over its competitors. Nearly 22% of them feel Maruti Cars re-sale value has an edge over its competitors. It can be inferred from the table that concluded Maruti's pricing strategy is better than its competitors and consistently gaining resale value are its unique features. The second hand sales segment of Maruti car may also add to the advantages of Maruti over other cars.

WEIGHTED AVERAGE BRAND PREFERENCES

An analysis of the ranks given by the customers for different factors influencing the customers' satisfaction is given below. Weighted averages of the ranks are calculated using the following formula:

Weights

Rank 1 = 5 points, Rank 2 = 4 points, Rank 3 = 3 points

Rank 4 = 2 points and Rank 5 = 1 point

Table 12
Weighted Averages Values

Ranks/Attributes	*Price*	*Mileage*	*Brand Image*	*After sales*	*Safety*
Rank 1	84	18	36	6	6
Rank 2	27	9	90	12	12
Rank 3	9	87	6	24	24
Rank 4	15	21	9	15	90
Rank 5	15	15	9	93	18
Total &	150	150	150	150	150
Total weightage score	600	445	585	273	348
Weighted Average	40	29.7	39	18.2	23.2

Source: Primary Data.

The observation of the Table 12 reveals that based on highest weighted average, customer chooses price as main factor while buying Maruti 'B' segment car followed by Brand Value, after sales services, mileage, and finally safety features. Modern consumers prefer the price and brand of the product to be proportionate to its quality as well as the quantity. Hence, price and brand preference gets the maximum weightage. As Maruti's price and brand preference are more competitive in comparison to others it is able to dominate the market.

FINDINGS

- Men in the age group of 30-50 years prefer Maruti Brand. All of them are married and belonging the middle income group.
- 'B' segment cars of Maruti have high percentage of Alto because of its innovative model and comfortable to all.
- The family and relatives are the considered to be the main motivators to purchase the Maruti cars.
- Around 40% of the respondents are mostly influenced by Television.
- Nearly 60% of the respondents are more brand loyalty towards Maruti cars.
- Preference towards Price and Brand Image of Maruti cars influence the people to choose this Brand.
- Maximum 60 % of the respondents feel about the Maruti Cars are good.
- Almost 64% of the respondents feel that maintenance cost of Maruti cars is at moderate level.
- 80% of the respondents' maintenance expenses are less than Rs. 5,000.

SUGGESTIONS

- The company's management should put in more efforts to increase the market share in terms of introducing more innovative colours of cars, new models in 'B' segment to cover the middle income groups of the people for providing new schemes in the loan arrangements and reduced down payment etc.
- More customers prefer the Maruti because of its moderate price only. So the management has to fully concentrate on the price for ever in the long run aspect.
- Since majority of the customers are influenced by Television it is highly important for the management to keep in constant touch with the existing loyal customers. Keep on advertisements in the Television and Magazines to retain the customers.
- Special marketing strategies should also be undertaken to convince the customers to go in for majority of colours while choosing Maruti B Segment cars.
- 80% of the customers are going for bank loan to buy a car, therefore company's management can strive for having a better relationship with all the leading banks providing car loan like conducting frequent meeting with them, creating promotional package deals for those plans etc.
- Since most of the customers are of the feeling that maintenance cost is pretty high, the management should take efforts in reducing and create awareness among customers by showing them how cheap it is to maintain Maruti B Segment cars when compared to its competitors.

CONCLUSION

Maruti Suzuki is No. 1 automobile industry in India and has changed over the time to suit the needs of their customers. Maruti is the only company in India with a lots of small car models. It holds more than 50% market share in India.

Maruti paves the way to customers in all walks of life to buy the car with many models to choose. As the interest rate are heading and as it is easy to avail car loans in the present trend, the demand for cars is increasing and many two wheelers customers are switching to basic car like Maruti 'B' Segment car like Alto, Wagon R, and Zen.

With its present infrastructure and capital, Maruti should take the initiative to introduce new models according to the choice of the customers at regular intervals which will pave the way to be No.1 Company throughout in India in the near future.

The customer benefits from the brand and the brand marketer benefits in terms of profits. While the customer gets satisfaction and is able to improve his/her standard of living and quality of life, the marketer profits from the brand experience that the customer gets and is able to generate a surplus after having satisfied the consumer. The more the consumer is satisfied, the greater is the chance of selling large volumes and therefore making large profits.

References

Dick, Alan S. and Kunal Basu (1994), "Customer Loyalty: Toward an Integrated Conceptual Framework," *Journal of the Academy of Marketing Science,* 22 (2), 99-113.

Jagdeep Kapoor, '9 Brand Shaastras',(Response Books, 2nd edn 2005), Sultan Chand Publication, New Delhi.

Jones, Michael A., David L. Mothersbaugh, and Sharon E. Beatty (2002), "Why Customers Stay: Measuring the Underlying Dimensions of Services Switching Costs and Managing Their Differential Strategic Outcomes," *Journal of Business Research,* 55, 441-50.

P. Kotler, 'Marketing Management ' (Prentice-Hall, 7th edn., 1991).

Reichheld, Frederick F. and W. Earl Jr. Sasser (1990), "Zero Defections: Quality Comes to Services," *Harvard Business Review,* (September-October), 105-11.

Reichheld, Frederick F. (1993), "Loyalty-Based Management," *Harvard Business Review,* 71 (2), 64-73.

MANIFESTATIONS OF QUALITY OF WORK LIFE PATTERNS: EMPIRICAL STUDY OF INDIAN MANAGERS

UPASNA JOSHI*

INTRODUCTION

The term 'Quality of Work Life' was first introduced at an international conference in New York in 1972. It was used to describe the conditions that create 'humane working life'. It is focused on work environment that leads to workers satisfaction and motivation. It is concerned with replacing repetitive and boring jobs based on Taylor's principles by more interesting and human task that ultimately leads to happiness at work place. Davis (1981) defined QWL as favorableness or unfavorableness of a job, environment for people. The purpose of QWL is to develop jobs that are excellent for people as well as for production. It provides careful balance of human imperative and the technological imperative.

Luthans (1981) defined QWL as a "process of joint decision making, collaboration and building mental respect between management and employees. It is concerned with overall climate at work. The basic idea is to change the climate at work place so as to boost cooperation between technological human organizational interfaces."

Quality of work life (QWL) consists of opportunities for active involvement in group working arrangements or problem solving that are of mutual benefit to employees and employers (Johnston *et al,* 1978; Mills, 1981). It requires employee commitment to the organization and an environment in which this commitment can flourish (Walton, 1974). Part of the commitment to the organization is the various attitudes or value judgments of people to their jobs and to their total work environment (Kolodny *et al,* 1979; Skinner, 1979). Organization-wide policies, practices and procedures send implicit and explicit messages to employees about the organization's stance toward the allocation of opportunities to remain competitive. Organizations must be willing to create an environment that supports teamwork in which work teams can find new and creative ways to meet the societal and employee expectations. Organizations

* Associate Professor, Punjabi University Patiala, (India), (*e-mail: upasna_sethi@yahoo.com*)

must renew their commitment in communicating accurate information in a timely manner so that all can do their jobs effectively. In creating a teamwork-based environment, organizations must ensure that the methods of communication they use are timely, accurate and effective in communicating to empowered work teams the information they must have in order to contribute effectively and efficiently. Organizational culture shapes the environmental stimuli and experiences to which one is exposed and to which one will react. As such, it directly and indirectly influences QWL for employees and influences individual attitudes concerning outcomes such as commitment, motivation, satisfaction, morale and power (Harris & Mossholder, 1996). A human relations culture emphasizes cohesion and morale through means such as training and human resource development. Organisations have to put less emphasis on formal coordination and control systems and a greater emphasis on decentralized decision making, horizontal communications and teamwork. Cordial interpersonal relations tend toward higher levels of trust, morale and leader credibility and relatively low levels of conflict and resistance to change.

RESEARCH OBJECTIVES OF THE STUDY

(1) To find out whether any significant difference exists between the quality of work life as perceived by the manager and the subordinates.

(2) To examine the influence of individual-centered variables, viz., age, educational qualification of the managers and the subordinates on QWL as perceived by self and the subordinates.

Research Hypotheses

1. There is a significant difference in terms of perceived quality of work life among the managers and the subordinates working in the same organisation.
2. There is a significant difference in terms of perceived quality of work life among the managers above 35 years of age from the managers below 35 years of age.
3. There is a significant difference in terms of perceived quality of work life among the managers with post-graduate qualifications from the managers with graduate qualifications.
4. There is a significant difference in terms of perceived quality of work life among the subordinates above 35 years of age from the subordinates below 35 years of age.
5. There is a significant difference in terms of perceived quality of work life among the subordinates with post-graduate qualifications from the subordinates with graduate qualifications.

RESEARCH DESIGN

For the present study, the descriptive research method was considered appropriate. The data was collected on the basis of convenience-cum-quota sampling wherein 425 employees working in consumer durable industry were contacted. The quota was drawn in terms of age, and educational qualifications. 398 response sheets were found complete in all respects and were finally analysed.

The domain of the study was restricted to employees serving in the geographical area of North India. The break up of the responses finally analysed is as under:

Managerial Cadre comprising of Branch Managers, Regional managers, Territory Managers, Zonal Managers, Assistant General Managers and above.

Subordinates comprising of Salesman, Sales officers, Regional Sales officers, Sales Executives, Regional Sales Executives etc.

Total Managerial cadre who responded to the survey and whose responses were finally included in the analysis was 151.

Total Subordinates who responded to the survey and whose responses were finally included in the analysis were 247.

The Quality of Work Life Inventory by Sinha & Sayeed (1980) is a scale having 17 dimensions to measure various aspects of work life. In all there are 85 items in the inventory measuring 17 dimensions of Quality of Work Life. The alpha reliability of the inventory was found to be 0.97.

ANALYSIS AND FINDINGS OF THE STUDY

The results of this survey were intended to assist decision makers in identifying key workplace issues, as perceived by employees, in order to develop strategies to address and improve the quality of working conditions for staff within consumer durable industry in particular and business enterprises as a whole. The Quality of Work Life inventory developed by Sinha and Sayeed (1980) was considered appropriate as it has been extensively used in Indian conditions.

Table 1 summarises various statistical parameters on the quality of work life index as computed for the managers and their subordinates. The findings reveal that the subordinates perceive their quality of work life to be much better than the perception of the managers. Thus, subordinates rate organizational culture and work environment to be much more conducive than the managers who do not express higher scores on the quality of work life index.

Table 1
Statistical Parameters of Quality of Work Life (QWL) Index as Perceived by Managers and their Subordinates

	Cadre	
	Managers	*Subordinates*
average	378.623	402.56
Stdev.	72.612	79.883

The quality of work life index was computed for both managers and Subordinates for different age groups (Table 2). Within the managerial cadre, younger age group expressed higher QWL scores as compared to the higher age group managers. One possible explanation could be the exposure to many different organizations which the elderly aged managers have served spanning across their careers thereby having a good idea of working conditions of many organisations, whereas the experiences of the younger managers may have been limited to few organizations. Another explanation could be higher expectations of the senior aged managers arising out of family compulsions, stress levels due to comparative inability to move to different organizations and locational constraints etc. On the other hand, senior aged Subordinates were more satisfied with the Quality of work life in their present organisation than the younger aged subordinates. This could arise with the satisfaction, reconciliation with their present status, understanding of the job market imperfections, family liabilities making them more realistic etc.

Table 2
Statistical Parameters of Quality of Work Life (QWL) Index as Perceived by Managers and their Subordinates (Classified on the Basis of Age Below 35 Years and Above 35 Years)

	Managers		*Subordinates*	
	Below 35 yrs	*Above 35 yrs*	*Below 35 yrs*	*Above 35 yrs*
average	166.362	150.833	195.986	247.238
stdev	9.898	8.846	6.789	9.967

The quality of work life index was also compared across different levels of educational qualifications (Table 3) Managers with Graduate qualifications had a higher perceived quality of work life scores compared to the managers with post graduate qualifications. Similar pattern was observed for Subordinates. One possible explanation could be the enhanced expectancy levels due to higher qualification, leading to increased dissatisfaction with present state of affairs. Another reason could be the difficulties in switching jobs which are in consonance with one's academic excellence. While job insecurity and declining working conditions are of paramount importance to employee groups, perceived employee dissatisfaction and the concomitant effects on productivity and on-costs are of concern to employers.

Table 3
Statistical Parameters of Quality of work life (QWL) Index as Perceived by Manager and their Subordinates (Classified on the Basis of Graduate and Post Graduate Qualifications)

	Managers		*Subordinates*	
	Graduate	*Post Graduate*	*Graduate*	*Post Graduate*
average	291.130	249.217	237.083	160.988
stdev	13.561	18.379	21.033	20.294

Each of the seventeen constituent elements of the quality of work life index was statistically analysed. The comparisons on the basis of age as well as academic qualifications were also undertaken.

Table 4 highlights the perception on the Economic Benefits component of the quality of work life index. Managerial cadre with Postgraduate qualifications and age above 35 years exhibited highest scores on the economic benefit component. Invariably such managers occupied the positions of divisional heads or equivalent. For Subordinates, graduates in the age group of below 35 years had the highest scores. One explanation could be realism that salaries and perks are in consonance with one's caliber and expertise.

Table 4

Statistical Parameters of Economic Benefits Component of Quality of Work Life (QWL) as Perceived by Managers and their Subordinates (Classified on the Basis of Age Below 35 Years and Above 35 Years as well as Graduate and Post Graduate Qualifications

	Managers					*Subordinates*				
	Total	*Below 35*	*Above 35*	*Grad*	*Post Grad*	*Total*	*Below 35*	*Above 35*	*Grad*	*Post Grad*
average	24.565	22.142	25.837	22.667	25.857	22.726	23	20.254	23.877	20.4375
stdev	6.8395	5.133	7.1356	6.244	6.3658	4.7550	4.990	4.6036	4.512	5.84718

Table 5 summarizes the Physical Working Conditions (PWC) component of the quality of work life index as perceived by managers and their subordinates. Managers expressed higher scores on the Physical Working Conditions index than the Subordinates. Within the managerial cadre, managers in the higher age group and with graduate qualifications expressed higher scores. Subordinates with younger age group and with graduate qualifications were more satisfied with the working conditions.

Table 5

Statistical Parameters of Physical Working Conditions (PWC) Component of Quality of Work Life (QWL) as Perceived by Managers and their Subordinates (Classified on the Basis of Age Below 35 years and Above 35 Years as well as Graduate and Post Graduate Qualifications)

	Managers					*Subordinates*				
	Total	*Below 35*	*Above 35*	*Grad*	*Post Grad*	*Total*	*Below 35*	*Above 35*	*Grad*	*Post Grad*
average	15.043	13.678	16.189	17.111	12.286	13.964	14.274	12.125	14.041	13.824
stdev	7.912	6.526	7.823	6.642	7.507	5.378	5.1562	5.3201	5.240	5.723

Table 6 highlights the perception of the managers and the subordinates on the Mental State component of the quality of work life index. It can be noticed that the managers perceive themselves to be in a better mental state than the subordinates. Within managers, the managers who are below the age of 35 years have better scores on the Mental state component. Similarly, managers with Graduate qualifications have better scores than the managers with Postgraduate qualifications. One possible cause could be the higher levels of the job responsibilities associated with the senior positions. Also, the family life positions and responsibilities of senior aged managers could be the contributing factors towards lowering the scores on the mental state component. Within the subordinates' category, those subordinates who were below the age of 35 had better perception about their mental state than the older age group subordinates. Subordinates with Graduate qualifications had better scores on the mental state component.

Table 6

Statistical Parameters of Mental State Component of Quality of Work Life (QWL) as Perceived by Managers and their Subordinates (Classified on the Basis of Age Below 35 Years and Above 35 Years as well as Graduate and Post Graduate Qualifications)

	Managers					*Subordinates*				
	Total	*Below 35*	*Above 35*	*Grad*	*Post Grad*	*Total*	*Below 35*	*Above 35*	*Grad*	*Post Grad*
average	33.522	33.679	31.189	35.222	31.750	31.762	33.438	31.275	33.204	30.147
stdev	7.563	6.527	7.824	6.476	6.850	4.998	5.847	5.150	4.920	5.188

These increasing levels of dissatisfaction reflected in lower scores on the mental state in part, reflect the changing nature of work and the manner in which these issues are linked. Dissatisfaction with career prospects amongst prime age and mature age workers was perhaps not surprising given the extent of downsizing in organisations in the late 1990s. By the late 1990s, almost half of consumer durable organisations had downsized. A consequence of this dramatic downsizing has been the demise of traditional career paths that employees could once have expected.

Table 7 summarises perceptions of the employees on the Career Orientation (CO) component of quality of work life (QWL). The findings reveal that managers perceive that their organization is more conscious towards their need for careers than the perception of the subordinates. This feeling is even more pronounced in the subordinates in younger age groups, especially with

Table 7

Statistical Parameters of Career Orientation (CO) Component of Quality of Work Life (QWL) as Perceived by Managers and their Subordinates (Classified on the Basis of Age Below 35 Years and Above 35 Years as well as Graduate and Post Graduate Qualifications)

	Managers					*Subordinates*				
	Total	*Below 35*	*Above 35*	*Grad*	*Post Grad*	*Total*	*Below 35*	*Above 35*	*Grad*	*Post Grad*
average	14.652	14.964	13.189	14.00	14.071	12.452	13.125	11.176	13.204	11.235
stdev	8.201	4.435	8.082	7.00	7.750	6.272	5.320	4.844	5.427	7.329

graduate qualifications. This disillusionment requires urgent attention of the human resource managers as career planning must incorporate justifiable aspirations of the employees. Older workers were also more likely to have higher levels of dissatisfaction with the amount of work they had to do, their career prospects and their level of pay relative to other employees doing similar work in other industries.

Table 8 reveals surprising findings on the Advancement on Merit (AM) component of Quality of work life (QWL) as perceived by managers and their subordinates. Findings reveal that almost 33% of the employees, whether managerial or subordinates feel that merit is not the only consideration for promotions. Extraneous factors play a predominant role in deciding the promotions. Managers in younger age groups, especially with Graduate qualifications are even more pronounced in their feelings. Subordinates in the senior age group and with Post Graduate qualifications are still more pessimistic in their expressions. This is contrary to the general perception that merit is the predominant factor in the private sector, especially in the multinational organizations.

Table 8

Statistical Parameters of Advancement on Merit (AM) Component of Quality of Work Life (QWL) as Perceived by Managers and their Subordinates (Classified on the Basis of Age Below 35 Years and Above 35 Years as well as Graduate and Post Graduate Qualifications)

	Managers					*Subordinates*				
	Total	*Below 35*	*Above 35*	*Grad*	*Post Grad*	*Total*	*Below 35*	*Above 35*	*Grad*	*Post Grad*
average	22.899	25.429	21.784	24.444	20.179	24.107	23.906	20.235	24.898	20.971
stdev	7.871	5.217	8.213	6.483	7.418	6.157	6.337	6.163	5.569	6.926

Table 9 highlights the effect on Personal Life (EPL) component of quality of work life (QWL) as perceived by managers and their subordinates. Subordinates had higher average score than the managers. Within the subordinates, respondents in the age group upto 35 years and with Graduate qualifications had the highest scores.

Table 9

Statistical Parameters of Effect on Personal Life (EPL) Component of Quality of Work Life (QWL) as Perceived by Managers and their Subordinates (Classified on the Basis of Age Below 35 Years and Above 35 Years as well as Graduate and Post Graduate Qualifications)

	Managers					*Subordinates*				
	Total	*Below 35*	*Above 35*	*Grad*	*Post Grad*	*Total*	*Below 35*	*Above 35*	*Grad*	*Post Grad*
average	10.681	10.143	10.351	10.24	10.231	11.488	11.969	11.020	12.796	10.853
stdev	0.247	0.508	0.371	0.225	0.870	0.403	0.255	0.617	0.930	0.046

Table 10 summarises perceived union-management relations. The managers perceived that the relations are cordial to a greater degree than the perception of the subordinates. Within the managerial cadre, younger age group managers were even more strong in their conviction that the union management relations are cordial than the managers in senior age groups. Similarly, managers with graduate qualifications gave higher scores on the relations within the organisation than the manners with Postgraduate qualifications. In the subordinates category also, similar pattern was observed.

Table 10
Statistical Parameters of Union Management Relations (UMR) Component of Quality of Work Life (QWL) as Perceived by Managers and their Subordinates (Classified on the Basis of Age Below 35 Years and Above 35 Years as well as Graduate and Post Graduate Qualifications)

	Managers					*Subordinates*				
	Total	*Below 35*	*Above 35*	*Grad*	*Post Grad*	*Total*	*Below 35*	*Above 35*	*Grad*	*Post Grad*
average	11.884	13.393	11.351	12.333	12.214	09.464	10.688	09.961	10.939	09.794
stdev	1.835	1.374	1.480	1.387	1.665	1.184	1.881	1.885	1.308	1.309

Self respect component of the quality of work life index was also computed for both managers as well as subordinates. The findings reveal that subordinates felt that self respect was enhanced by association with the organisation to a greater extent than the feelings of the managerial cadre. The subordinates with graduate qualifications gave higher scores on self respect component than the Postgraduate qualifications. Such self esteem augurs well with the consumer durable industry as it reflects pride felt by the subordinates for being associated with the organization (Table 11).

Table 11
Statistical Parameters of Self Respect (SR) Component of Quality of Work Life (QWL) as Perceived by Managers and their Subordinates (Classified on the Basis of Age Below 35 Years and Above 35 Years as well as Graduate and Post Graduate Qualifications)

	Managers					*Subordinates*				
	Total	*Below 35*	*Above 35*	*Grad*	*Post Grad*	*Total*	*Below 35*	*Above 35*	*Grad*	*Post Grad*
average	21.855	23.964	20.757	24.778	21.714	22.798	23.375	20.059	24.265	20.118
stdev	3.548	3.660	3.711	3.167	3.241	3.581	3.470	3.743	5.074	2.333

The perceived relations with their supervisors was analysed for both the managerial as well as subordinate cadre (Table 12). On a positive note, the survey found that the majority of workers believed that relationships amongst co-workers *were* positive. In total 70 per cent of employees indicated that they either agreed or strongly agreed that people at their workplace got on well together Managers perceived that their relations are cordial with their subordinates whereas the perception of the subordinates is not to the same intensity. Average scores of the managerial cadre were around 77% whereas subordinates gave much lower averages.

Table 12

Statistical Parameters of Supervisory Relationship (RS) Component of Quality of Work Life (QWL) as Perceived by Managers and their Subordinates (classified on the Basis of Age Below 35 Years and Above 35 Years as well as Graduate and Post Graduate Qualifications)

	Managers					*Subordinates*				
	Total	*Below 35*	*Above 35*	*Grad*	*Post Grad*	*Total*	*Below 35*	*Above 35*	*Grad*	*Post Grad*
average	60.217	62.893	59.703	61.444	59.518	54.857	58.563	52.078	56.143	51.508
stdev	3.711	3.065	3.353	4.157	3.800	3.666	3.701	3.764	2.934	3.440

Table 13 highlights another related factor on intragroup relations in organizations. Here again, managers perceptions about cordial nature of relations in the organizations is much higher than the perceptions of the subordinates. The feeling of bon home in the organizations is more in the younger age group and with Graduate qualification, whether they are managers or subordinates.

Table 13

Statistical Parameters of Intra-group Relations (IGR) Component of Quality of Work Life (QWL) as Perceived by Managers and their Subordinates (Classified on the Basis of Age Below 35 Years and Above 35 Years as well as Graduate and Post Graduate Qualifications)

	Managers					*Subordinates*				
	Total	*Below 35*	*Above 35*	*Grad*	*Post Grad*	*Total*	*Below 35*	*Above 35*	*Grad*	*Post Grad*
average	52.290	54.607	50.973	53.444	51.393	48.298	52.156	43.490	53.510	43.147
stdev	4.169	4.779	4.269	3.747	3.143	3.971	3.604	3.649	3.442	3.382

Researchers have highlighted important factors that make work a positive experience are *'co-workers getting along together'* and *'interesting and satisfying work'*. Most of the workers believed that having interesting and satisfying work was as important an factor as getting on well together at the workplace in contributing to a positive work experience These two indicators complement the factors typically attributed to employee satisfaction such as having your efforts recognized, having control over the way you do work, being treated well by your immediate supervisors or even having fair and reasonable pay. The implication of these results is that Human Resource managers can with a high degree of confidence, direct attention towards these two aspects of working life that can make a substantially greater difference to employee satisfaction than other general issues.

Managers and the subordinates expressed similar sentiments regarding feeling of achievement by being associated with their present organizations (Table 14). Here again, higher sense of elation was noticed in the younger age group an the Graduate qualifications, irrespective of whether it was managerial or subordinate cadre.

Table 14
Statistical Parameters of Sense of Achievement Vs Apathy (A) Component of Quality of Work Life (QWL) as Perceived by Managers and their Subordinates (Classified on the Basis of Age Below 35 Years and Above 35 Years as well as Graduate and Post Graduate Qualifications)

	Managers					*Subordinates*				
	Total	*Below 35*	*Above 35*	*Grad*	*Post Grad*	*Total*	*Below 35*	*Above 35*	*Grad*	*Post Grad*
average	10.565	11.393	10.054	11.889	10.250	10.750	11.656	10.765	11.735	10.706
stdev	3.889	2.934	3.592	2.339	3.426	2.338	3.723	3.827	3.807	3.248

Confidence in Management index was computed for both the categories of employees (Table 15). Managers expressed greater confidence in their superiors as compared to the subordinate cadre. This feeling was more pronounced in the managers below 35 years and with Postgraduate qualifications. Managers need to cultivate trust of their subordinates by involving them more in the decision making, decentralizing and developing teams etc.

Table 15
Statistical Parameters of Confidence in Management (CM) Component of Quality of Work Life (QWL) as Perceived by Managers and their Subordinates (Classified on the Basis of Age Below 35 Years and Above 35 Years as well as Graduate and Post Graduate Qualifications)

	Managers					*Subordinates*				
	Total	*Below 35*	*Above 35*	*Grad*	*Post Grad*	*Total*	*Below 35*	*Above 35*	*Grad*	*Post Grad*
average	17.072	18.464	16.189	16.889	17.214	14.929	14.531	15.294	15.061	14.912
stdev	0.305	0.474	0.141	0.555	0.422	0.485	0.229	0.723	0.403	0.751

Another parameter analysed was the development of employees in the organization (Table 16). The feeling about meaningful developments in the organisation is almost identical in both managerial and the subordinate cadre. Younger age workers felt that there are more avenues for learning than the older aged employees. Existence of a certain set of organizational conditions and practical such as enriched positions, participation of the employees in the processes of decision taking, safe conditions of work all contribute to make the development of individuals more meaningful.

Table 16

Statistical Parameters of Meaningful Development (MD) Component of Quality of Work Life (QWL) as Perceived by Managers and their Subordinates (Classified on the Basis of Age Below 35 Years and Above 35 Years as well as Graduate and Post Graduate Qualifications)

	Managers					*Subordinates*				
	Total	*Below 35*	*Above 35*	*Grad*	*Post Grad*	*Total*	*Below 35*	*Above 35*	*Grad*	*Post Grad*
average	16.188	17.143	15.595	17.556	15.393	16.679	17.719	15.627	17.918	15.294
stdev	0.531	0.973	0.871	0.307	0.309	0.825	0.158	0.747	0.129	0.553

Table 17 highlights the perception of employees in terms of control, influence and participation they undertake in their organizations. Here, the comparison is more stark. There is a marked difference in the way managers and the subordinates perceive. Managers below the age of 35 and having graduate qualifications feel more involved. On the other hand, subordinates with Postgraduate qualifications and above the age of 35 more disillusioned as compared to subordinates with lower Qualifications or younger age group.

Table 17

Statistical Parameters of Control, Influence and Participation (CIP) Component of Quality of Work Life (QWL) as Perceived by Managers and their Subordinates

	Managers					*Subordinates*				
	Total	*Below 35*	*Above 35*	*Grad*	*Post Grad*	*Total*	*Below 35*	*Above 35*	*Grad*	*Post Grad*
average	70.087	71.607	69.432	71.889	70.125	56.726	59.000	51.941	60.347	51.471
stdev	2.020	3.618	2.500	2.723	2.229	2.607	2.385	2.546	3.812	2.335

Table 18 summaries the employee commitment component of quality of work life. There is not much perceived difference in the scores of managers or subordinates. Similarly, there is not a substantial difference on the basis of age or educational Qualifications.

Table 18

Statistical Parameters of Employee Commitment Component of Quality of work life (QWL) as perceived by Managers and their Subordinates (classified on the Basis of Age Below 35 years and Above 35 years as well as Graduate and Post Graduate Qualifications)

	Managers					*Subordinates*				
	Total	*Below 35*	*Above 35*	*Grad*	*Post Grad*	*Total*	*Below 35*	*Above 35*	*Grad*	*Post Grad*
average	14.594	16.107	14.216	14.111	15.179	14.929	14.031	15.471	14.612	15.353
stdev	2.690	2.672	2.537	2.541	2.242	2.728	2.337	2.398	2.348	1.913

Table 19 highlights findings of General Life Satisfaction (GLS) component of quality of work life (QWL) as perceived by managers and their subordinates.

The findings reveal there is no significant difference on the general satisfaction level among the managers or the non-managers. Similarly, there is not much influence of educational qualifications.

Table 19

Statistical Parameters of General Life Satisfaction (GLS) Component of Quality of Work Life (QWL) as Perceived by Managers and their Subordinates (Classified on the Basis of Age Below 35 Years and Above 35 Years as well as Graduate and Post Graduate Qualifications)

	Managers					*Subordinates*				
	Total	*Below 35*	*Above 35*	*Grad*	*Post Grad*	*Total*	*Below 35*	*Above 35*	*Grad*	*Post Grad*
average	33.464	35.964	32.324	33.667	33.929	34.464	33.875	34.824	34.449	34.471
stdev	2.806	2.941	2.519	2.471	2.368	2.917	2.517	2.635	2.497	2.210

Table 20 reveals that the non-managers do not consider organizational climate to be as conducive as the strong feelings of the managers. This feeling of disillusionment is more pronounced among the senior aged subordinates. The subordinates with Postgraduate qualifications are equally pessimistic.

Table 20

Statistical Parameters of Organisational Climate (O.C.) Component of Quality of Work Life (QWL) as Perceived by Managers and their Subordinates (Classified on the Basis of Age Below 35 Years and Above 35 Years as well as Graduate and Post Graduate Qualifications)

	Managers					*Subordinates*				
	Total	*Below 35*	*Above 35*	*Grad*	*Post Grad*	*Total*	*Below 35*	*Above 35*	*Grad*	*Post Grad*
average	34.943	36.929	32.297	36.556	33.250	31.667	32.219	30.980	32.429	30.059
stdev	2.546	2.218	2.156	2.055	2.269	2.948	2.250	2.875	2.283	2.628

MANAGERIAL IMPLICATIONS

The impact of restructuring which most of the consumer durable organizations have undertaken was also reflected in the older employee's level of dissatisfaction with the amount of work they are expected to do. Work intensification and longer hours were other legacies of corporate restructuring as survivors of downsizing efforts felt that they have to do the work of those who were retrenched. Normally full-time employed persons in consumer durable industry usually work more than 1010 hours per week. Furthermore, one third of those working more than 109 hours per week do so as they feel it is an expectation of the job and another one in five say that extra hours are necessary to get the job done. Dissatisfaction with the amount of work also goes some way to explaining dissatisfaction with the organizations policies and procedures and the compensation packages. Almost 70% workers feel that the amount of work they have to do is more and they expected that they could be more adequately remunerated for their efforts.

References

Davis, K. (1981), *Human Behaviour at Work – Organisational Behaviour,* New York: McGraw Hill.

Harris, S. G. and K. W. Mossholder (1996), "The Affective Implications of Perceived Congruence with Culture Dimensions During Organizational Transformation." *Journal of Management,* Vol. 22(4), pp. 527-547.

Johnston, M.W., A. Parasuraman, C.M. Futrell and W.C. Black (1990), "A Longitudinal Assessment of the Impact of Selected Organizational Influences on Salespeople' Organizational Commitment During Early Employment." *Journal of Marketing Research,* Vol. 27, pp. 333-34.

Kolodny, H. F., C.P. Johnston and W. Jeffery, (1979), "Job Design and Socio-technical Systems." in *Quality of Working Life Series,* Ottawa: Labour Canada.

Lau, R. S. M., and E. M. Bruce (1998), "A Win-Win Paradigm for Quality of Work Life and Business Performance". *Human Resource Development Quarterly,* 9(3), 211-226.

Luthans, F. (1981), *Organizational Behaviour,* McGraw- Hill International Book Company, New York.

Mills, T. (1981), *"What is the Quality of Working Life?"* Ottawa: Labour Canada.

Skinner, W. (1979), "The Impact of Changing Technology on the Working Environment" in *Work in America: The Decade Ahead,* Clark Kerr and Jerome R. Rosow ed., New York, Van Nostrand Reinhold Company.

Sinha, P. & Sayeed, O.B. (1980), "Measuring QWL: Development of an Inventory." *Indian Journal of Social Work,* Vol. 41(3), pp. 219-226.

Walton, R. E. (1974), "Improving the Quality of Work Life." *Harvard Business Review,* Vol. 52(3), May-June, pp. 12, 16, 155.

Walton R. E. (1975), 'Criteria for Quality of Working Life' in Davis, L. & Cherns, A. (eds) (1975) *The Quality of Working Life,* Vol. 1, Free Press, New York, 91-104.

SAVING AND ECONOMIC GROWTH IN SOUTH ASIA: EVIDENCE FROM TIME SERIES ANALYSIS

UDAYA RAJ REGMI*

INTRODUCTION

Various empirical studies have shown that there is a causal relationship between savings and growth. First, savings can stimulate economic growth. Capital accumulation or physical investment is the most important source of economic growth. Increasing savings would accelerate growth. To facilitate the process of structural transformation, the saving rate should be raised from 4-5 per cent of the national income to 12-15 per cent of national income (Lewis, 1955) but We now know from the East Asian and the Chinese experience that the right ratio is 30 to 35 per cent of GDP (Naqvi, 1999). The relationship between saving and growth plays a vital role in the neoclassical growth models of Solow (1956) and Cass (1965), Koopmans (1965). It also features prominently in the AK models starting with Harrod (1939) and Domar (1946), and then more recently by Romer (1986). Bacha (1990), Jappelli and Pagano (1994), Alguacil, Cuadros and Orts, (2004) and Singh (2009) empirically support this hypothesis. All these growth models emphasize that higher saving rates should foster growth because higher savings imply higher capital investment. Agrawal (2001) has shown that there is a relationship between saving rates and growth. During 1984-94, 31 countries had average annual per capita GDP growth rates of 2.5% or higher where the median saving rate was more than 24%, but the median saving rate stood at 16% in the 59 countries in which per capita income grew at less than 1% a year.

Second, many recent studies have concluded that economic growth affects its saving rate (Sinha and Sinha, 1998; Salz, 1999; Agrawal, 2001; Anoruo and Ahmad, 2001; Narayan and Narayan, 2006. There is growing evidence that causation may run from growth to saving. Edwards (1995) found that per capita growth is one of the most important determinants of both private and public savings. Caroll, Overland, and Weil (2000) demonstrated that if utility depends partly on how consumption compares to a habit stock determined by past

* Associate Professor in Management, Tribhuvan University, Nepal.

consumption, an otherwise-standard growth model can imply that increases in growth can cause increased saving. Studies by Sinha and Sanha (1998), Saltz (1999), and Agrawal (2001) revealed that economic growth rates pave the way for savings growth rates. The lifecycle theory of saving and consumption foretells that changes in an economy's rate of economic growth will affect its aggregate saving rate.

REVIEW OF LITERATURE

Bacha (1990), and Jappelli and Pagano (1994) conducted Ordinary Least Squares regression on cross-section data and concluded that a higher savings rate led to higher economic growth.

Caroll and Weil (1994) used five year averages of the economic growth rate and savings for OECD countries and found that economic growth Granger caused savings. However, the reverse was obtained when dummies were included in their estimation.

Sinha and Sinha (1996) presented evidence that economic growth Granger causes growth rate of savings in Pakistan. Further, Sinha and Sinha (1998) found that causality was from the economic growth rate to growth rate of savings in Mexico. Sinha and Sinha (1999) examined the relationship between the growth rate of savings and economic growth in Sri Lanka. Sinha and Sinha (2000) did similar studies in the Philippines and found causality from economic growth rate to growth rate of domestic savings.

Saltz (1999) in a study of 17 third world countries, using the Vector Error Correction (VEC) model for eight countries and Vector Auto Regressive (VAR) model for the other nine countries found that for nine countries the causality was from the economic growth rate to growth rate of savings. For only two countries was the direction of causality reversed. There were four countries where no causality was identified, and for the other two countries bidirectional causality was detected. The author concluded that higher growth rates of real GDP contribute to a higher growth of savings.

Anoruo and Ahmad (2001) investigated the causality of savings and economic growth in seven African countries using VEC. The authors found that in four out of seven countries, economic growth Granger causes the growth rate of domestic savings. However, they obtained a bi-directional causality in two countries. Only in one country, the growth rate of domestic savings Granger caused economic growth.

Mavrotas and Kelly (2001) tested Granger causality among gross domestic product, gross domestic savings, and private savings, using data from India and Sri Lanka, and found no causality between GDP growth and private savings in India. However, bi-directional causality was found in Sri Lanka.

Krieckhaus (2002) in a study of 32 countries finds that a higher level of national savings led to higher investment and consequently caused higher economic growth.

Baharumshah *et al.* (2003) investigated growth rate of savings behavior in five Asian countries: Singapore, South Korea, Malaysia, Thailand, and the Philippines for 1960-1997, using VEC. It was found that growth rate of savings does not Granger cause economic growth rate in the countries except for Singapore.

Alguacil, Caudros and Orts (2004), found evidence in favour of Solow's model prediction that higher savings leads to higher economic growth for Mexico.

Mohan (2006) concluded using cross section data from 1960 to 2001 and Granger causality methodology, that economic growth rate Granger caused savings growth rate in eight high income countries except in one county, 3 lower-middle income countries except two countries, 2 low income countries except one country. There was bi-directional causation in all upper-middle income countries except one country.

MATERIALS AND METHODS

Unit Root Test

Up to the present days, regression analysis based on time series data assumes that most macroeconomic time series are stationary. But it is now a well-known fact that most macroeconomic time series are non-stationary (Dickey-Fuller, 1979; Gujarati, 1995:729). In such a case, applying standard regression models to non-stationary data is inappropriate because of the possibility of obtaining spurious relationship, which makes hypothetical test results unreliable. Hence, to avoid a spurious relationship, detecting the stationary or non-stationary of time series is crucial. For this purpose, Phillips-Perron unit root test has been conducted on each variable. The Phillips-Perron test (Phillips and Perron, 1988) gives robust estimates in comparison with the ADF test. Hence, Phillips-Perron test has also been used in addition to the conventional ADF test. The test detects the presence of a unit root in a series, say Y_t, by estimating,

$$\Delta Y_t = \alpha + \rho^* Y_{t-1} + e_t$$

The PP test is the t-value associated with the estimated coefficient of ρ^*. The series is stationary if ρ^* is negative and significant.

Johansen Co-integration Test

After confirming the non-stationary of time series in their levels, the next step is the investigation of presence of cointegration between GDP and Saving. It is used to ascertain the long run relationship between GDP and Saving. For this purpose, Johansen cointegration procedure has been utilized (Johansen, 1988; Johansen and Juselius, 1990). Cointegration and Error Correction techniques are suitable for investigating the statistical relationship among non-stationary data and help exploring the dynamics of short run changes and the long run equilibrium relationship of time series variables (Ahmed *et al*, 1993).

Then, hypothesis of existence of zero cointegration vector (r = 0) and more than respectively tested with the likelihood ratio test statistics (λ_{trace}) and maximal eigenvalue test (λ_{trace}). The likelihood ratio test statistic (trace test) is computed as:

$$\lambda_{trace} = -n \sum_{i=r+1}^{k} \ln(1 - \lambda i)$$

In this case the null hypothesis that there are r cointegrating vectors against the alternative of more than r cointegrating vectors is tested and when accepted which trace statistic is lower than critical value suggested with Johanson and Juselius. Other test is maximal eigenvalue test which us following:

$$\lambda_{max} = -n \ln(1+\lambda_{r+1}) \; r = 0, 1,..., k - 1$$

This statistic tested for all the null hypothesis of r cointegrating vectors against the alternative of r + 1 cointegrating vectors. When existence of r cointegrating vector is accepted that maximal eigenvalue statistic is lower than critical value. Then it has been suggested that the likelihood ratio test statistics and maximal eigenvalue test deterministic presence or absence the long run relationship between variables in model.

Granger Causality Test

In this analysis, test for Granger test of causality has been used to study the causal relationship between Economic Growth (Y) and Saving (S) in south Asian countı. .s. The Granger test of causality will be used here because it is a very simple test, which has been widely accepted as a reliable test for causality between two variables. It states that a variable *Y* Granger-cause *S* if the prediction of *S* is improved solely by the past values of *Y* and not by other series included in the analysis. Vice versa is true for *S* Granger-causing *Y*. If Economic Growth can be better explained on the basis of past growth and past saving than on the basis of past growth alone, a causal relationship exists from savingto growth according to Granger (1969). Threc other possible results are the cases of unilateral causality from growth to savinge, bi-directional causality (or feedback), and independence. The procedure here is used to detect the causality between economic growth and saving in the context of the bivariate model, which is defined as follows:

$$Y_t = a_o + \sum_{i=1}^{n} \alpha_i S_{t-i} + \sum_{i=1}^{n} \beta_i Y_{t-j} + \varepsilon_1$$

$$S_t = a_1 + \sum_{i=1}^{n} \delta_i Y_{t-j} + \sum_{i=1}^{n} \lambda_i S_{t-i} + \varepsilon_2$$

Where Y is Gross domestic product, S is gross domestic saving and ε_1 and ε_2 are white-noise residuals. The null hypothesis to be tested here would be that S does not granger cause Y. The corresponding null hypothesis will be that Y does not granger cause S. If both the hypotheses are subject to rejection, then we can conclude the presence of feedback effect between *S* and *Y*. And, if only one of the hypotheses is subject to rejection, we can construe the unidirectional causality from that variable to the independent variable of the equation. An unidirectional causality from TR to GE will be found if $\Sigma\alpha_i \neq 0$ and $\Sigma\delta_i = 0$, that is, the set of estimated coefficients of lagged *TR* are significantly different from zero in S equation and cluster of estimated coefficients of lagged *GE* are not significantly different from zero in *Y* equation. Conversely, an unidirectional causality from S to Y will be found if $\Sigma\delta_i \neq 0$ and $\Sigma\alpha_i = 0$, that is, the set of estimated coefficients of lagged S are significantly different from zero in *Y* equation and cluster of estimated coefficients of lagged *Y* are not significantly different from zero in S equation. There will be bi-directional causality or feedback between Y and S if both the conditions $\Sigma\delta_i \neq 0$ and $\Sigma\alpha_i \neq 0$ simultaneously hold, that is the set of estimated coefficients of lagged *Y* and lagged S are significantly different from zero in both S and *Y* equation. Y and S will be determined independently if $\Sigma\delta_i = 0$ and $\Sigma\alpha_i = 0$, that is there is no causal link between these two variables.

The Granger Causality test is very sensitive to the selection of appropriate lags. The arbitrary choice of the appropriate lags cannot be justified *a priori* and generate biased results and lead to a potential model misspecification. The distribution of a test statistic is sensitive to the order of lags used. If the lag order used is less than the true lag, the regression estimates will be biased and the residuals will be serially correlated. If the order of lags used exceeds the true order, the power of the test is likely to be reduced. Therefore, the Akaike Information Criterion (1969) and Schwarz Criterion (1978) are adopted to determine the appropriate lag lengths for Saving and GDP. Both these tests suggest that a model with the least value of AIC and/or SC should be chosen. To overcome this problem, this paper adopts the Akaike Information Criterion and Schwarz Criterion.

The Akaike Information Criterion (AIC) is computed as:

$$AIC = -2l/T + 2k/T$$

Likewise, the Schwarz Criterion (SC) is computed as:

$$SC = -2(l/T) + (k\log T)/T$$

Where *l* is the value of the log of the likelihood function with the k parameters estimated using T observations. The various information criteria are all based on –2 times the average log likelihood function, adjusted by a penalty function. The optimal lag length corresponds to the lowest value of the AIC and SC.

Vector Error Correction Modeling

The next stage is determinant of short run and long run causality. If the variables are co-integrated or if the null hypothesis of no co-integration is rejected, the residuals from the equilibrium regression can be used to estimate the error correction term. If there is one or there are more than one cointegrating vectors between variables, one can use error correction model for testing Granger causality. Simple contemporaneous correlation based tests assume that the causation is unidirectional—from Saving to GDP. This is, as a matter of fact, unrealistic since the causation may even be bi-directional—from GDP to Saving and Saving to GDP—given the level and degree of economic structure. A necessary precondition to causality testing is to check the cointegrating properties of the variables under consideration, since standard tests for causality are not valid if there exists cointegration (Granger, 1988; Bahmani-Oskooee and Alse, 1993). Standard tests for causality (i.e. Granger/Sims tests) are only valid if the original time series, from which growth rates are obtained, are not cointegrated (Ghatak *et al,* 1997). So, the relevant error correction term is included in the standard causality tests, if the variables are found to be cointegrated. The error correction model for these variables can be written as:

$$\Delta Y_t = \alpha_1 + \rho_1 z_{t-1} + \sum_{i=1}^{p} \beta_i \Delta Y_{t-i} + \sum_{j=1}^{q} \delta_j \Delta S_{t-j}$$

$$\Delta S_t = \alpha_2 + \rho_2 z_{t-1} + \sum_{i=1}^{p} \beta_i \Delta Y_{t-i} + \sum_{j=1}^{q} \delta_j \Delta S_{t-j}$$

Where, z_{t-1} is an error correction term, representing the long run relationship. If both coefficients (ρ_1 and ρ_2) are significant, this will suggest the bi-directional causality. But, if only ρ_1 is significant, this will suggest a unidirectional causality from S to GDP, implying that gross domestic saving drives economic growth toward long run equilibrium. If only ρ_2 is significant, this will suggest a unidirectional causality from GDP to S, implying that economic growth drives gross domestic saving toward long run equilibrium. The ECM allows for the finding that gross domestic saving cause economic growth as long as the error correction term ρ_1 carries a significant coefficient with a negative sign.

This study uses annual data on gross domestic saving and Gross Domestic Product for five South Asian countries viz. Bhutan, India, Pakistan, Nepal and Sri Lanka, covering the period 1981 through 2008 for all countries except Bhutan for which 1981 to 2006 has been taken as a study period. All the data are collected from the Key Indicators for Asian and Pacific countries published by Asian Development Bank. The data are expressed in real terms, deflated by the GDP. deflator (1995=100).

RESULTS AND DISCUSSION

At the outset, Phillips-Perron (PP) unit root test is used to test the null hypothesis of unit root. The results of the PP Unit Root statistic for Gross Domestic Product (GDP) and gross domestic saving (S) of south Asian countries are presented in Table 1.

Since the computed PP test statistics of Y and S are higher than any of these MacKinnon Critical values at level forms, the null hypothesis that these variables exhibit a unit root cannot be rejected. Phillips–Perron test does not

Table 1
Phillips-Perron Unit Root Test

		Phillips-Perron Unit Root Test	
Countries	*Form*	*GDP*	*Saving*
Bhutan	Level	-1.770947	-1.387063
	First Difference	-7.656811*	-6.602527*
India	Level	1.552218	1.809330
	First Difference	-4.987914*	-4.963852*
Nepal	Level	-2.637917	-1.028307
	First Difference	-4.841054*	-5.511256*
Pakistan	Level	-1.232442	-1.859898
	First Difference	-3.362285**	-5.222600*
Sri Lanka	Level	1.280548	-0.036012
	First Difference	-5.218343*	-6.617769*

Source: Author's Calculation based on Data from the Key Indicators for Asian and Pacific Countries (Various issues), Asian Development Bank.

reject the null hypothesis of unit root for Y and S in the level form and rejects the null hypothesis in the first difference form of the series. Because of the presence of unit root in the variables, they are non-stationary implying no statistically meaningful relationship between them. However, after first differencing, the null hypothesis of unit root is rejected in all of the cases since the PP test statistic is smaller than MacKinnon critical values. That is, the first differenced Y and S do not exhibit a unit root, meaning that these variables are stationary. The results show that one could not reject the null hypothesis of unit root (non-stationarity) for both variables in level forms. The first differences of Y and S are stationary indicating that these variables are integrated of the first order *I* (1). Hence, PP test have shows that all the variables have unit root in level forms and no unit root in the first difference.

Having determined the non-stationary of time series in their levels, and they are also of the same order of integration I (1), Johansen procedure has been applied to ascertain whether S and GDP are cointegrated or not, assuming no deterministic trend in data. Because in the case of nonstationarity in the time series data, the most appropriate procedures are cointegration and error-correction models. The results of the Johansen cointegration tests are presented in Table 2.

The null hypothesis of no cointegration between GDP and S is rejected in the case of India and Nepal, since both Trace and Max-Eigen statistics are larger than the critical values at 1 per cent significance level in the case of India and at 5 per cent significance level in the case of Nepal. In other words, for cointegrating regression GDP = f (S), one can reject the null hypothesis $r = 0$ against the alternative hypothesis $r = 1$ since both Trace and Max-Eigen statistics are larger than the critical values at 1 per cent significance level but cannot reject the null $r \leq 1$ against the alternative $r = 2$ since both Trace and Max-Eigen

Table 2
Johansen Cointegration Test

Eigen Value	*Trace Value*	H_o	H_1	*Max-Eigen Statistic*	H_o	H_1
Sri Lanka						
0.274	8.658	r = 0	r ≥ 1	8.320	r = 0	r = 1
	(15.41)			(14.07)		
013	0.338	r ≤ 1	r ≥ 2	0.338	r ≤ 1	r = 2
	(3.76)			(3.76)		
India						
0.593	32.298*	r = 0	r ≥ 1	25.50*	r = 0	r = 1
	(30.45)			(23.65)		
0.324	9.798	r ≤ 1	r ≥ 2	9.798	r ≤ 1	r = 2
	(16.26)			(16.26)		
Bhutan						
0.226	6.784	r = 0	r ≥ 1	5.906	r = 0	r =1
	(15.41)			(14.07)		
0.037	0.879	r ≤ 1	r ≥ 2	0.879	r ≤ 1	r = 2
	(3.76)			(3.76)		
Nepal						
0.601	24.458**	r = 0	r ≥ 1	19.312**	r = 0	r = 1
	(19.96)			(15.65)		
0.217	5.145	r ≤ 1	r ≥ 2	5.145	r ≤ 1	r = 2
	(9.24)			(9.24)		
Pakistan						
0.232	6.894	r = 0	r ≥ 1	6.893	r = 0	r = 1
	(15.41)			(14.07)		
0.00002	0.0005	r ≤ 1	r ≥ 2	0.0005	r ≤ 1	r = 2
	(3.76)			(3.76)		

Note: *indicates significance at 1 per cent level and **indicate significance at 5 per cent level. Figures in parenthesis indicate Critical Value at 5% level for Sri Lanka, Bhutan, Nepal and Pakistan and at 1% level for India.

Source: Author's Calculation based on Data from the Key Indicators for Asian and Pacific Countries (Various issues), Asian Development Bank.

statistics are less than the critical values even at 5 per cent level. The fact that the presence of cointegration between S and GDP suggest (i) that there is a long run equilibrium relationship between the two time series and (ii) the existence of causality in at least one direction. All this indicates that GDP and S is cointegrated, which is sufficed to indicate that saving bears a long run equilibrium relationship with GDP in these two South Asian countries. However, the null hypothesis of no cointegration between GDP and S cannot be rejected in the case of Pakistan, Bhutan and Sri Lanka, since both Trace and Max-Eigen statistics are smaller than the critical values at 1 per cent significance level.

There are some difficulties regarding the selection of appropriate lags. First, although Granger causality test seems to have a greater appeal than most other alternative techniques, the issue concerning the optimal lag length still remains elusive. The distribution of a test statistic is sensitive to the order of lags used. If the lag order used is less than the true lag, the regression estimates will be biased and the residuals will be serially correlated. If the order of lags used exceeds the true order, the power of the test is likely to be reduced. To overcome this problem, this paper adopts the minimum final prediction error criterion based on Akaike Info criterion (AIC) and Schwartz criterion (SC). The optimal lag length corresponds to the minimum AIC and SC. The outcomes of the procedure for the selection of optimal lag have been presented through the following table.

Table 3
Selection of Optimal Lag Length

Country	*Dependant Variable*	*Lag of GDP*	*Lag of Sav*	*AIC*	*SC*
Bhutan	GDP	1	–	**-2.998553**	**-2.901043**
		2	–	-2.519013	-2.420842
		3	–	-2.245719	-2.147010
		4	–	-2.046835	-1.947650
	Sav	–	1	**0.401209**	**0.498719**
		–	2	0.663047	0.761218
		–	3	1.022364	1.121549
		–	4	1.062816	1.162002
Pakistan	GDP	1	–	**5.035855**	**-4.939078**
		2	–	-4.036535	-3.939025
		3	–	-3.528505	-3.430334
		4	–	-3.228585	-3.129846
	Sav	–	1	**-0.685458**	**-0.588682**
		–	2	-0.201296	-0.104519
		–	3	-0.124843	-0.027333
		–	4	-0.168371	-0.070199
Sri Lanka	GDP	1	–	**-4.962620**	**-4.866632**
		2	–	-4309375	-4.212598
		3	–	-3.885617	-3.788177
		4	–	-3.714522	-3.616350
	Sav	–	1	**-0.857849**	**-0.761861**
		–	2	-0.473873	-0.377097
		–	3	-0.609451	-0.511941
		–	4	-0.359073	-0.260902

Source: Author's Calculation based on Data from the Key Indicators for Asian and Pacific Countries (Various issues), Asian Development Bank.

This paper applies the technique of bi-variate Granger Causality estimated in the previous section to examine the causal relationship between GDP and saving, using annual data over the period 1981-2008. The results appeared in Table 4 were obtained using first lag as optimum lag length for each variable.

Table 4
Granger Causality

Country	*Null Hypothesis*	*Obs*	*Lag*	*F-Statistic*	*Conclusion*
Bhutan	Saving does not Granger Cause GDP	25	1	0.60849 (0.44367)	Accept
	GDP does not Granger Cause Saving			4.17502 (0.05318)	Reject
Pakistan	Saving does not Granger Cause GDP	27	1	0.17765 (0.67715)	Accept
	GDP does not Granger Cause Saving			1.56397 (0.22314)	Accept
Sri Lanka	Saving does not Granger Cause GDP	27	1	0.16736 (0.6861)	Accept
	GDP does not Granger Cause Saving			10.0786 (0.00408)	Reject

Note: Figures in parenthesis indicate probability values.
Source: Author's Calculation based on Data from the Key Indicators for Asian and Pacific Countries (Various issues), Asian Development Bank.

The results of Bhutan show that the null hypothesis of saving does not Granger Cause GDP cannot be rejected because F statistic is statistically insignificant. However, the null hypothesis that GDP does not Granger Cause Saving is rejected since the F statistic is statistically significant at the 10 per cent level. From the results, it can be inferred that there is unidirectional causality from GDP to Saving.

Similarly, the results of Sri Lanka show that the null hypothesis of saving does not Granger Cause GDP cannot be rejected because F statistic is statistically insignificant. However, the null hypothesis that GDP does not Granger Cause Saving is rejected since the F statistic is statistically significant at the 1 per cent level. From the results, it can be inferred that there is unidirectional causality from GDP to Saving.

However, so far as the result of Pakistan is concerned, it is quite different. The results of Pakistan show that the null hypothesis of saving does not Granger Cause GDP cannot be rejected because F statistic is statistically insignificant. Likewise, the null hypothesis that saving does not Granger Cause GDP cannot be rejected because F statistic is statistically insignificant. From the results, it can be inferred that there is no causal relationship between GDP and Saving.

After confirming that saving and GDP are cointegrated in the case of Nepal and India, it is appropriate to find out the direction of causality between them through estimating the Vector Error Correction Model. The results of the Vector Error Correction Estimates are presented in Table 5.

Table 5
Vector Error Correction Estimates

	GDP Equation (GDP)			*Saving Equation (S)*	
Z_{t-1}	$\Delta S(-1)$	$\Delta S(-2)$	Z_{t-1}	$\Delta GDP(-1)$	$\Delta GDP(-2)$
India					
-0.243***	0.078	0.097	-0.445	-1.448	-1.383
(-1.874)	(0.769)	(1.254)	(-0.858)	(-1.582)	(-1.438)
Nepal					
-0.012*	0.039	0.005	-0.038	1.701	-3.406
(-2.850)	(1.466)	(0.172)	(-0.995)	(0.804)	(-1.690)

Source: Author's Calculation based on Data from the Key Indicators for Asian and Pacific Countries (Various issues), Asian Development Bank.

The significance of the error correction coefficient (Z_{t-1}), which is determined by the t-ratio given below the coefficient, with a negative sign indicates Granger causality in at least one direction The results show that the error correction term in the GDP equation is statistically significant with a correct negative sign in India and Nepal, indicating that Saving has significantly contributed to economic growth in these countries. While that the error correction in the saving equation is not significant and a wrong positive sign, which indicates that economic growth has not significantly contributed to saving in these countries. The error correction term of GDP equation is significant and of saving equation is not significant, which indicates the absence of bi-directional causality in both these countries. Thus, it can be inferred that saving has promoted economic growth in India and Nepal.

CONCLUDING REMARKS

This study makes an attempt to assess causal relationship between GDP and saving, using the Phillips-Perron unit root test, Cointegration, Granger Causality, and Vector Error Correction models. Since the GDP and saving are not cointegrated in Bhutan, Sri Lanka and Pakistan, Granger causality test is conducted. The analysis discovers a firm unidirectional causality running from GDP to Saving in Bhutan and Sri Lanka and no causal relationship between these variables in Pakistan. Since Saving and GDP are cointegrated in the case of Nepal and India, the result is estimated through the Vector Error Correction model. It indicates that saving has significantly contributed to economic growth in India and Nepal.

References

Agrawal, P. (2001), "The Relation between Savings and Growth: Cointegration and Causality Evidence from Asia." *Applied Economics*, 33, 499-513.

Agrawal, P. and Sahoo, P. (2009), "Saving and Growth in Bangladesh." *The Journal of Developing Areas*, 42(2), 89-110.

Alguacil, M., Cuadros, A. and Orts, V. (2004), "Does Saving Really Matter for Growth? Mexico (1970-2000)." *Journal of International Development,* 16(2), 281-90.

Anoruo, E. and Ahmad, Y. (2001), "Causal Relationship between Domestic Savings and Economic Growth: Evidence from Seven African Countries." *African Development Bank,* 13(2), 238-49.

Bacha, E. L. (1990), "A Three-Gap Model of Foreign Transfers and the GDP Growth Rate in Developing Countries." *Journal of Development Economics,* 32, 279-96.

Baharumshah *et al.* (2003), "Savings Dynamic in Asian Countries". *Journal of Asian Economics,* 13, 827-845.

Cass, D. (1965), "Optimum Growth in an Aggregative Model of Capital Accumulation." *Review of Economic Studies,* 32, 233–40.

Caroll, C. D., Overland, J. and Weil, D. N. (2000), "*Saving and Growth with Habit Formation.*" *American Economic Review,* 90(3), 351-55.

Dickey D. A. and Fuller, W. A. (1979), "Distributions of the Estimators for Autoregressive Time Series with a Unit Root." *Journal of The American Statistical Association,* 74, 427-31.

Domer, E. D. (1946), "Capital Expansion, Rate of Growth, and Employment." *Econometric,* 14, 137-147.

Engle, R. F. and Granger, C. W. J. (1987), "*Cointegration and Error Correction: Representation, Estimation and Testing.*" *Econometrica,* 55, 251-71.

Granger, C. (1969), "Investigating Causal Relations by Economic Models and Cross-Spectral Methods." *Econometrica,* 37, 3, 424-438.

Granger, C. (1988), "Causality, Cointegration, and Control." *Journal of Economic Dynamics and Control,* 12, 511-59.

Gujarati, D. (1995), *Basic Econometrics,* Singapore: Mcgraw–Hill Book Company.

Harrod, R. (1939), "An Essay in Dynamic Theory." *Economic Journal,* 49, 14-33.

Japelli, T. and Pagano, M. (1994), Savings, Growth and Liquidity Constraints, *Quarterly Journal of Economics,* 109, 83-109.

Johansen, S. (1988), Statistical Analysis of Cointegrating Vectors, *Journal of Economic Dynamics and Control,* 12, 231-54.

Johansen, S. and Juselius, K. (1990), "Maximum Likelihood Estimation and Inference on Cointegration- with Applications to the Demand for Money." *Oxford Bulletin of Economics and Statistics,* 52(2), 169-210.

Koopmans, T. C. (1965), "On The Concept of Optimal Economic Growth." In *The Econometric Approach to Development Planning.* Amsterdam: North-Holland.

Krieckhaus, J. (2002), "Reconceptualizing the Developmental State: Public Savings and Economic Growth." *World Development,* 30 (10), 1697-1712.

Lewis, W. A. (1955), *The Theory of Economic Growth.* Homewood, III: Irwin.

Mavrotas, G. and Kelly, R. (2001), "Old Wine in New Bottles: Testing Causality between Savings and Growth." *The Manchester School,* Vol. 69, 97-105.

Mohan, R. (2006), "Causal Relationship between Savings and Economic Growth in Countries with Different Income Levels." *Economic Bulletin,* 5(3), 1-12.

Narayan, P. K. and Narayan, S. (2006), "Savings Behavior in Fiji: An Empirical Assessment Using the ARDL Approach to Cointegration." *International Journal of Social Economics*, 33(7), 468-480.

Romer, P. M. (1986), "Increasing Returns and Long-Run Growth." *Journal of Political Economy*, 94, 1002-37.

Salz, I. S. (1999), "An Examination of the Causal Relationship between Savings and Growth in the Third World." *Journal of Economics and Finance*, 23(1), 90-98.

Sinha, D. and Sinha, T. (1998), "Cart Before Horse? The Saving-Growth Nexus in Mexico." *Economics Letter*, 61, 43-47.

Sinha, D., and Sinha, T. (1999), "Saving and Economic Growth in Sri Lanka." *Indian Journal of Applied Economics*, 8 (3), 163-174.

Singh, T. (2009), "Does Domestic Saving Cause Economic Growth? A Time-series Evidence from India." *Journal of Policy Modeling, doi:10.1016/j.jpolmod.2009.08.008.*

Solow, R. M. (1956), "A Contribution to the Theory of Economic Growth." *Quarterly Journal of Economics*, 70, 65-94.

STRESS AND ACCIDENTS – ARE THEY RELATED?: A CASE STUDY OF BMTC

VEENA K. N.[*], *S. J. MANJUNATH*[**] & *ASHA PATIL*[***]

INTRODUCTION

> *"Nothing gives one person so much advantage over another as to remain always cool and unruffled under all circumstances."*[1] – **Thomas Jefferson**

The above statement says that a person who stays cool and calm in all circumstances and who doesn't face stress has an advantage over other person. But today's modern world, which is said to be a world of achievement, is also a world of stress. One feels stress everywhere, be it a family or work place. Stress is an inevitable consequence of socio-economic complexity and to some extent it's a stimulant as well. People experience stress as they can no longer have complete control over what happens in their lives. The delay or denial of expected promotion and posting, job pressure, behavior of section commanders/peers, sickness, marital disharmony, poor performance of children at school etc could be the causes of stress. Even trifles such as telephone going out of order, power shut down and irregular water supply can give rise to stress.[2]

According to the Health and Safety Executive (HSE) (2001) there are three main reasons why organizations should take action towards work-related stress: the ethical argument emphasizes the negative effects of work-related stress; the legal argument highlights the employer's legal duties to prevent stress; and the economic argument focuses on the vast cost ascribed to work-related stress.[3] Lot of study has been made on workplace stress but very limited study has been made in the transportation area, regarding bus drivers stress level

* Assistant Professor, Department of Management Studies - MBA , Acharya Institute of Management and Sciences, Bangalurur.

** Reader, B. N. Bahadur Institute of Management Sciences, University of Mysore, Manasagangotri, Mysore.

*** Ex student of Department of Management Studies - MBA, Acharya Institute of Management and Sciences (AIMS).

and the effect of such stress on their performance. Bus is one of the most popular modes of public transport in worldwide. Bangalore Metropolitan Transport Corporation (BMTC) is a public transport corporation in Banagalore which provides transport service to the people in and around Bangalore. More than 500 accidents were reported where BMTC buses are involved in the last two years (2007 & 2008). Recent research has indicated that there are a number of factors that may lead to accidents and number of studies that have looked at the relationship between fatigue and the occurrence of accidents. Fatigue can be due to the stress of prolonged and/or irregular working hours. In this situation, bus drivers must successfully balance the competing demands of safety, customer-focused service and company operating regulations. The physical and psychological health of the bus driver is a critical factor in his performance. Any impairment can have undesirable consequences for passengers, other on the road and bus operating companies alike.

This study is focused on how stress leads to accidents and what is the extent of the relationship between stress and accidents.

MEANING AND DEFINITION OF STRESS AND ACCIDENTS

Stress : Hans Selye first introduced the concept of stress in the life science in 1936. He defined stress as "The force, pressure, or strain exerted upon a material object or person which resist these forces and attempt to maintain its original state." Stress is ubiquitous in our society. Growth of industries, pressure in the urban areas, quantitative growth in population and various problems in day to day life are some of the reasons for increase in stress. Stress is a condition of strain that has a direct bearing on emotions, thought process and physical conditions of a person.[4]

Stress is derived from the Latin word "Stringer" (to draw tight) and was popularly used in the seventeenth century to mean 'hardship', 'straits', 'adversity', or 'affliction'. The concept of stress is also explained in the traditional texts of Indian culture and tradition. There are two Sanskrit words *'klesha'* and *'Dukha'* which approximates modern concept of stress. The word *klesha* has its origin in the root *'khis'* which means to 'torment', 'cause pain', or to 'afflict'. *Klesha* are not mental processes but are a set of 'hindering load' on our mental process. Thus, *dukha* refers to the phenomena of stress itself and *'klesha'* is the stressor aspect.[5] The term 'stress' has been used in so many different contexts, few more definitions[6] of stress are given below; and they are useful according to scope and clarity.

"Stress is any condition that disturbs normal functioning" - Arnold, 1960.

"Stress is the state of an organism where he perceives that his well-being is endangered and that he must divert all his energies to its protection" - Cofer and Appley, 1964.

"Stress is a stimulus or situation to which man reacts with learned coping mechanism activated by homeostasis principle and fuelled by energies which are in finite supply." - Caplan, 1964, Marshal and Cooper, 1979.

There is no single satisfactory definition of stress which encompasses the social, psychological and biological issues as they pertain to individual. Stress is multifaceted in nature and stress response arousal involves every set of organs and tissues in our body.

Accident: Meaning of accident as given in Encyclopedia is 'An **accident** is a specific, identifiable, unexpected, unusual and unintended external event which occurs in a particular time and place, without apparent cause but with marked effects. It implies a generally negative probabilistic outcome which may have been avoided or revented had circumstances leading up to the accident been recognized, and acted upon, prior to its occurrence'[7].

Accident, is unintended and unforeseen event, usually resulting in personal injury or property damage. In law, the term is usually limited to events not involving negligence (that is, the carelessness or misconduct of a party involved) or to a loss caused by lightning, floods, or other natural event (*See Act of God*). In popular usage, however, the term "accident" designates an unexpected event, especially if it causes injury or damage, without reference to the negligence or fault of an individual. The basic causes of such accidents are, in general, unsafe conditions of machinery, equipment, or surroundings, and the unsafe actions of persons, caused by ignorance or neglect of safety principles.[8]

Causes of Stress: Stress is not independent, there are some causes which are called stressors which stimulate and leads to stress. These causes of stress are as follows:

Environmental Factors: Environmental factors viz working in a place under tough climatic conditions, technological changes, new machinery, equipment and inventions can make employees' skill and experience obsolete in a very short period of time and this induces stress.

Organisational Factors: Pressure to avoid error, completion of task in limited time, work overload, demanding and insensitive section commander and unplanned workers are a few examples of organisational factors. Poor inter-personnel relationship and lack of support from colleagues can cause considerable stress especially among persons with high social need.

Individual Factors: Individual factors generally encompass factors in the employee's personal life. These could be marital difficulties, family issues, economic problems, inherent personality characteristics, medical problems of relatives etc that create stress for employees when they arrive at work.

Effects of Stress: Stress may have both positive and negative effects. The positive stress is called as Eustress. Eustress is often viewed as a motivator which helps in taking action to get things accomplished. Distress or negative stress occurs when your level of stress is either too high or too low and the body and/or mind begin to respond negatively to the stressors which can lead to heart-disease, alcoholism, drug abuse, marital breakdown, absenteeism and a host of other social, physical, organizational and emotional problems.

Behavioral scientists are of the opinion that stress has behavioral, cognitive and physiological consequences. Behavioral outcomes may be satisfaction, performance, absenteeism, turnover, accidents, substance abuse etc. Cognitive outcomes may be poor decision - making, lack of concentration, forgetfulness etc. Finally, physiological outcome may be increased blood, high cholesterol, heart disease, burnout etc.

Causes of Accidents: The causes of the accidents may be divided into two types: Human Factors, and Environmental Factors. These factors are as follows:

Human Factors: Carelessness, Intoxication, Daydreaming, Inability to do the job, Other human deficiencies can be considered as Human factors.

Environmental Factors: Other than human factors are environmental factors. Environmental factors may be Tools, Equipment, General work environment, Condition of plant.

Effects of Accidents: The occurrence of accidents harms the person and the property. There are mainly three types of harms causes by accidents.

Fatality: In the United States, for example, the definition used in the Fatality Analysis Reporting System (FARS) is death of a person within 30 days of a crash on a US public road involving a vehicle with an engine, the death being the result of the crash.

Injuries: Minor injuries, which can be cured in a short period and Major injuries, which require a long time to heal. Usually small injuries are not at all reported, hence it is very difficult to know the exact number of minor injuries.

Property Damage: vehicles involved in the crash gets damaged in many accidents. In some cases building and other infrastructure also gets damaged due to the impact of a crash.

IMPORTANCE OF PUBLIC TRANSPORT IN BENGALURU

Bengaluru is the 5th largest city in India and one of the fastest growing cities in the world. As per 2001 report, the population is about 62 lakhs and the city covers about 531 sq. kms and is expected to touch 800 sq. kms area under Greater Bengaluru Project. The number of registered vehicles is about 28 lakhs of which 88% are personal vehicles and 72% of the total vehicles are two wheelers. This has led to congestion on roads, increased travelling time, pollution level and other related problems on Bengaluru roads. Increasing fuel prices is expected to add to the agony of Bangaloreans. Good public transport system can improve the conditions and can contribute to the growth of the city.

BENGALORE METROPOLITAN TRANSPORT CORPORATION - B M T C

BMTC provides an affordable way of transit in the Bangalore city. It is an undertaking of the Government of Karnataka. BMTC is the fourth biggest Public City Transport Corporation in India, catering the needs of passengers with cost effective and reliable public transportation.

B M T C came into existence in August 1997 after bifurcating from Karnataka State Road Transport Corporation - KSRTC. There are 31 depots operating more than 4850 buses in 4735 schedules covering 10.44 lakhs service kilometers carrying about 37 lakh passengers per day. An organization which is realizing a good profit has given employment to more than 22,000 people.

Mission: To provide Efficient, Economic, Safe, Reliable and Punctual services to the commuters of City and Sub-urban areas of Bangalore.

The only profit[9] making public sector urban transport corporation in the country, uses returns in operations in a strive to improve quality of service not only in providing comfort to the travelling public but also in other vital aspects like containing pollution, easing traffic congestion, saving fuel, introducing latest technologies in operations to save precious time and money as it will ultimately benefit the people since it is a public undertaking.

Patrick Sherry *et. al.* (1996): In a study conducted by Patrick Sherry, Allison Gaa, Scott Thurlow- Harrison, Kimberly Graber, Julianne Clemmons, Michelle Bobulinski, on "Traffic Accidents, Job Stress, and Supervisor Support in the Trucking Industry", Park City, Utah, April, 1996, the correlation between Job Stress and Traffic Accidents was tested. Parker *et al.* (1996): A survey of over 1600 drivers by Parker *et. al.* revealed that lapses in concentration were one of the major sources of driving errors. In addition, another study, revealed that driver fatigue was a major factor in car driving accidents but less of a factor in truck driving accidents. Brown (1994): A study by Brown revealed that fatigue played a role in driving accidents. However, this was due to the stress of prolonged and irregular working hours. Thus, despite inconsistent results with the role of fatigue there seems to be some acknowledgment of the role of the unpredictability of work hours as a source of fatigue.

Statement of The Problem: In India very little study has been made on the relationship between stress and accidents in transportation. An attempt has been made here to know the relationship. In this study the relationship between stress and accidents is assessed by using statistical tools.

Sample: A convenient sample of 30 drivers was considered for the study. Participants were invited to complete a survey prior to going on duty. Drivers from four depots viz. depots No. 8, No. 9, No. 22, and No. 26 are taken for study. A list of drivers who have caused accidents is used for the study.

The data for research was collected using a questionnaire designed on 5 point scale to measure different aspects related to stress and accident.

Some important questions asked included *How many injuries have you had in the last 4 years? How many collisions have you been involved in during the last 4 years? and How many traffic tickets have you received in the last 4 years?*

Individuals perceived level of stress, General level of interest in getting along with others, Interest in taking risks or adventure, perceived level of concentration, distraction or lack of attention, opinion about, if the supervisor has established clear safety goals, supervisor has given the individual feedback on their safe job performance, the supervisor is perceived as supportive were measured using questionnaire which contained 5 items for each parameter. 5 items were used to determine the individual's belief that accidents and injuries are under the control of the individual and not just due to chance.

The objectives of the study are:

- To know the perception of the drivers of BMTC about stress.
- To study the relationship between stress and accidents.
- To know the techniques employed by the organization to reduce the stress.

ANALYSIS AND INTERPRETATION

Table 1
Descriptive Statistics about Stress

	Stress at Home or life	*Stress at Work (Daily hassles)*	*Stress at Work (Interpersonal Relation)*	*Stress at Work (Career Development)*	*Stress at Work (Organizational Culture)*
N I Valid	30	30	30	30	30
Mean	15.6333	50.4333	4.1333	2.9000	2.4667
Mode	7.00 (a)	34.00 (a)	5.00	2.00	0.00
Std. Deviation	9.4193	17.1136	1.5253	1.2134	2.5695
Minimum	3.00	27.00	2.00	1.00	0.00
Maximum	36.00	99.00	8.00	7.00	8.00

(a) Multiple modes exist. The smallest value is shown.

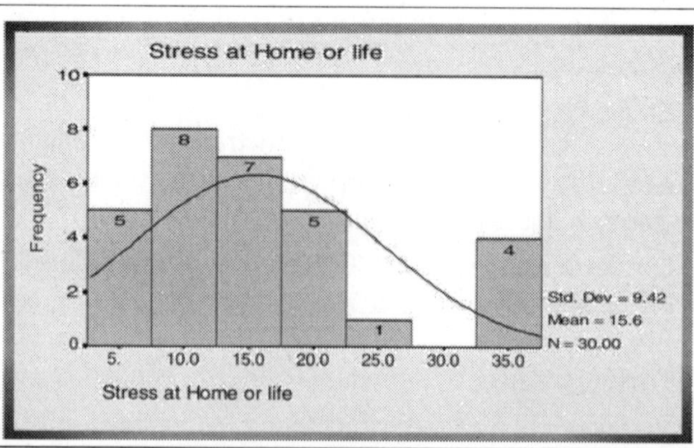

Figure 1

Stress at Home or life: Nineteen parameters are included to measure stress at home. The maximum score could be 76 for a respondent. But the maximum observed value is 36 with mode equal to 7. This indicates that the stress level at home is very low but with positively skewed distribution. One of the reasons for this could be that 23 out of 30 [77%] respondents are unmarried.

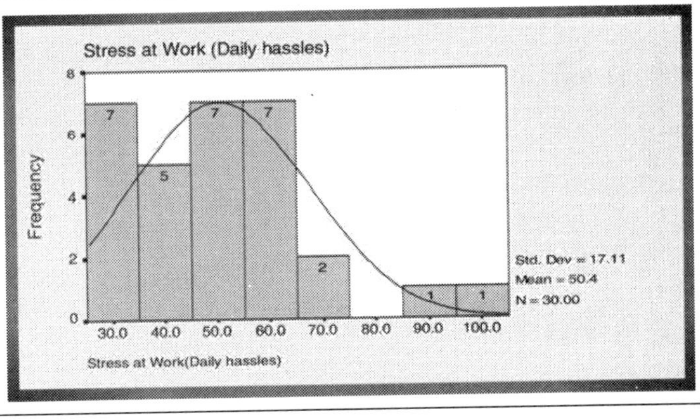

Figure 2

Stress at work (Daily Hassles): Thirty eight parameters are included to measure stress at home. The maximum score could be 152 for a respondent. But the maximum observed value is 99 and minimum is 27 with mode equal to 34 (multi-modal case) This indicates that the stress level at work due to daily hassles is low but with positively skewed distribution.

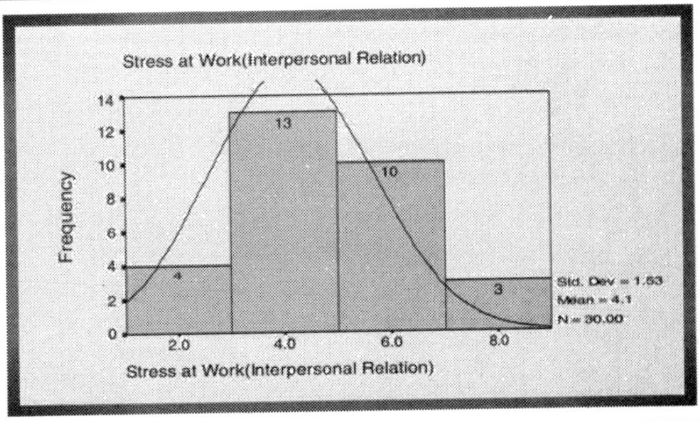

Figure 3

Stress at work (Inter personal relation): Three parameters are included to measure stress at home. The maximum score could be 12 for a respondent. But the maximum observed value is 08 and minimum is 02 with mode equal to 05. This indicates that the stress level at work due to Inter personal relation is HIGH with positively skewed distribution.

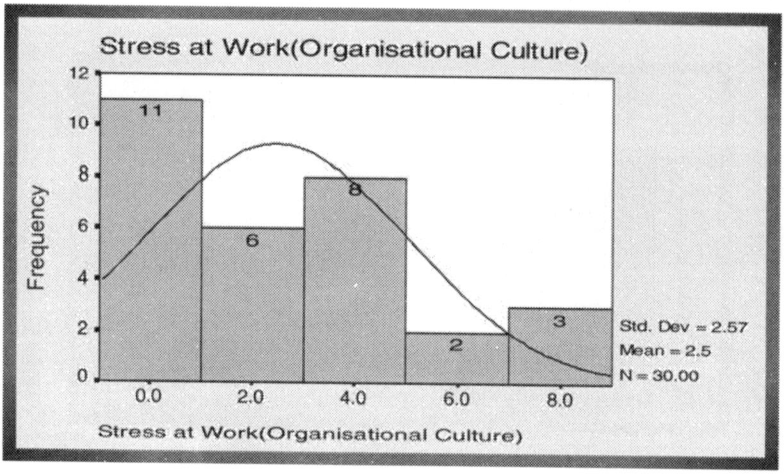

Figure 4

Stress at work (Organisational Culture): Two parameters are included to measure stress at home. The maximum score could be 08 for a respondent. But the maximum observed value is 08 and minimum is 00 with mode equal to 00. This indicates that the stress level at work due to organizational culture is LOW but with highly positively skewed distribution.

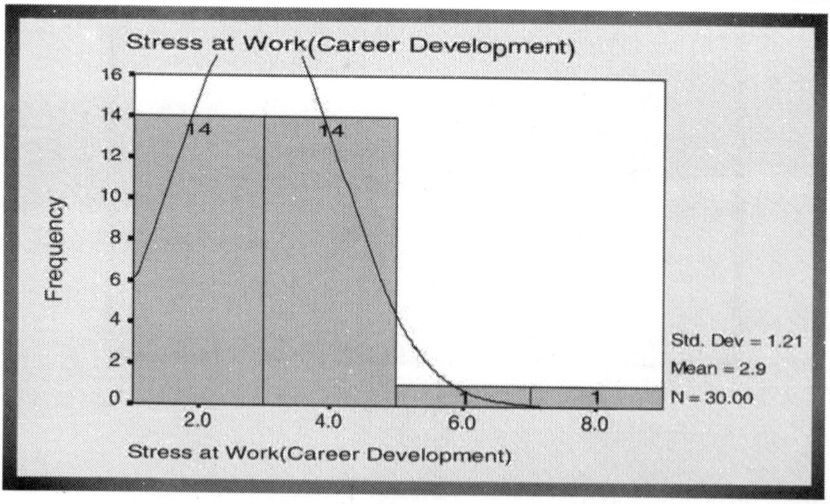

Figure 5

Stress at work (Career Development) : Two parameters are included to measure stress at home. The maximum score could be 08 for a respondent. But the maximum observed value is 07 and minimum is 01 with mode equal to 02. This indicates that the stress level at work due to organizational culture is LOW but with Leptokurtic distribution.

Table 2

Correlations between Stress Level and No. of Accidents

		No. of Accident	*Over all Stress Level*
No. of Accident	Pearson Correlation	1.000	0.111
	Sig. (2-tailed)	.	0.559
	N	30	30
Over all Stress Level	Pearson Correlation	0.111	1.000
	Sig. (2-tailed)	0.559	.
	N	30	30

Table 2 indicates that the correlation coefficient between stress level and number of accidents caused by drivers is not significant.

Table 3

Linear Equation for Relation Between Stress Level(X) and No. of Accidents(Y)

Variable	*B*	*SE B*	*Beta*	*T*	*Sig T*
STRESSLEVEL (X)	0.002616	0.004422	0.111108	0.592	0.5589
Constant (K)	1.135639	0.352440		3.222	0.0032**

** Significant at 1% level of significance

Therefore the equation is $Y = 0.0026X + 1.1356$

Further from Table 3, in the linear relation between stress level and number of accidents caused by drivers, the slope of the curve is not significant but the Constant is significant at 1% level.

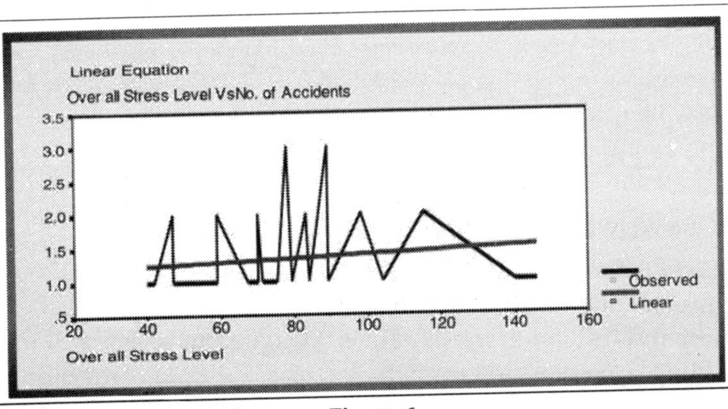

Figure 6

Figure 6 indicates that the number of accidents increase as the stress level increases even though.

Their correlation coefficient is statistically not significant.

Table 4
Age of Respondents

Age [yrs]	*25-30*	*30-35*	*35-40*	*40-45*	*45-50*	*50-55*	*Total*
No. of drivers	6	9	11	1	2	1	30

The AVERAGE Age of drivers is 35.33 years. Low average age can also be one of the reasons for low stress level.

Table 5
Experience of Drivers

No of years	*5-10*	*10-15*	*15-20*	*20-25*	*25-30*	*Total*
No. of drivers	10	7	8	4	1	30

The AVERAGE experience of drivers is 14 years. Among respondents 2 are Graduates, 7 have cleared 2nd PU examinations, 17 have cleared SSLC and 4 are 7th standard pass. 26 out of 30 [87 %] are of the opinion that TRAINING helps in reducing stress.

Table 6
Descriptive Statistics
Top 20 factors which lead to STRESS based on Mean score given by drivers

S. No.	*Parameter*	*Mean*	*S. No.*	*Parameter*	*Mean*
1.	Traffic	3.5517	11.	Location of the Bus stops	2.3704
2.	Other private transporters	3.3	12.	Poor working conditions	2.3571
3.	Pollution	3.1071	13.	Trouble with higher officers	2.3333
4.	Excess heat	3.0667	14.	Changing of routs	2.2857
5.	Varying work time table	2.88	15.	Road crossers	2.2143
6.	Roads condition	2.8462	16.	Firing employees	2.2105
7.	Having to work late	2.6296	17.	Department Policy	2.2
8.	Shift work	2.5	18.	Mobile phones interruptions	2.1875
9.	Getting fired at work	2.4762	19.	Self growing older	2.1429
10.	Poorly maintained buses	2.44	20.	Work overload	2.1429

PRACTICES ADOPTED BY BMTC TO PREVENT ACCIDENTS

Driver Selection: Candidates should be SSLC Pass, Holding HPV License, Must passes physical standards 160cm height, 50 kg weight. *Selection through test:* driving test and test about traffic rule is taken before selection. *Training:* Class room training by senior driver instructors & RTO BMTC & Police officers are held. Practical Training on Vehicles, Documentary films on Good Driving habits, Alert on roads, Accidents Almanac (case studies) and Fuel Conservation are shown regularly. *Incentives for safe driving:* Silver Medal award for three years accidents free service, and Chief Minister's Gold Medal for five years accidents free service. *Compulsory Medical check up & Eye checkup for drivers after 45 years.*

CONCLUSIONS AND RECOMMENDATIONS

Analysis of data indicates that, even though stress and number of accidents are not significantly correlated, Inter Personal Relation is one of the major factors which leads to Stress. Traffic, Private Transporters, Pollution, Heat, Variation in working hours are some of important parameters influencing Stress Levels.

In this context, BMTC can try to improve relationship among employees by creating a platform where they can discuss issues freely. Also, BMTC can request for separate lanes for its buses, at least on some roads and during peak hours, with concerned authorities. Training to improve Physical and Mental stamina [Yoga, Meditation etc.,] can be introduced.

Notes

1. Quoted in "Stress – Stress Busters at Work" *www.lifepositive.com*
2. "Stress and Stress Management" *http://mod.nic.in/Samachar/1aug2000/html/ch2.htm*
3. Gyllensten Kristina and Palmer Stephen, "The relationship between coaching and workplace stress: A correlational study", *"International Journal of Health Promotion and Education"*, Vol. 43, Number 3, 2005, pp. 97-103.
4. Prof. Dileep Kumar. M, "A Study on Job Stress of Nationalized and Non Nationalized Bank Employees", *http://www.indianmba.com*
5. Dr. Kaila H L, Dr. Pai Satish, Dr. Ravishankar S and Dr. Dhar Upinder, "Stress Management – Western and Indian Techniques", Mumbai: Himalaya Publishing House, 2001, p. 9.
6. Definitions are quoted in Dr. Kaila, Supra note-5, pp. 3-4.
7. Wikipedia, the free encyclopedia
8. "Accident," *Microsoft® Encarta® Encyclopedia 2000.* © 1993-1999 Microsoft Corporation. All rights reserved.
9. BMTC Annual Administrative Report 2007-08.

References

Aswattappa, K. (2006), *Organisational Behaviour*, 6th ed, Himala Publishing House, India.

Aswattappa, K. (2006), *Human Resource and Personnel Management*, 4th ed, Tata McGraw-Hill Publishing Company Ltd., New Delhi.

Cooper, D. R. and Pamela, S. Schindler (1995), *Business Research Methods*, 6th ed, Tata McGraw – Hill Publishing Company Ltd.

Curry, A. (1999), "Innovation in Public Service Management", *Managing Service Quality*, Vol. 9, No. 3, pp. 180-190.

Gaster, L. (1995), *Quality in Public Services* , Open University Press, Buckingham.

Kaila, H. L. Pai, Satish and Ravishankar, S. *Stress Management-Western and Indian Techniques,* Himala Publishing House, India.

Vohra, N. D. (2005), *Quantitative Techniques in Management,* 2nd ed., Tata McGraw–Hill Publishing Company Ltd.

www.bmtcinfo.com

IS CORPORATE GOVERNANCE REALLY A KEY TO NATIONAL DEVELOPMENT?

*VVR Raman** & *Veena Tewari***

INTRODUCTION

Although prior work has provided some insight into the role of corporate governance, the results of similar studies are frequently contradictory and a consistent set of results has yet to emerge regarding the importance of corporate governance for understanding managerial behavior and organizational performance. There are also many organizations that sell governance ratings (e.g., Governance Metrics International, Institutional Shareholder Services, Investor Responsibility Center, and Standard & Poor). The growth in this type of service offerings attests to the perceived importance of corporate governance issues. Although the precise computation of these ratings is proprietary, the scores seem to be based on board independence, distribution of ownership, and other structural characteristics. Despite considerable claims by these organizations, we are not aware of rigorous evidence regarding the ability of these ratings to predict managerial behavior or organizational performance (with the possible exception of Gompers, Ishii, and Metrick, 2003; but note the discussion in Cremers and Nair, 2003 regarding the sensitivity of the Gompers, Ishii and Metrick results).

Prior Research: Seven features of prior research that makes it difficult to draw substantive conclusions.

First, most studies use a small set of convenient (easy to collect) set of indicators for corporate governance, as opposed to developing a more comprehensive set of governance variables. Second, each study tends to use a different set of governance variables which makes integration across studies extremely difficult. Third, there is very little analysis regarding the measurement

* Asst. Professor, Head (Computer Sciences) Asmara College of Health Sciences, Eritrea, (*e-mail: raman.vvr@gmail.com*)

** Lecturer, Department of Management, College of Business & Economics, Asmara University, Eritrea, (*e-mail: veenatewari@yahoo.com*) properties for the selected indicators of corporate governance (e.g., the traditional psychometric properties of reliability and construct validity).

Moreover, we do not have detailed insight into the number of dimensions (or constructs) that are necessary to provide a comprehensive assessment of corporate governance.

Fourth, single indicators are used as measures for ill-defined and complex corporate governance constructs (e.g., percentage of external board members). Such single indicators are likely to have substantial measurement error for the construct of interest (e.g., board independence) which will bias the estimated coefficients in typical methodological approaches. Fifth, the sample size and specific firms included in the sample vary considerably across studies depending on the dependent variable examined and the source of the governance variables. These differences make it problematic to compare results across studies. Sixth, most studies focus on the statistical significance, as opposed to the incremental explanatory power, of the governance indicators. While statistical significance is necessary, it is also important to demonstrate explanatory power in order to draw substantive conclusions about corporate governance. Finally, the methodological approach used is typically restricted to some type of linear model where complex interactions among governance are not considered. Since empirical governance research is at an early stage in its evolution, it would be useful to use more exploratory methods as a complement to traditional linear model approaches.

The Concept: Defined broadly, "corporate governance" refers to the private and public institutions, including laws, regulations and accepted business practices, which together govern the relationship, in a market economy, between corporate managers and entrepreneurs ("corporate insiders") on one hand, and those who invest resources in corporations, on the other. Investors can include suppliers of equity finance (shareholders), suppliers of debt finance (creditors), suppliers of relatively firm-specific human capital (employees) and suppliers of other tangible and intangible assets that corporations may use to operate and grow.

Specifically, what are the institutions of corporate governance? Not only do they vary from country to country – in form and substance and, importantly, in how they mutually interact in a given country – they evolve over time. An indicative, hypothetical, list can nevertheless illustrate the main institutions of corporate governance. Comprising key "actors" and relevant legislation, regulations, other formal and informal rules, and generally accepted business practices.

Perhaps most important to understanding the concept, however, is to understand the purpose of corporate governance. In all countries, the institutions of corporate governance serve two indispensable and ultimately in dissociable objectives: enhance the performance and ensure the conformance of corporations. They facilitate and stimulate the performance of corporations – the principal generators of economic wealth and growth in society – by creating and maintaining a business environment that motivates managers and entrepreneurs to maximize firms' operational efficiency, returns on investment and long-term productivity growth.

Why Corporate Governance Matters For Development: A good illustration of the importance of this question, and of its challenging nature, is the fact that for 30 years or more, until mid-1997, developing East and Southeast Asia achieved very impressive, sustained, high rates of growth – growth that significantly raised their populations' standards of living – in a context that most people would now describe as one of poor corporate governance. How was that possible? If corporate governance has an important role to play in the process of development in a country, one must be able to explain the apparent paradox that the Asian growth "miracle" occurred in conjunction with poor corporate governance.

- *The Importance of Productivity Growth:* Part of the explanation was suggested, albeit in highly provocative and caricaturized fashion, by Paul Krugman in his notorious 1994 Foreign Affairs article (three years before the onset of the crisis) when he compared the success of growth in East and Southeast Asia to the Soviet model, and predicted a similar outcome. His point was that experience (in this case Soviet experience) shows that it is not impossible for a country to achieve and sustain high rates of output and income growth for long periods of time – many decades even – by engaging in a process of massive mobilization of factors of production. Such factor mobilization can be achieved through various kinds of forced saving, significant and sustained investment in the education of the country's population, high rates of rural-urban migration, mobilization of the female population into the modern manufacturing as well as the agricultural and services sectors, and so on. It should perhaps be emphasized more clearly than Krugman did, there is nothing illegitimate about the output and income growth that stems from such factor mobilization; on the contrary, it is rarely easy to accomplish, and it is very real.

The further point, however, is that because decreasing returns to continued factor mobilization must ultimately set in, growth based on factor mobilization alone cannot be sustained indefinitely. It can last for years and should not be seen as anything less than a vitally important source of economic growth, but the key to achieving sustainable development in the long run is productivity growth.

- *Relationship-based vs. Rules-based Regimes:* To the importance for development of productivity growth can be added another important observation. It is that a predominantly clientelistic relationship-based system of corporate and political governance and poor corporate governance are quite compatible with a national development strategy based on massive factor mobilization. Clientelistic relationship-based governance systems and poor corporate governance – ubiquitous in the developing world (including East and Southeast Asia at the time of the crisis) – appear rather less amenable to the move from a strategy of massive factor mobilization to sustained productivity growth.

The country studies illustrate this observation well. All seven countries are in the midst of a dual transition, from predominantly relationship-based to more rules-based systems in their economic and political spheres of governance. In the economic sphere the movement is from relatively closed or inward-oriented and market-unfriendly to much more open and market-friendly systems. In the political sphere the transition is from relatively undemocratic to much more democratic systems.

Some countries are of course more advanced in their transition processes than others. Chile, for example, is more advanced than many in its move to rules-based governance in both the economic and political spheres, though its move in the political sphere is recent. Argentina and Brazil have both made very significant moves in both spheres, roughly simultaneously, since the debt crisis of the 1980s. India has long been a political democracy but in most respects effectively began its move to a more open and market-friendly economy in 1991. China began its economic transition in the late 1970s but is not yet a political democracy. Malaysia emerged from its colonial status in the1960s as a political democracy, and soon moved to relatively outward-oriented and market-friendly economic governance, yet questions have risen in recent years about the depth of its rules-based system of political governance. South Africa began its challenging move from inward-oriented economic and undemocratic political governance to more open and democratic economic and political governance with the abolition of apartheid in the early 1990s.

- *Agency and Expropriation Costs:* Much of the literature on corporate governance focuses on the "principal-agent" relationship between shareholders (the principals) and managers (the agents) that stems from the separation of ownership and management in the "publicly" owned corporation of the kind that prevails in the United States and the United Kingdom, in which no single shareholder owns more than a small fraction of a corporation's stock. Many authors argue, or assume, that the raison d'être of corporate governance, in any country, is to protect the interests of shareholders because the interests of other investors can adequately be protected through contractual relations with the company, leaving shareholders as the "residual" claimants whose interests can adequately be protected only through the institutions of corporate governance4. They thus tend to see the role of corporate governance in development as one of helping to ensure the supply and lower the cost of the financial resources that corporations in developing countries require from extra-firm sources to finance their investment activity.

- *Vested Interests:* The seven countries in this project also tend to suffer from the destructive, often highly negative-sum-game, behavior of powerful vested interests entrenched in highly concentrated oligopolistic structures of local economic and political power. That behavior tends greatly to weaken or undermine healthy price competition and the proper functioning of markets – indispensable for the move to sustained productivity growth – as well as to weaken or undermine the development and consolidation of democratic political institutions.

Indeed, in any market-based economy – developed or developing, national or global – the firm, or corporation, is society's principal agent of economic activity and development. The institutions of corporate governance, combined with those of market competition and government regulation, are society's principal means of inducing corporations collectively to behave in ways that are good for society as a whole. There is, in other words, a principal-agent relationship between society (the principal) and corporations as a group (the agents) embodied in the institutions of corporate governance. Society provides corporations with the incentive to act (notably the right to earn profits) and the means to do so (the right to exist, and act, as "legal persons", and the benefit from limited liability) and seeks, through the institutions of corporate governance, along with those of market competition (Adam Smith's "invisible hand") and government regulation, to ensure that corporations collectively serve its best interests.

FACTORS OR FORCES WORKING FOR AND AGAINST IMPROVED CORPORATE GOVERNANCE IN DEVELOPING COUNTRIES

- *Factors and Forces Working for Improved Corporate Governance:* In OECD countries, interest in corporate governance has grown rapidly in conjunction with the current wave of globalization. In the United States, the interest mushroomed in the 1980s when major US corporations suffered a number of widely publicized losses of home-market shares to foreign competitors, followed by the advent of "junk bonds" which led to the first big wave of hostile takeovers. More recent in Europe, the interest has been fuelled by deepening regional integration and the growth of cross-border mergers and acquisitions. Also important in OECD countries has been the spectacular growth of portfolio investments in corporate equities both at home and abroad by rapidly growing pension funds and other major institutional investors, along with concerns by corporate investors about establishing a "level playing field" for their international investment activity.

The rapid growth of international portfolio investments by OECD-based (particularly US and UK) institutional investors is in turn reflected in, and largely responsible for, the significant growth of foreign portfolio investment in "emerging market" economies in the 1990s. Portfolio equity investment flows going to developing countries rose from insignificant levels prior to the late 1980s to an annual average of $2.7 billion in1989–1990 and then surged to an annual average of some $43 billion during the years 1993–1996. Dropping to about $16 billion in 1998 in conjunction with the East Asian crisis, they are estimated to have risen again to about $48 billion in 2010. Foreign portfolio investors, in particular the major institutional investors, have thus been an important force working in favor of improved corporate governance worldwide.

The combined result is a marked decrease in the supply of extra-firm investment finance from traditional domestic sources precisely at a time when corporate extra-firm financial needs in those countries, as elsewhere, have risen substantially. The result is thus also to increase domestic pressures, within governments as well as among corporate insiders, in favor of improved corporate governance in order to facilitate the flow of investment finance to local corporations.

- *Obstacles to Improved Corporate Governance:* There is also, however, considerable resistance to changes needed significantly to improve corporate governance. Particularly important in this regard are the actions of the oligopolistic coalitions and powerful vested interest groups, mentioned earlier, who operate simultaneously in the marketplace, notably as corporate insiders, and in the sphere of domestic politics. They are sometimes referred to as "distributional cartels" because, in seeking to maintain or increase their share of a country's wealth (e.g. market share), they often invest significant corporate-controlled (as well as government- controlled) resources not in the creation of new wealth but in actions of strategic rivalry among themselves. Those actions tend to result not in healthy inter-firm price competition but in significant wastage and misallocation of a country's resources. They tend often to reduce aggregate wealth and thus constitute, from society's point of view, highly negative-sum games.

Distributional cartels undertake actions that not only hinder healthy inter-firm price competition and often reduce aggregate wealth, but also help to resolve certain apparent "paradoxes" of the development process. A good example is the extent to which corporations undertake large investments in highly capital-intensive production facilities that remain unused or significantly under-used (i.e. large investments in overcapacity) in countries that not only have significant supplies of unemployed or under-employed workers (i.e. surplus labor) but, virtually by definition, suffer from capital scarcity. Such "distortions" – and huge wastage of capital from an economy-wide perspective – reflect behavior typical of distributional cartels.

POLICY IMPLICATIONS

- *In the Financial Sector:* The considerable growth in the needs of corporations for extra-firm finance, due to the combined effects of accelerated global change and significant domestic policy liberalization precisely at a time when the availability of long-term investment funds from traditional sources (e.g. national development banks) has declined markedly, means that the institutions of corporate governance have a significant potential role to play in helping to channel investment finance to firms. While this role can be described as one of factor mobilization, it has become more important in recent years, as reflected in the spectacular increase in the extent to which firms in "emerging markets" have turned to domestic and especially foreign portfolio investors as suppliers of funds.
- *Stock Markets:* Understood by many as the raison d'être of corporate governance, the increased importance of improved corporate governance is reflected in the spectacular growth in the size of the stock market – i.e. in the value of shares listed, referred to as "market capitalization" – in all the case studies. South Africa and Malaysia, for example, have seen their market capitalization rise in 1999 to over 150 per cent of GDP.

While a weakening of stock-market activity is not necessarily indicative of weaker corporate governance, these contrasting experiences raise important questions for policymakers in developing countries: What is the importance of country's having a vibrant local stock market for the country's long-term development? How important are stock markets as a source of investment finance for corporations in developing countries? Is it reasonable to expect many of the small and medium-size firms that account for the bulk of local employment and constitute a significant source of local dynamism and flexibility, but which are unlikely ever to be able to sell their shares in New York or London, to be able to generate significant financing on the local stock market.

The more serious problem from a development policy perspective may thus not be a shortage of corporate finance as such, but the extent to which the ubiquitous use of devices to separate corporate ownership rights from the control of corporate resources serves to facilitate and camouflage self-dealing and related rent-seeking behavior, and the negative-sum-game dynamics reflected in such behavior, by corporate insiders.

The costs to society as a whole, in terms of wasted resources, lost growth opportunities and foregone development, though difficult to measure, undoubtedly go well beyond those incurred by expropriated minority shareholders alone.

- *The Importance of Liquidity:* The separation of ownership from management in the United States also made it possible for shareholders, often led by corporate founder-owners and their heirs, to diversify

> their corporate equity holdings – spreading their investment risk, and reducing their level of portfolio risk, in the process. The further result was a self-reinforcing process, a virtuous circle, which greatly increased not only the size but also the liquidity of the stock market in the United States.

Its significant liquidity in turn made it possible for the US stock market to play an important role in strengthening the entire financial system, and process of development, of the US economy. As recent studies of the positive correlation across countries between the degree of local stock-market liquidity (more than its size per se) and the strength of a country's subsequent economic growth further suggests, the key to understanding the potential importance for a country's long-term development of the country's having a vibrant stock market appears to be the latter's potential contribution to enhancing the liquidity of the country's financial system as a whole.

Banks and Stock Markets: Complements: Measures to strengthen a country's stock market and its corporate governance as a whole, should thus be understood as a potentially important complement to, but not as a substitute for, measures needed to strengthen its banking sector. A country cannot have a strong and vibrant stock market without a strong, healthy, commercial banking sector. Indeed, for small and medium-size local firms in particular, and for assuring liquidity in a country's financial system – including in low-income countries – a healthy banking system is sine qua non for development.

An important implication for policymakers and regulators – as Chile's experience points up most clearly, for example – is thus the need for careful attention to the quality of bank supervision and prudential requirements, as well as to bankruptcy rules and procedures. Often equally important is the need to enhance the corporate governance of local financial institutions, notably including that of banks. The latter implies a need for attention not only to disclosure requirements, the quality of auditing, etc., but to such questions as whether business groups should be prohibited from having a bank as one of their group firms (as Chile's experience would also seem to recommend) and whether a developing country should or should not require a separation between commercial and investment banking activities.

Minority Shareholders' Rights: What about stock markets per se, and corporate governance as a whole? Here there can be no doubt of the need to strengthen the effective protection of minority shareholders' rights in many of the countries covered in our study. The best means to achieve that protection will not only vary from one country to another; they will usually require the enhancement or modification in a given country of several, perhaps many, of the institutions listed in the annex. Certain key issues can nevertheless be pointed up as requiring policymakers' careful attention.

Two of the most crucial are the questions of how best to combine (and where to draw the line between) voluntary and mandatory mechanisms of corporate governance, and the use of judicial versus regulatory means of enforcement. Many countries have found, for example, that mandatory disclosure requirements — including mandatory disclosure of a firm's compliance or non-compliance with key (specified) voluntary codes or standards, and of its reasons for eventual non-compliance — combined with an otherwise heavy reliance on voluntary mechanisms is a good approach. Whether such an approach is appropriate where institutions are relatively weak nevertheless leads straight to the issue many see as the single most important: enforcement. There is some evidence, for example, that in countries with weak judicial systems (to enforce contracts as well as laws) a regulatory approach to enforcement of securities laws by an independent and motivated securities commission can be more effective than judicial enforcement. We touch on this issue again below.

A third issue is the importance to avoid significantly increasing agency costs as the price of trying to reduce the expropriation of minority shareholders. China's experience with its move since 1992 to "corporatism" state-owned companies highlights this danger, as managers have reportedly gained considerable new autonomy to "manage badly" in some of those companies. Concerns have also been raised that calls for greater professionalism of management in some countries may be more reflective of desires there to increase managers' autonomy than of any commitment to increase their level of professional standards.

In the "Real" Sector: Equally if not more important than the potential contribution of improved corporate governance to financial development is its potential contribution to "real" economic development. Significant wastage and misallocation of human and physical capital in countries that suffer critical shortages of both, and volatility often combined with resistance to needed change, widely constitute serious constraints on development, as noted earlier. These are problems towards whose solution improved corporate governance can also make a significant contribution. It can do so by helping to discipline corporate insiders — in private business groups and state-owned corporations alike — in the way they allocate and especially in the way they use, or waste, the sizeable real resources they control.

In the "real" as in the financial sector the institutions of corporate governance cannot operate alone. In the financial sector, policymakers must, as noted earlier, give careful attention to ensuring a sound banking system (including bankruptcy procedures, etc.) along with measures to enhance protection of minority shareholders' rights and others to strengthen corporate governance per se. In the real economy, policymakers must simultaneously give attention to three sets of institutions: (a) the institutions of corporate governance per se; (b) the institutions of market competition; (c) the institutions of regulation that are required in some specific sectors (e.g. telecommunications, air transportation, etc.) including many where major state-owned corporations have recently been privatized.

Similarly, it is difficult to overstate the importance for policymakers to give adequate attention to the need for regulatory reform and the establishment of competent regulatory bodies in those specific sectors (in addition to financial services) that require regulation. This importance is considerably amplified, moreover, by the risk of regulatory "capture" (which occurs when those with responsibility to regulate a given market are corrupted or otherwise unduly influenced by one or a number of participants in that market) especially where there are strong distributional cartels.

Political Governance: Negative-sum-games can rarely be eliminated without close attention to the institutions of political governance. The very strength of resistance to many of the changes needed significantly to enhance the protection of minority shareholders' rights and to improve corporate governance as a whole, as noted earlier, often exerts itself most strongly (even where corporate insiders may give lip service to the need for better corporate governance) through clientelistic relationship-based systems of political governance. The relative weakening or collapse of such systems in recent years, widely visible in the greatly reduced capacity of state-controlled providers of investment finance (such as national development banks) to supply such finance, can thus be seen as a "window of opportunity" for countries to achieve change that is needed as much in the institutions of political governance as in those of corporate governance.

Indeed, the close interaction between the institutions of political governance and those of corporate governance is clearly reflected in at least three ways: in the central roles of the legislative, regulatory and judicial bodies listed among the institutions of corporate governance in Annex 1; in the extent to which distributional cartels exert their power in both the economic and political spheres of activity in a country; and in the importance of the enforcement issue. It is therefore virtually impossible to move to an essentially rules-based system of governance in one of those sets of institutions without doing likewise in the other. Ultimately, they are inseparable.

CONCLUSION

Corporate governance matters for development. It has a central role to play in helping to increase the flow and lower the cost of the financial capital that firms need to finance their investment activity. The importance of this role has grown considerably in recent years, and is likely to continue to grow, as the needs of corporations for extra-firm finance has grown precisely at a time when the capacity of traditional sources of such finance to supply those needs has greatly diminished.

The significant growth of portfolio equity flows from OECD to developing countries, especially by institutional investors, points to the potential for improved corporate governance in developing countries and emerging markets to contribute to the stability of international financial markets. The potential benefits of such stability are also significant.

Equally important are the potential benefits of improved corporate governance for achieving productivity growth in the real economy of many developing countries. Volatility combined with excessive rigidities and huge wastage of real investment resources, both human and material, reflects the actions of distributional cartels in many developing countries. Reflected in ubiquitous self-dealing and rent-seeking behavior by corporate insiders in a context of clientelistic relationship-based systems of local governance, those actions widely constitute a serious obstacle to sustained productivity growth.

Improved corporate governance has an important potential role to play in helping to limit that behavior and overcome the obstacles to productivity growth.

Forces working in favor of improved corporate governance in developing countries include those operating both on the demand and on the supply side of portfolio equity flows to corporations there. Those on the demand side include corporations whose extra-firm financial needs have grown as their traditional sources of supply have shrunk; they also include governments responsible for those traditional sources in some cases. Those on the supply side include major institutional investors, especially pension funds and other long-term investors, in OECD and some developing countries. Forces working against significantly improved corporate governance (which may give lip service to the need for such improvement) include many dominant shareholders and other corporate insiders – in the private and public sectors alike – in entrenched distributional cartels.

The importance of distributional cartels in developing countries, as obstacles to development as well as to improved corporate governance, and the heightened risk of regulatory capture in countries with clientelistic relationship-based systems of governance, only reinforces the fact that good corporate governance requires good political governance, and vice-versa. As John Locke might have put it if he were writing today, development requires moving from the rule of man, or woman, to the rule of law – in the institutions of corporate and political governance together.

References

Ashbaugh, H., D. W. Collins, R. LaFond (2004), The Effects of Corporate Governance in Firms' Credit Ratings. Working Paper, University of Iowa.

Bartov, E., F. A. Gul, and J. S. L. Tsui (2001), Discretionary Accruals Models and Audit Qualifications. *Journal of Accounting and Economics*, 30, 421-452.

Baysinger, B. D., R. H. Kosnik, and T. A. Turk (1991), Effects of Board and Ownership Structure on Corporate R&D Strategy. *Academy of Management Journal*, 34, 205-214.

Bhagat, S. (2004), Goverance and Performance. Working paper, University of Colorado.

Bhagat, S. and B. Black (2002), The Non-correlation between Board Independece and Long-term Firm Performance. *Journal of Corporation Law*, 27, 2, 231-273.

Bhoraj, S. and P. Sengupta (2004), Effect of Corporate Governance on Bond Ratings and Yields: The Role of Institutional Investors and Outside Directors. Working Paper, Cornell University.

Conyon, M. J. and A. Florou (2004), Does Governance Quality Mitigate Horizon Effects? Investment Patterns Surrounding CEO Departures, Working Paper, University of Pennsylvania.

Core, J. E., R. W. Holthausen, and D. F. Larcker (1999), Corporate Governance, Chief Executive Officer Compensation and Firm Performance. *Journal of Financial Economics*, 51, 371-406.

Cremers, M. and V. B. Nair (2003), Governance Mechanisms and Equity Prices. Working Paper, Yale School of Management.

Hall, B. J. and J. B. Liebman (1998), Are CEOs Really Paid Like Bureaucrats? *Quarterly Journal of Economics*, 113, 653-691.

Hallock, K. (1997), Reciprocally Interlocking Boards of Directors and Executive Compensation. *Journal of Financial and Quantitative Analysis*, 32, 331-44.

Harford, J. (1999), Corporate Cash Reserves and Acquisitions. *Journal of Finance*, 54, 1969-1997.

Hubbard, R. G. (1998), Capital-market Imperfections and Investment. *Journal of Economic Literature*, 36, 193-225.

Jenkins, Nicole T. (2002), Auditor Independence, Audit Committee Effectiveness and Earnings Management. Working paper, Washington University.

Klein, April (2002), Audit Committee, Board of Director Characteristics, and Earnings Management. *Journal of Accounting and Economics*, 33, 375-400.

Klock, M. S., S. A. Mansi, and W. F. Maxwell (2004), Corporate Governance and the Agency Cost of Debt. Working Paper, George Washington University.

Stickel, S. E. (2000), Analyst Incentives and the Financial Characteristics of and Returns to Wall Street Darlings and Dogs, Working Paper, La Salle University.

Stulz, R. M. (1990), Managerial Discretion and Optimal Financing Policies. *Journal of Financial Economics*, 26, 3-27.

Sundaramurthy, C., J. M. Mahoney, and J. T. Mahoney (1997), Board Structure, Antitakeover Provisions, and Stockholder Wealth. *Strategic Management Journal*, 18, 231-245.

Yermack, D. (1996), Higher Market Valuation of Companies with a Small Board of Directors. *Journal of Financial Economics*, 40, 185-211.

INDEX

T